INTO THE
LAND
OF
DARKNESS

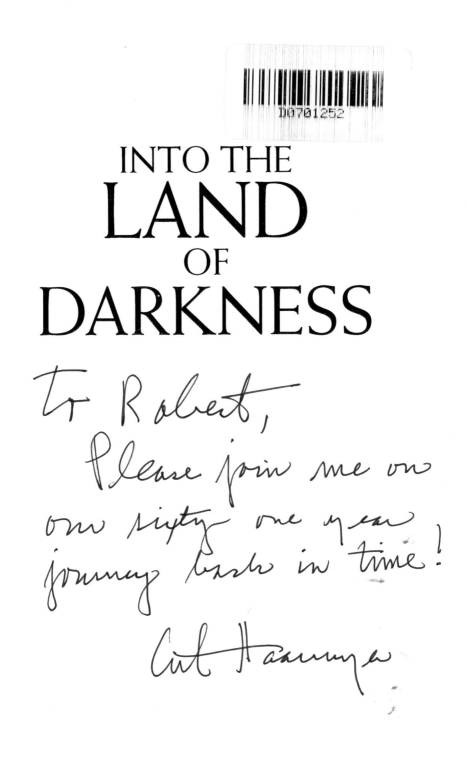

To Robert,
Please join me on
our sixty one year
journey back in time!

Cut Haumya

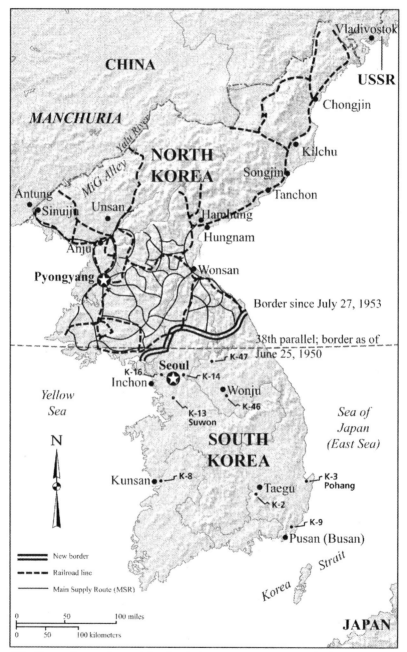

The Korean Peninsula, with borders before (June 25, 1950) and after (July 27, 1953) hostilities.

ABOUT THE BOOK

On a cold December morning in 1952, young Lt. Arthur L. Haarmeyer reported for duty in Korea as a B-26 bombardier-navigator to Colonel Delwin D. Bentley, Commander, 95th Bomb Squadron, 17th Bomb Group, K-9 Air Force Base, Pusan. Haarmeyer was immediately challenged by the colonel: "You've got an MBA . . . from a high-priced university. You could be riding a desk at the Pentagon right now. So why the hell are you here?" His reply— "I always wanted to be here, sir. I can be an accountant later"—was apparently convincing. But over the next seven months, flying fifty missions, mostly low-level nighttime bombing and strafing raids over mountainous North Korea, there were many times when he had reason to question the sanity of both his response and his decision.

Most of Haarmeyer's combat missions were single-ship sorties flown during hours of darkness with his crew, with the others being daylight formation bombing missions with his crew or as lead bombardier for Colonel Bentley. In this book Haarmeyer recalls with clarity and economy of style just what it was like to fly these missions. He puts the reader in the B-26, flying into deep valleys to find and attack communist freight trains and truck convoys carrying men and materiel to the front lines, and then unexpectedly caught in the sudden and blinding glare of enemy searchlights that triggered multiple streams of deadly and upward-arcing green or white tracers. And he recalls instances of agony, guilt, and terror, such as the times when he was unable to advise his pilot to "break right" or "break left" because the flak was so heavy on all sides that a quick and accurate decision was impossible—so their B-26 just simply plowed straight through it. He also recalls moment of breathtaking beauty and poignancy, and it is this artful juxtaposition that makes Haarmeyer's work more than just another wartime memoir.

Although Haarmeyer left the Air Force upon completion of his three-year contract of military service, the recurring and troubling memories of Korea never left him. Hence, the start of this manuscript fifty years after the restoration of freedom to the people of the Republic of Korea. Just as telling these stories was therapeutic for the author, so reading them will be healing for any reader who is a veteran of that or any war, as well as their family members and friends. The book also provides a valuable perspective on the United Nations Command's tactical approach to Korea, namely, the aerial interdiction of

North Korean troops and materiel, and so it will be of interest to students of the war, as well as military personnel and historians.

ABOUT THE AUTHOR

Born in Chicago in 1928, Arthur L. Haarmeyer earned an MBA from the University of Chicago before volunteering for service in Korea in Douglas B-26 bombers. After completing a fifty-mission combat tour of duty in Korea with the 95th Bomb Squadron, 17th Bomb Group, he served as a first lieutenant and as Project Officer in design and development of bombing tactics and devices until his honorable discharge in 1955. His earned military awards and citations include the Distinguished Flying Cross, Air Medal with three Oak Leaf Clusters, two Presidential Unit Citations, and a Republic of Korea Presidential Unit Citation. After earning a law degree at Northwestern University in 1958, he practiced law and then engaged in the development and management of commercial properties in Sacramento, California. He is currently working on his second manuscript, a compilation of biographical sketches featuring twelve Korean War combat veterans, representing every branch of our military services, whom he knew during or after that oft-forgotten United Nations effort.

1953   2013

INTO THE
LAND
OF
DARKNESS
A BOMBARDIER-NAVIGATOR'S STORY

ARTHUR L.
HAARMEYER

DEDICATION

I DEDICATE THIS COLLECTION OF NONFICTION SHORT stories to the memory of Colonel Delwin Dale Bentley, a gifted command pilot, a fearless and courageous warrior, and a truly inspirational leader. I also make this dedication to Captain Robert Crow, the finest pilot, officer, and gentleman I ever had the privilege of knowing and serving.

I further dedicate this book to over seventeen hundred USAF combat crewmen of the Korean War (pilots, bombardier-navigators, air gunners, and flight engineers) and, in too many cases, only to their collective memory. These brave airmen flew and fought tenaciously and effectively, usually by night and over sixty years ago, with each of them planning and executing fifty bombing and/or strafing missions, or dying in the attempt. These volunteers willingly strapped their bodies to high-performance twin-engine Douglas B-26 Invaders that took them deep into hostile North Korean skies throughout a geopolitically and historically significant regional war. Diminished by being insultingly designated officially as merely a "police action," this intense and deadly conflict took the lives of over 34,000 Americans during the course of its thirty-seven month duration. (This staggering number of fatalities far exceeds the combined total of American military deaths in the countries of Afghanistan and Iraq to the current date.)

To be remembered with respect and honor are those unseen and unsung heroes, our crew chiefs, aircraft mechanics, bomb/rocket loaders, and flight instrument technicians of that distant and deadly war. These dedicated and skilled airmen/technicians achieved amazing results, delivering the highest levels of quality of aircraft repair and maintenance services under frequently brutal weather conditions and continually sub-standard living circumstances.

Finally, I dedicate this book to the people and the military forces of the Republic of Korea who had never known freedom and independence until they joined with the United Nations Command in 1950 and fought for their nation, culture, and language.

CONTENTS

PART IV

OVER THE HUMP

PART V

COMING HOME

PREFACE

THE STORIES IN THIS BOOK PORTRAY THE LONG SUP-
pressed but still startlingly vivid recollections of my personal
experiences in Korea from late December 1952 until the last days of
July of the following year. They are far more than bits and pieces of
vague and distant memories. They are vivid recollections, stark and
clear visual images, and implacable impressions of the most meaningful
personal experiences of a lifetime that I have long and subconsciously
suppressed, probably much too long for the good of my psyche. They
are as accurate and specific as my eighty-four-year-old mind and memory can recall them and my writing skills can portray them. They are
narratives of actual events and happenings during my seven months of
air-ground combat over North Korea. And they are about the men of
the 95th Bomb Squadron, 17th Bomb Group, Far East Air Force, who
were then stationed at the USAF's K-9 Air Force Base (AFB), located
ten miles east of the teeming seaport city of Pusan near the southern tip
of the rugged Korean peninsula during 1952 and 1953. They are about
the things that these volunteers did and the things that happened to
them during the course of flying fifty bombing and strafing missions.

These "single ship" missions, flown mostly at night, were low-level,
low-speed armed reconnaissance raids against moving and stationary
targets located in the eastern half of North Korea. In several cases, these
stories are about what happened before takeoff from the weatherworn,

cracked, and undulating asphalt runway (15/33) of K-9 AFB, or just after landing. And several stories are about significant events and happenings on the ground in Pusan, the second largest city in South Korea, or in one of several major cities or USAF air bases in Japan.

The events described in these narratives were, and continue to be, in varying degrees, the dominating elements of numerous dreams that I have experienced over the decades since returning to the United States during the last days of the Korean hostilities in late July 1953. The frequency and intensity of these dreams have diminished as the months and years have relentlessly marched by. But now, more than sporadically, they still come back to occupy, or most often, to haunt my nightly three to four hours of uneasily induced unconsciousness. Quite simply, they constitute the deep, pervasive, and ever-hardening psychological scar tissue that has not sufficiently lessened with the passage of time.

I have not attempted to thoroughly research or verify the accuracy of the happenings herein described. And not from 1954 until 2007 did I attempt to contact my pilot, Captain Robert Crow. And to this day I have never attempted to contact our gunner, Sergeant Jerry Davis. I have periodically and seriously considered such contacts so that I could not only determine the degree of accuracy of the happenings that I describe, but also to reach out and reconnect with these two skillful, brave, and patriotic men. I did attempt, on Memorial Day of 2004, to make contact via telephone with Colonel Delwin D. Bentley, our 95th Bomb Squadron commander. I flew with Colonel Bentley as his bombardier-navigator on less than seven missions when he "drafted" me for dangerous and deep penetrations into the distant northeastern corner of North Korea, and those few missions constitute the most memorable, exhilarating, and terrifying experiences of my entire life. Simply stated, he was the most fearless, most aggressive, and most innovative individual I have ever known. Unfortunately, I learned from his son that day that the colonel had died on September 3, 1992, at the age of seventy-three in Wilson, Wyoming.

I had also thought, on many occasions, to reach out and attempt to thank Major John Fortner, a highly skilled USAF senior pilot, an outstanding officer, and a sensitive and caring human being, who stuck his neck out a country mile for my gunner and me. But for some reason, I could not bring myself to reach out to anyone from that most eventful and traumatic period of my life until May of 2007. During the three years prior to that time I had been remembering and recording, intermittently in rough draft, the nonfiction short stories that constitute the totality of this book, as self-imposed and long past due mental and emotional therapy. A few days before, I had written about my recurring dreams of Captains Doolittle and Hall. They had flown their last mission into North Korea in the spring of 1953 and had been classified as "missing in action," so I finally did an Internet search to determine whether their status had ever been changed.

It had not. However, incident to that research, well over fifty years after the completion of our crew's fiftieth and final mission over North Korea, I stumbled into a vast reservoir of print data and photography about the 17th Bomb Group. I discovered that for decades there had been published a sixteen-page quarterly newsletter, titled *The Sortie,* partly written and solely and ably published and distributed by a talented gentleman named Ted Baker and targeted to veterans of the Korean War who had served with the 17th Bomb Group and to their surviving family members. I contacted Ted Baker by telephone, and he graciously offered to mail to me multiple and recent copies of *The Sortie.* I learned that Ted had been a gunner with the 17th Bomb Wing at Pusan and had completed his combat tour the year before I arrived at K-9 AFB. He invited me to participate in an upcoming and combined annual reunion (17th Bomb Group/World War II, the

17th/452nd Bomb Wing/Korea, and the 319th Bomb Group/World War II), to be held in St. Louis, Missouri, later in the year. I did attend and, as the expression goes, "the rest is history." For me, it was most significant history, as I met in St. Louis many of the brave and talented men who flew the uncertain skies over North Korea, as well as those on the ground at K-9 AFB who enabled them to get to the target and back, in most cases.

This manuscript would never have been written were it not for Ted Baker, *The Sortie,* and many of the people with whom I was once again in direct contact, not having had any contact with any of them since we had served at K-9 AFB during the thirty-seven months of the "Korean hostilities." I have shared my Korean experiences and writings with them, and collectively, they have made many valuable and insightful observations, corrections, and recommendations, as well as suggestions for additional chapters. Almost all of these veterans have contributed constructively in the drafting or editing of this manuscript, and/or by their permission to use their photographs of the aircraft, its bomb loads and weaponry, and related photography.

I have never joined any veterans' organization (except for the Disabled American Veterans Association) since being honorably discharged from the USAF during 1955, although I admire and respect them and appreciate their efforts on behalf of all American veterans. Nor have I ever participated in any parade or ceremony on the Fourth of July, Memorial Day, or Veterans' Day, or even attended such an event, as I know that I will uncontrollably choke up and break down upon seeing American flags and military uniforms, and hearing stirring but haunting military music. I am unable to even display the American flag or wear a patriotic lapel pin, or to manifest in any way the strong and enduring sense of duty to country and patriotism that I feel but cannot outwardly express. This is a direct consequence of psychological trauma resulting from the conflicted emotions resulting from my intense and suppressed Korean experiences.

Rather than attempt to express my pride in flag and country in any public way, or attempt to reveal the overwhelming gratitude that I feel for this great country and the benefits of freedom and opportunity that it has bestowed upon me and my progeny, I have attempted instead to record, according to my very best recollections and writing abilities, my own personal experiences in a very distant but necessary regional war. Although I have only recently extracted and carefully reconstructed these stories from mind and memory, I am confident that they will closely approximate the recollections of other B-26 crewmen who served in these combat operations. Without intending to be presumptuous, I have set forth these varied but often painful memories with the sincere desire and intention that they fairly and accurately convey the nature, extent, and character of that intense, brutal air-ground combat. My hope is that our children and grandchildren can thus better understand and appreciate the efforts expended and the sacrifices made by our USAF combatants, and thereby derive enduring courage and pride.

So, to the survivors and descendants of those skillful and self-sacrificing, but much too long forgotten or unknown USAF air combat volunteers, I can only say that I hope and trust that I have adequately recalled, and effectively and fairly described, my own Korean combat experiences. My desire is that my narratives be truly representative of yours, and that they will enable other Americans to remember or learn about the efforts and contributions of a relatively small number of USAF air crews and their dedicated ground support crews. These men served in a war that advanced the cause of freedom by ensuring the survival of a vibrant and democratic South Korea, a war that has been too long forgotten by too many and remains totally unknown to far too many others: Nobody's War.

ANY ERRORS IN THIS BOOK ARE MY OWN, AND I SUSPECT there would have been many more were it not for the help of many good friends and helpful readers. I wish to acknowledge and express my heartfelt gratitude and sincere appreciation to George Singer of Danbury, Connecticut; Ted Baker of Almont, Michigan; Dick Uyehara of Grand Junction, Colorado; Paul Geidel of Las Vegas, Nevada; Gordon Cooper of Aleto, Illinois; and Wayne Knowles of Reddick, Florida. All of them served with the 95th Bomb Squadron at K-9 AFB, Pusan, South Korea. Several of them read and edited the entire manuscript, and their corrections, recommendations, suggestions, and encouragement were invaluable. George was exceptionally helpful over a year's time during which we exchanged over 250 emails in improving and augmenting the accuracy, character, and content of the book. George performed admirably in Korea as both flight engineer and gunner on B-26s during 1951 and 1952. Dick Uyehara excelled as a B-26 bombardier-navigator during 1953. He often sat in the right seat of the 26, and he has provided me with invaluable technical knowledge and expertise as to its controls, instrument panel, and related systems and equipment. Paul Geidel fought as a B-26 gunner and generously provided combat photography that dramatically brought the manuscript to life. Gordon Cooper ably served as crew chief for the ill-fated B-26 (tail number 449) in 1952 and 1953. Wayne Knowles was a skilled flight engineer and gunner in 1952 and 1953.

I also wish to express my heartfelt gratitude to Curt Gentry, who read a major portion of the manuscript at an early stage of its development and encouraged me by offering to write a book jacket endorsement. Curt also served with the 17th Bomb Wing at K-9 AFB in Korea during 1952–1953. His encouragement was truly motivating as he has achieved many exceptional literary successes by authoring or co-authoring such memorable books as *Operation Overflight: A Memoir of the U-2*

Incident, John M. Browning: American Gunmaker, J. Edgar Hoover: The Man and his Secrets, and *Helter Skelter, The True Story of the Manson Murders.*

I am grateful to Peter Decker of Greenwood, California, a Korean combat veteran with the 11th Regiment, 1st Marine Division, who contributed immensely by way of insightful critiques and valid recommendations. And I wish to thank Robert Fischer of Sacramento, California, who served in Korea as a medic with the 36th Air Rescue Squadron (MATS) stationed at K-55 AFB, Osan, South Korea. Bob critiqued the manuscript and provided perspective and accuracy all along the way.

I also wish to recognize and thank Dr. Gary Leiser, editor of the *Jimmie Doolittle Air & Space Museum Foundation News* and curator and director of the Travis Air Museum, Fairfield, California, who accorded me unlimited access to the museum's archives, as well as presenting two of my stories in its publication. I would like to further recognize bombardier-navigator William Chatfield (452nd Bomb Wing) and gunner Antonio Fucci (37th Bomb Squadron) for their insight and valuable contributions.

I wish to express my appreciation particularly for the major contributions of Major General William C. Lindley, Jr., who read an advanced copy of the manuscript and provided multiple corrections and recommendations. In the rank of colonel, General Lindley served at K-9 AFB as deputy wing commander of the 17th Bomb Wing and as wing commander upon the loss of Wing Commander Colonel Glenn Nye in 1953. Colonel Nye was leading a sixteen-ship daylight mission over a factory complex along the west coastline of North Korea when it was struck by triple A on the bomb run over the target area.

I wish to express my heartfelt appreciation to members of the medical staffs at the VA Hospitals in Reno, Nevada, and Sacramento,

California, specifically to John Van Biber MD and Beverly Parker MD in Reno and Narinder S. Dhaliwal MD in Sacramento, as well as the PTSD counselors at the Vet Centers in Sacramento and Citrus Heights, California, especially to Mike Cohen and Edna Gabaldon in Sacramento and Ugo Punteri in Citrus Heights.

I wish to thank Lt. Charles W. Hinton, who completed his fifty-mission tour of duty in 1952 as a B-26 navigator, 13th Bomb Squadron, 3rd Bomb Group, K-8, Kunsan, South Korea. Charley later served as the first president of the 13th Bomb Squadron Association and for decades as its historian.

Last but foremost, I acknowledge and thank, with affection and respect, Patricia Heinicke, Jr., my developmental editor, who brought me, figuratively, kicking and screaming into the strange and demanding world of book publication. She graciously taught me much about the beauty and necessity of brevity, clarity, and accuracy of expression.

And to our gunner, "Sarge" Jerry Davis (wherever you are), I truly regret that I never found you.

PART I
INTRODUCTION

AUTHOR'S NOTE

ON THE FIFTIETH ANNIVERSARY OF THE LAST DAY OF the Korean hostilities, a prominent newspaper of general circulation referred to the Korean War as a "needless war." In fact, over the years this war has been wrongfully and insultingly diminished, even labeled a "police action" or merely a "conflict," by the politician, the revisionist, and the faint of heart who never have nor ever will appreciate or make the personal commitment that proves once again that "freedom isn't free."

This deadly war was definitely not fought in vain, despite the fact that the border between South Korea and North Korea has been long stabilized close to where it was on June 25, 1950. On that early Sunday morning, the communist hordes from North Korea, the so-called Korean People's Army, without cause or provocation, began to swarm across the sparsely defended northern border of South Korea to launch a massive invasion of death, destruction, rape, and plunder upon the outnumbered and outgunned Republic of Korea Army and the populace of that small, new, and struggling democracy.

Overwhelmingly, the millions of South Koreans who survived this unprovoked and vicious regional war and are alive today, living and working in that prospering free democratic nation, and many of their children and grandchildren, do not consider the Korean War to have been "needless." In point of fact, for over the past half-century the

Republic of Korea has been totally free from communist rule and occupation in large measure because of the constant vigilance of its government and that of the United States. Specifically, the Republic of Korea has continued since 1953 to benefit from the ongoing presence of over 30,000 American military personnel who serve as a trip wire, with a preponderance of our airmen and aircraft being stationed within very close proximity to South Korea's common border with North Korea.

The Republic of South Korea has become steadily more democratic, more heavily industrialized, and more economically successful. It now has the tenth largest economy in the world, and it has a standard of living light years above that of their starving and dwindling neighbors to the north. In North Korea today, the people continue to struggle, suffer, and die under the heel of a mad communist dictator, who pours 35 percent of North Korea's gross national product each and every year into weapons for and support and maintenance of a 1.1-million-man standing army almost totally massed along its common border with the Republic of South Korea.

As conditions in North Korea worsen and the fragile regional stability becomes more uncertain, it is perhaps time to revisit our involvement in the Korean War. It was undoubtedly a deadly undertaking. According to the *Encyclopedia of the Korean War* (Spencer C. Tucker, editor) this fiercely fought regional war took the lives of almost 34,000 American combatants, 185,000 South Korean combatants, 800,000 to 1,100,000 North Korean and Chinese foot soldiers, and over 1 million Korean civilians.

Known as the "first shooting war" of the USAF, the Korean War was certainly fought just as fiercely in the air as on the ground. According to a long-suppressed Russian General Staff Report (G. F. Krivosheev, ed. *Soviet Casualties and Combat Losses in the Twentieth Century*. Mechanicsburg, PA: Stackpole Books, 1997, p. 281), at least one hundred and twenty highly experienced and skilled Russian pilots were killed over North Korea in opposing our United Nations air forces while flying the swift Russian-made MiG-15 jet fighters that treacherously carried the markings of the communist North Korea Air Force. In the USAF's *Air University Quarterly Review* (Spring, 1954 edition, p. 74), the major strategic and tactical significance of the air operations of USAF aircraft during the three years of the Korean War was demonstrated "by the cumulative effect of interdiction" as documented by the confirmed destruction or damaging of 33,081 railroad cars, 2,134 locomotives, and 1,002 rail and road tunnels, as well as 28,621 rail cuts. And the number of enemy trucks carrying men or materiel that were destroyed or damaged by such interdiction is staggering; based upon recent discussions with other B-26 crew members then stationed at K-9 AFB, I can estimate that the number of enemy trucks that were destroyed or damaged in North Korea (June 1950 to July 1953) was conservatively a multiple of five to fifteen times the number of the 33,081 railroad cars that were confirmed as destroyed or damaged, as reported in the USAF's *Air University Quarterly Review*'s Spring edition of 1954.

Much of this "interdiction" was undoubtedly carried out by the only light bomber that was flown in that theatre of operations by the USAF—the Douglas B-26. The B model had a hard nose and eighteen .50 caliber Browning machine guns, and the C model had a soft nose (the bombardier-navigator's Plexiglas nose compartment), and ten .50 caliber Browning machine guns. Both models carried varied loads of up to 6,000 pounds of bombs, napalm, and rockets on each mission. This fast and highly maneuverable twin-engine light bomber was used by only three bomb groups of the United States Far East Air Force: the 452nd Bomb Group and its successor, the 17th Bomb Group, both stationed at K-9 AFB, Pusan, South Korea, and the 3rd Bomb Group, first stationed at Iwakuni, Japan, and later, after July of 1951, at K-8 AFB, Kunsan, South Korea.

Each of these three groups was comprised of three squadrons, and generally sixteen B-26 bombers were assigned permanently to each squadron. Therefore, there was a maximum of only ninety-six B-26s available at any time during the Korean War, to detect, interdict, destroy, and suppress the heavy communist troop reinforcements and weapons/munitions replacements streaming relentlessly via train, truck, oxen, and human backpack to the brutal battlefields of Korea. These relatively few aircraft were also tasked by Fifth Air Force Headquarters in Tokyo to deliver proficient and frequent close air support for the usually far outnumbered ground forces of the United Nations Command.

The Douglas B-26 is often cited by noted military historians as the "backbone" and the "workhorse" of the USAF over North Korea. It ceaselessly and proficiently crossed over the front lines at eight to twelve thousand feet of altitude and then dropped down to fifty to five hundred feet of terrain clearance. At these dangerously low levels, particularly during hours of darkness, the B-26 bombed and strafed communist truck convoys, frontline and rear echelon troop concentrations, Russian-made T-34 tanks, munitions and fuel dumps, troop and freight trains, bridges, viaducts, and coastal freighters that carried men and materiel from China, Manchuria, and Russia to the killing fields at or near the contested 38th Parallel. The deadly B-26 relentlessly continued the fight until the long-negotiated signing on July 27, 1953, of the cease-fire agreement that de facto ended this seemingly endless Asian war.

To my knowledge, no factual and comprehensive book has been written by a former USAF B-26 bombardier-navigator from K-9 AFB who was directly engaged in air-to-ground combat operations in North Korea during the thirty-seven months of that forgotten war. That which follows is my attempt to fill the void.

IGNORANCE AND APATHY

The danger's passed, the wrong is righted,
The veteran's ignored, the soldier's slighted.
—Author unknown

W E WERE FLOWN FROM K-9 AFB JUST EAST OF PU-
san, South Korea, to a big, barren, and gray relocation compound, commonly known as Fuchu, near the heart of Tokyo, Japan, the same way we had arrived over seven months earlier. We had been transported to Fuchu in the cold and empty belly of a lumbering C-119 cargo plane, the then famous Fairchild C-119 "Flying Boxcar." We were two veteran B-26 crews from the 95th Bomb Squadron coming back to the world from air-ground combat, each crew comprised of a pilot, a bombardier-navigator, and an air gunner. We had just completed our fifty-mission tours of duty together and were finally escaping that unwelcoming Korean peninsula in the dying days of July 1953. Each of us was without physical injury, but we had mixed emotions and haunting memories of comrades left behind in North Korea who would never leave that brutal land of jagged, deadly, and unforgiving mountain ranges with narrow, deep, and treacherous river valleys.

We were denied the daytime sights and nocturnal pleasures of Tokyo, as on the same day as our unheralded arrival we had been quickly and hurriedly loaded upon a chartered Canadian Pacific Douglas C-54 transport, at nearby Tachikawa AFB, for a long two-stop, over-water flight to Vancouver, British Columbia, Canada. I climbed the ramped steps into the cabin of the transport, stuffed my heavy duffel bag into a cramped overhead compartment, and slumped into a comfortable reclining seat, anxiously awaiting the start of the long takeoff roll. As I sat there, through engine run-up, I began to shudder uncontrollably, not really believing that it was all nearly over.

In my head was a veritable kaleidoscope of vivid recollections—the multitude of events, many uncomprehended and some incomprehensible, that impacted my young American life as a volunteer aircrew member in a vicious regional Asian war that was then commonly referred to back home as merely a "police action." I remembered from those eventful months of service too many moments of sheer terror, when flak was suddenly arcing upward toward us and I had to make an immediate and agonizing decision as to what I should be shouting into the intercom—for my pilot to either "break left" or "break right"—to escape the deadly and multiple arcs of green or white tracers, the flaming "golf balls," rushing at and by us.

I remembered the hard and empty faces of the disheveled and gaunt Korean refugees who passed before us in seemingly endless lines as they trudged along the sides of an icy road while we rode by in a new, warm, enclosed jeep. I remembered the exquisite and absolute beauty of a summer tropical sky at sunset as we flew back toward the northwest coast of Honshu, the main island of Japan, for aircraft repair and our rest and recuperation. I remembered being totally mesmerized by the soaring multicolored clouds on all sides, gawking at the ever-changing permutations of light, configuration, and color, and forgetting for the moment that I was in the Plexiglas nose of a light bomber as a navigator with substantial crew responsibilities.

I remembered the barren, primitive shelter that I shared with a passing array of B-26 crewmembers whom I thought I knew well but did not really know at all. I remembered the expression on our innocent young Korean house girl's face the last time I saw her, both of us knowing that we would never see each other again. These were among many fast and fleeting recollections of K-9 Air Force Base and its people that I had on that air-cooled C-54 transport. I remember particularly the overwhelming sense of relief from anxiety, tension, and terror as the wheels left the dark runway along Tokyo Bay and I stared out at the receding nightlights of Tokyo. I also left the Far East with a feeling of regret and the nagging conviction that we had not finished the mission we had inherited upon our arrival, and an uneasy feeling of guilt for having failed to volunteer for an extended tour of duty. But I also knew that I simply could not psychologically handle twenty-five more flights into those dark and dangerous North Korean skies.

After brief refueling stops in the Aleutian Islands and at a major air base near Anchorage, Alaska, we landed at Vancouver International Airport, tired, hungry, and dirty. We arrived with our heavy duffel bags jammed with Air Force clothing, a few Asian souvenirs of questionable value, and little else. There was no one to meet or assist us upon our arrival in Vancouver, and we soon learned there were no arrangements for us to reach the city of Seattle, where, we had been informed just prior to take-off, we would receive full base pay and combat pay for our months of military service in Korea. So we shared the cost of a limousine and together we rode the approximately ninety miles to Seattle in comparative comfort, but in silence, total fatigue, and with some substantial measure of loneliness and disappointment.

In Seattle we were rudely informed that our military pay records had not yet been received and that we would not be paid until their arrival. So we went our separate ways. My pilot, Captain Robert Crow, and I took adjacent rooms in a major downtown Seattle hotel where we reasonably expected to be quartered for just a day or two. At this point I felt financially comfortable as I had hoarded well over three hundred dollars that I had won in a series of chess games in Korea, playing against mostly USAF air and ground crewmen whose self-confidence and competitive spirit far exceeded their recently acquired chess skills.

By happenstance, I discovered that a dark and intimate bar in this hotel was the hangout for reporters who worked for the *Post-Intelligencer,* one of Seattle's major daily newspapers. And it was my good luck and good fortune to meet there a petite and veritably sparkling brunette who was referred to by her older male colleagues as a "cub reporter." I was twenty-five years old, single, and reasonably presentable in my newly pressed blue gabardine dress uniform, well adorned, I thought, with a number of brightly colored fabric bars representing the awards and decorations I had earned in Korea.

In view of our mutual attraction and by way of many fine restaurants and alluring wharf-side cocktail lounges along Puget Sound, my three hundred dollars almost totally disappeared within four days. Unfortunately, my USAF pay records had not yet arrived to enable me to replenish my dwindling cash reserves. At the same time the weekend arrived, and to my joy and discomfort, this adventurous young lady suggested that we junket to a ski lodge on the slopes of nearby Mount Rainier. She further suggested that I wear casual civilian attire for the occasion. Having no other option, I informed her that I was temporarily broke, that I had nothing but military apparel in my possession, and that consequently, my purchase of civilian clothing or my financing of a weekend trip to a ski lodge was not within the range of possibility. She quickly and rudely stated that military dress uniforms (and combat awards and decorations) made but slight impact upon the war-weary citizens of Seattle. World War II had just eight years prior left major and lasting impressions upon the local populace, in contrast to the recent events and happenings of the comparatively limited and seemingly unremarkable Korean War, despite the grim reality that close to thirty-four thousand mostly young American lives were brutally and abruptly terminated in Korea over three years of intense warfare.

She then described something that had happened at her newspaper just a few months before. It seems that every day this newspaper printed a summary of the "battle actions" that had occurred the previous day in Korea. Such reports generally summarized the significant military happenings, such as enemy planes shot down, coastal supply ships sunk, front line positions overrun, and combat casualties. According to her account, one day her paper inadvertently ran, word for word, the very same story of death and destruction that it had run the previous day. Remarkably, not a single newspaper reader contacted the newspaper to report this negligent duplication. The city editor was so intrigued by this lack of readership reaction that he decided to run it a third consecutive day. Only then, after these two days of total content duplication, did the paper receive three or four observations or complaints from its readers.

This significant absence of awareness or interest on the part of the newspaper's large "big city" readership in the combat actions of the Korean War reminded my young and cynical companion of that long-forgotten but still somewhat amusing question: "What is the difference between ignorance and apathy?" Answer: "I don't know and I don't care!"

So then and there I became brutally aware that what I had experienced in Korea, what I had personally accomplished, and what I had thought was vital, meaningful, and important was considered rather insignificant back here in the States. Few people seemed to know or care that we were enabling the South Korean people (horribly enslaved and brutalized by the Japanese from 1910 until the end of World War II in 1945) and their new and struggling democratic government to survive and ultimately prosper, by our dominant role in holding back the hordes of relentlessly attacking and brutal invaders from communist North Korea and China.

Then and there I further and finally acknowledged to myself the depressing and disillusioning reality that what I had thought was morally responsible and patriotic was not so considered by an overwhelming majority of Americans. This conclusion was confirmed several days later upon my arrival home in Chicago, where it seems that no one really knew or cared about a distant war on a small peninsula in eastern Asia unless they had a close family member whose life was threatened directly by being so involved. Simply stated, to them the war in Korea was little more than an annoyance: a distraction from normal life and business as usual. So I deliberately suppressed the compulsive need to talk about my experiences, my beliefs, and my feelings about what I still believed was a very necessary war. And I substantially succeeded over the next five decades in the attempt to bury and suppress the types of memories that really never leave a survivor of intense and sustained combat action, no matter how hard and long the efforts to forget.

I DON'T EVEN KNOW
HER NAME

LATE ONE SATURDAY MORNING IN AUGUST OF 2003 I sat alone at my desk cleaning up sundry paperwork. I was basically retired by that time but maintained a small office where I performed various writing services. I did not have any appointments scheduled that morning so I was startled when I heard the exterior door to my reception room open and close. I then realized that I had forgotten to lock the door when I had arrived several hours before.

I closed the file I was working on and rose slowly from my desk, intending to walk toward the reception room to greet my unknown visitor. But when I looked up I saw a trim and vivacious young lady standing just outside my open office door. She was looking at me with a wide, happy, and impish smile. I assumed that she was in my office for the purpose of selling something or other, or simply soliciting monies for some local charity.

Before I could say a word she stated: "Oh, you're one of those old guys."

Seeing that she seemed harmless and pleasantly playful, I quickly decided to play along. So I simulated the careful and awkward movement of a crippled old man, walking slowly toward her, holding an imaginary walker in front of me with both hands. She laughed easily and heartily as this exaggerated display of decrepitude.

I asked how I could be of assistance to her. She responded, "I'm here to inquire about a business plan, its cost, and when it could be completed." And then she added quickly:

"But we should talk about your problem first."

"I don't have any problem."

"Yes, you do. I can see it in your eyes."

"You can see *what* in my eyes?"

"You were in combat in World War II or Korea, weren't you?"

"I don't know what you're talking about. . . . Let's get back to the business plan."

"It's difficult to even talk about it, isn't it?"

"What's difficult to talk about?"

"Your combat experiences. Was it World War II or Korea?"

"Well, I was in Korea in '52 and '53. That's a long time ago."

"It may have been a long time ago, but it's still with you and probably has been with you every day of your life since."

At this point, this perceptive and outspoken young lady suddenly had my full attention: her accuracy of observation and insight made me feel exposed and vulnerable.

So I had the urgent need to end this startling and much too self-revealing conversation.

"Okay, look, it's difficult to talk about and now is certainly not the time. I was just about to leave for the day when you walked in. I have a time problem. I really have to get going. So please tell me why you need a business plan."

She then offered a direct and concise description of an intended professional partnership or association involving her, several other psychologists, and a psychiatrist. She stated that she had just left the position that she held in southern California at a medical facility where she was involved in treating patients afflicted by PTSD. This acronym was somewhat familiar to me, but I did not know its literal meaning. I returned to my desk and reached for a yellow writing pad and scribbled these four letters as well as her first name. It was the only name she gave me. Looking at the writing pad several days later, the letters "PTSD" were clearly printed. However, her scribbled name was indecipherable. It looked like Jane or Janice.

I asked her a series of questions. From her answers I quickly concluded that the financial needs of their prospective office practice did not require the borrowing of any substantial sum of money for their start-up and initial working capital requirements. In fact, her group could satisfy all or practically all of its short-term financing needs by taking advantage of their collective borrowing capacity, simply by using their personal credit cards. And this I so advised her.

As I stood up to conclude our discussion and to bid farewell, she remained seated and blandly stated: "Now it's my turn."

"Your turn for what?"

"My turn to give you a possible solution to your problem."

"I don't have any problem."

"You certainly do. Your problem is PTSD. Probably you don't even know it."

"And how do you know that's what my 'problem' is?"

"It's in your eyes and your evasiveness in talking about your war."

"In the first place, a half a million Americans served in 'my war' in Korea so it is hardly my war, singular. Second, I certainly don't think eyes are that revealing."

"Well, I have dealt with enough of you old guys to be able to quickly detect the psychological scar tissue that you carry around with you every day of your lives. Let me describe your major and ongoing symptoms. You have recurring nightmares—you might call them 'bad dreams'—with their content being your personal combat experiences where sudden and violent death was always a possibility or a probability. You have had a long-term problem going to sleep and staying asleep. You probably have a history of alcohol or drug abuse starting during or soon after your combat experiences. You have attempted suicide or have seriously considered suicide as an option, probably more than once. You have long experienced a sense of loneliness or isolation. You tend to be a solitary person, even reclusive. You have difficulty in relating to others, in trusting them, and in maintaining long-term relationships. Also, you frequently or periodically experience the dreaded sense of being or becoming vulnerable or being out of control. You . . ."

"Okay, okay, you've made your point!"

"All right then, let's talk about a solution. You certainly have waited long enough to be ready for one. You've got to confront your demons, directly, head on, starting now. First, have an early, bland, and light dinner, tonight and every night. No alcohol before or after dinner. Work or read after dinner. Don't watch television: you want to actively engage your brain. Don't go to bed until you are really tired. Before you lie down place a writing pad beside your bed with an open ballpoint pen beside it. Lie on your back and try to concentrate upon absolutely nothing. Visualize a black void in your mind's eye. If you are not asleep within an hour after you retire, then get up, sit in a comfortable chair, and resume reading something pleasurable and relaxing. Repeat this process until you are really tired.

"If you are awakened suddenly in the middle of one of your recurring bad dreams, sit up immediately, take the writing pad and pen in hand, and record what you were experiencing. Write down everything that you were reliving in as much detail as your memory provides you. Don't be concerned about spelling errors or sentence structure: just scribble it down. Some guys perspire profusely when going through a particularly vivid and disturbing bad dream. Should that happen to you, replace the sweat-soaked pajama top or tee shirt when you're done writing and then do what you can to get back to sleep.

"If you are awakened again by that dream or some other bad dream, then record it as you did before and then try to get back to sleep again.

"Many of you old guys wake up three, four, or five times during the course of a night's sleep. Each time you are jarred to full consciousness, record the specifics of the dream that was just interrupted by your involuntary reaction to it.

"After you wake up for the last time, go directly to your computer and input these long suppressed recollections, editing and augmenting content as you proceed.

"Don't wait until later in the day because if you delay the recording and editing process for any substantial period of time you won't be able to understand and decode your scribbled notes. And remember to later review, amend, and correct what you wrote the preceding night. You will be amazed by how much more content will come back to you by way of thought associations. And then read aloud the finished product. This aids the venting and purging process."

She abruptly stopped talking. We sat there for over thirty seconds just looking at each other. I suddenly realized how hot my office had become: I had turned off the air conditioning system about fifteen minutes before her unscheduled arrival. I said, "Let's get out of here, the air conditioning is off."

She rose as I did and asked, "What's your fee for the financial advice?"

"What's your fee for the unsolicited psychological consultation?"

We both began to laugh, spontaneously and heartily. We shook hands, said our good byes, and she turned and walked briskly out the door to a shiny new red Ford Mustang parked a few steps away. I headed in the opposite direction. I took a couple of dozen steps and glanced back. She was waving good-bye as she backed up her car and turned and drove swiftly away.

I don't even know her name. But the stories that follow, remembered as completely and as accurately as I can relate them, are the direct result of her seemingly serendipitous office visit that hot summer day.

PART II
IN THE PIPELINE

WHY I JOINED
THE AIR FORCE

I WAS RUSHING DOWN A LONG AND CLUTTERED COR-
ridor of the hospital at Great Lakes Naval Air Station, Glenview, Illinois, searching frantically for my older brother, Jerry, whom I had
not seen or heard from directly for over three years of World War II.
Jerry was born fourteen months before me and two years after Evelyn,
our older sister. As well as being brothers, Jerry and I had been close
friends and constant companions throughout most of our early childhood years.

We played together and we worked together. One day when I was
nine and he was ten we went to the local agency that distributed the
Sunday morning edition of the *Chicago Tribune*. We had eighty-five
cents between us. We bought ten "surplus" newspapers, each costing
eight and a half cents. We walked up and down the quiet and deserted
streets of our northside neighborhood, shouting "Yoo-hoo, Sunday
morning paper." It took about an hour, but we sold all ten papers and
earned a grand profit totaling fifteen cents!

For over a year thereafter Jerry and I got up at 3 AM each Sunday morning and bought progressively larger numbers of *Tribunes* for a
growing number of our "regular customers" until we had a well-struc-
tured route of over one hundred newspaper readers. Along the way we

saved enough money to buy a new wooden wagon with removable side panels that transported our *Tribunes* so we did not have to carry them on our backs.

A year or two later Jerry and I got lucky. After too long crawling out of warm beds early every Sunday morning, shivering uncontrollably while getting dressed in a heatless room, and going out into the darkness to earn usually no more than a dollar each for a seven- or eight-hour workday delivering Sunday *Tribunes,* I got a "normal" six-day-a-week job. I began to sell all of the daily Chicago newspapers (*Tribune, Sun-Times, Daily News*) for three dollars a week, plus tips, from a large black metal newsstand on the southwest corner of Western and Lawrence Avenues, in front of the entrance to the Hollywood Restaurant, where they made truly delicious double malted milk shakes. I worked from 3:30 PM until 7:00 PM Monday through Friday after school and 10:00 AM until 7:00 PM on Saturdays.

There were four other news stands at the convergence of Western, Lawrence, and Lincoln Avenues (now known as Lincoln Square), with a concrete "island" in the center where a red bearded, burly, and likeable old guy named Morrie presided over this cluster of newspaper retail sales. I persuaded Morrie to hire Jerry when some other kid failed to show up two days in a row (my brother just happening to be there and fully available for immediate employment). Again, Jerry and I quickly developed regular customers who changed streetcars at this busy intersection. Remembering them by their appearance and the newspapers they bought on their way to and from work each day, I provided fast and friendly service with a wide and happy smile. The tips that resulted were good and the chocolate milk shakes were even better!!

But after a year or so we quit the newspaper business, purchasing matching red and white Admiral bicycles (we had been giving half of our earnings each week to our mother, saving two dollars, and "squandering" the rest). It was now summertime and each day we would make peanut butter and jelly sandwiches, pack them away with spending money in the secret metal compartment between the bicycle seat and the handlebars, and explore the northern suburbs of the city along the Chicago River as well as the winding and hilly bike trails along its eastern bank.

We would be gone each day for the entire day! We had some great times and varied childhood adventures together that entire summer, just Jerry and me.

That autumn we went back to school. I got a job as a dishwasher and soda jerk at the Sugar Bowl, an excellent soda fountain and lunch counter at the corner of Sunnyside and Western Avenues and just across the street from my grade school. I was now earning ten to fifteen dollars for a twenty- to thirty-hour workweek. Jerry got a job somewhere else, and thereafter, we were always working part time during the school year and full time during summers. Our good times together were much fewer.

In November of 1942 my brother reached his sixteenth birthday and wanted to enlist in the Marine Corps. When he approached my mother to request that she sign the parental consent form then legally required, she flatly rejected the idea. As he was very disappointed and disturbed by her refusal, he proceeded to deliberately flunk out of high school. I remember sitting at the wooden desk directly in front of him while taking a test in a geometry class (as Arthur precedes Gerald on the customary alphabetical seating chart), I glanced over my shoulder at his answer sheet and noticed it was totally void of any writing. So I copied my answers and passed them back to him. He abruptly stood up and walked out the back door of the classroom. The period ended about five minutes later and I walked out the same door. To my surprise he was waiting for me. He grabbed the front of my shirt and sweater with one hand and held me at arm's length. He informed me quite forcefully what he would do to me if I ever did anything like that again.

Coming to the realization that Jerry was determined to fail at high school and was totally committed to military service with the Marines, our mother relented after two or three weeks and signed the consent. Then he was gone: first to Parris Island in South Carolina and eventually overseas to the South Pacific with the Second Marine Division. My brother did not write to me, nor did I write to him.

I am quite sure that my mother wrote frequent letters to him but I don't recall her mentioning any responses. I was a junior or senior in high school when Jerry came back from combat in the South Pacific, having participated in the brutal and bloody invasions of Tarawa, Saipan, and Okinawa. He was first hospitalized at the naval facility on Mare Island near the city of Vallejo in northern California. He was treated there for several months before being transferred to another naval hospital in Farragut, Idaho. Our mother was advised not to visit him as he still had serious physical and emotional issues during this period of recovery. She did, however, receive several telephone calls from Jerry's Marine buddies when they were changing trains and passing through Chicago. They informed her that Jerry had sustained multiple injuries in several island invasions but his left leg had been saved by surgery and his chances of full recovery were excellent. Finally, six months later, Jerry was transferred to the hospital at Great Lakes Naval Air Station, just a short ride from Chicago on the Illinois Central Railroad.

My mother was upset and agitated at the prospect of seeing her first son after this long separation and fearful as to his multiple and unknown physical injuries and mental problems. So before our first visit I convinced her to have a cup of coffee in the coffee shop while I acquired the information needed to locate and visit him. I had decided that I should see him first and alone, so I could prepare my mother for

WHY I JOINED THE AIR FORCE   **25**

the worst if such was necessary. I pushed open a large door that swung inward from left to right. I took a step or two inside a large rectangular room that contained six or eight beds, all occupied by seriously wounded Marines. Several were amputees. A number of them had arms and/or legs heavily bandaged and elevated by weights and pulleys. I looked at their faces and did not see Jerry among them. Two or three wore head bandages and I examined them more closely. But none of them were of my brother's body size or type.

Several of these men were now staring at me. I was about to say "Excuse me, I am looking for Jerry Haarmeyer" when a gruff voice to my right and from below said, "Art, get your ass in here." I took another step into the room and looked past the edge of the door and down, finally glimpsing the head and skinny, sun-tanned neck of someone I could hardly recognize. Jerry had his back to the door with his legs extending toward the sidewall. His left leg was fully encased in a plaster cast integrated with a strange type of full-length leg brace. He appeared to have lost forty to fifty pounds. There were deep and dark hollows under his eyes. He stared at me fixedly for several moments as I tried to conceal the shock and horror that his altered appearance had triggered in me.

Without a greeting of any kind, or even the blink of an eye, he deliberately and slowly stated: "If you enlist in the Marines or the Army I will break your fucking neck!"

FIVE YEARS LATER, UPON COMPLETING ALL REQUIRE-ments for an MBA in accounting and finance in December 1950, and six months after the start of the Korean War, I enlisted as a Basic Trainee in the United States Air Force.

THE PIPELINE TO KOREA

NORTH KOREA BRUTALLY INVADED SOUTH KOREA BY suddenly and unexpectedly pouring massive waves of battle-hardened ground forces across their common border during the early and quiet Sunday morning of June 25, 1950. Within two or three days, I applied for admission to the Aviation Cadet Training Program of the United States Air Force (USAF), along with thousands of other young American males, although I was still six months away from completion of an MBA program.

Many of those so applying for the USAF or Navy flight training programs had been too young for World War II. But in my case, on the day I had turned eighteen years of age in January of 1946 and was subject to the legally required Selective Service physical examination, I had been summarily classified 4-F (physically unfit for military service) due to a previously undetected heart murmur. This rejection was a big surprise and a major disappointment as I had already partially qualified by written examination for entry into a Naval Aviation Cadet Program.

So I graduated from high school in June of 1946 and started college five days later. By way of a program of intensive study, and while working various full-time or part-time jobs, I completed requirements for an MBA within two and a half calendar years after receiving an AA degree. Because a rigorous regime of running and progressively more demanding exercises had eliminated the heart murmur and I was no longer unqualified, I then enlisted in the USAF as a Basic Trainee to protect my status as a prospective Aviation Cadet.

I completed Airman's Basic Training at Sheppard AFB, Wichita Falls, Texas, in the late spring of 1951. Subsequently I began formal Aviation Cadet Training, completing the new six-month Single Observer Program of Basic Navigation Training at Ellington AFB in Houston, Texas, followed by four more months of Norden Bombing and Shoran Training at Mather AFB, at Sacramento, California.

I entered "the pipeline to Korea" when I arrived at Langley Field, Virginia, in the autumn of 1952 as a newly commissioned second lieutenant, a pair of shiny new gold bars carefully affixed to the epaulets on my new blue gabardine dress uniform. Then and there I was crewed with a World War II veteran, a "retread" B-26 pilot, Captain Robert Caulfield (a fictitious surname), and Gunnery Sergeant Jerry Davis, correctly designated in the new USAF as Airman First Class Gerald Davis.

After a brief ground school orientation focused on the flight characteristics and capabilities of the "hot" twin-engine Douglas B-26 light bomber, our new crew began combat training in the aircraft, flying both day and night bombing and strafing mission simulations over the rolling and wooded hills and valleys of Virginia and West Virginia. Unfortunately for Jerry and me, Captain Caulfield quickly proved to be a consummate incompetent both as pilot and aircraft commander, as well as acting like a total horse's ass whether he was in the left seat or not. He had been abruptly reactivated for Korean combat duty from his inactive air force reserve officer status at Long Beach Airport, California, where his reserve B-26 wing was permanently stationed. Apparently he had little prior flying time and/or inadequate training in B-26s, and he demonstrated his many deficiencies on just about every training mission we flew together while at Langley Field.

Jerry Davis, then about twenty-two years of age, had enlisted in the USAF shortly after I did. He completed Basic Training, I believe at either Lackland AFB in San Antonio, Texas, or Shepard AFB, Wichita Falls, Texas. He successfully completed Flight Mechanic's School at Sheppard and then Gunnery School, where he apparently excelled, as he had earned and received a third and extra stripe upon graduation. As Jerry and I became close friends, we talked over our mutual and growing concerns and anxieties about Captain Caulfield's piloting deficiencies and related personality issues. In fact, our aircraft commander nearly killed all three of us on several occasions while we were flying low-level, low-speed practice missions at night in rainy weather over undulating and heavily wooded terrain. He was particularly dangerous on landings.

I was always in the nose of the 26, as bombardier-navigator, from the start of taxiing from the hardstand along the flight line to the threshold of the runway before takeoff, and upon landing and until return to the hardstand after mission completion. So I got to see the Langley runways very up close and personal. The problem with Captain Caulfield was that our B-26 would often stop flying when we were still eight to ten feet above the runway. A fairly heavy aircraft for its size, the B-26 would then make a rapid sequence of multiple and violent "landings" with Captain Caulfield at the controls. The result would be that I was bounced around the Plexiglas nose of the 26 like a ping-pong ball! It was an absolute wonder that we never blew a tire and that I never suffered a concussion.

Captain Caulfield also had frequent difficulty in maintaining requested headings, altitudes, and airspeeds. These major and recurring problems made accurate navigation and precision Norden bombing extremely difficult for me. The result is that "we" got lost several times, and in his mind, our disorientation and my bombing CE (circular

error) was always my fault. Other such issues and concerns are too numerous to mention.

Exacerbating Caulfield's piloting and personality problems was the
unpleasant reality that he treated Jerry and me like we were some lower
form of animal life. Thus, there was minimal crew cohesion and our
morale was nonexistent. But there we were, in the pipeline together, as
B-26 replacement crews were much needed in Korea. When we were
amazingly designated as a "combat-ready" crew, each of us received a
ten-day leave of absence, after which we dutifully reassembled at Stead
AFB, just a few miles north of Reno, Nevada, to begin ten days of
survival training in the heavily snow-covered Sierra Nevada Mountains
surrounding Dog Valley, twenty miles further west and north.

During this program of rigorous training, accomplished on snow-
shoes in deep snowdrifts while traversing and paralleling the ridgelines
of this heavily wooded mountain range, our unstable Captain Caulfield
proceeded to quickly and thoroughly alienate everyone in our fifteen-
member "squadron" (five crews of three members each, led by a Lt.
Colonel Kurek) with his irrational conduct and emotional outbursts.
So upon completion of this last phase of training before departure for
combat operations, Jerry and I were both worried and pessimistic about
our prospects of even getting to Korea, not to mention our chances of
surviving a fifty-mission combat tour of duty with Captain Caulfield as
our pilot.

But then the benign face of good fortune smiled down upon us
in the form of Major John Fortner, an outstanding senior pilot from
our survival squadron and a true "superior officer" in every sense of
the word. He had observed Captain Caulfield's weird and erratic be-
havior as we collectively and painfully trudged back to Stead AFB
through heavy snows while diligently avoiding simulated "capture" by
defender forces patrolling the roads in the valleys below. Major Fortner

had expressed his concern and compassion for Jerry and me during our common struggles through the deep snowdrifts of northern Nevada. Later, while we were assigned to temporary quarters at a tactical combat crew-processing center at Camp Stoneman in Pittsburg, California, en route to South Korea, he took me aside. In a most friendly and fatherly manner he instructed me to confidentially convey to Jerry that he and Lt. Colonel Kurek were engaged in getting Jerry and me "out of this predicament" and that we should patiently forebear any negative, overt reaction to Captain Caulfield's irrational and totally unprofessional statements, conduct, and attitude.

And so it happened, just as Major Fortner had promised. Caulfield, Haarmeyer, and Davis departed Camp Stoneman as a three-man B-26 crew. We boarded a chartered Flying Tiger C-54 transport at Travis AFB in nearby Fairfield, California, and arrived in Tokyo three days later after refueling stops in Honolulu and the island of Guam. Our crew cabbed together to Fuchu, a huge and ugly gray crew-processing compound near downtown Tokyo, with Captain Caulfield continuing to gripe, grumble, and otherwise conduct himself as obnoxiously as before.

Upon arrival, Jerry and I quickly threw our duffel bags on our assigned beds in our separate and unequal sleeping quarters. By agreement, we hurriedly departed Fuchu on foot and separately. We caught a cab on a nearby street corner for a full night of Tokyo adventures. Just two mornings later, the names of AIC Gerald Davis and 2nd Lt. Arthur Haarmeyer were duly posted "on the board" for assignment to Pusan, Korea, together with air transport instructions. And Captain Caulfield's name was conspicuously absent! He soon accosted me as I feigned sleep in the cramped quarters that I shared with four or five other second lieutenants. With a blank but apparently unconvincing face, I pled total ignorance about the absence of his name from the shipment list, whereupon he stalked out of the room in silent rage, never to be seen again by either Jerry or me.

The late afternoon of the second day following, Jerry and I arrived, pilotless but together, at K-9 AFB, Pusan, South Korea, after riding uncomfortably but happily in the cavernous belly of a frigid and drafty Fairchild C-119 transport plane.

THE LAST LOOK BACK

FEAR WAS A CONSTANT AND NAGGING COMPANION on every mission I flew into the skies over North Korea. And fear had its many and varied manifestations: A thin and ever-present film of perspiration over the surface of the body on even the coldest of January and February nights when at altitude the temperature dipped and stayed over thirty degrees below zero. A strange coolness at the base of the stomach even under four thick layers of clothing and a well-functioning electrified flight suit. A sharply elevated awareness of time and place. Heightened senses of sight and sound. The relentless urge toward constant motion satisfied by ceaselessly swinging head and torso left and right and then left again, the better to see anything and everything that might be arching upward and toward us from concealed radar-controlled triple A batteries embedded in mountainsides along our line of flight, up and down deep valleys. The concentrated focus of my primary sight line centered by the curving ribbons of enemy main supply routes that our B-26s relentlessly bombed and strafed night after night. A dry mouth that impelled a chewing motion to stimulate the flow of saliva, by which I hoped to prevent the embarrassing "croaking" sound in my voice when transmitting to my pilot the heading changes that kept us more or less over the twisting and turning railroad tracks and roadways.

My first recollection of any semblance of fear of combat occurred long before I reached Korea. I gazed out a clear cabin window on the left side of a chartered Flying Tiger Airline C-54 as it climbed out on course from Travis AFB, California, and passed over the south tower of the Golden Gate Bridge. We were heading for Hawaii on the first leg of our long overwater flight to Tokyo, Japan.

Just moments before, when we were probably at no more than three or four thousand feet of altitude, I could clearly discern the lighted windows of the towering hotels and office buildings of downtown San Francisco surrounding the darkness of Union Square. The night before, and at about the same time, Major Fortner and I had shared several Seven and Sevens at a friendly, warm, and cozy cocktail lounge called the Yankee Doodle, on Powell Street just off the Square. We were joined by a couple of Air Force officers who had just returned from Japan, where they had been stationed and from where they had flown numerous C-46 (Curtis Commando) air cargo supply missions into South Korea from Brady AFB on the southern Japanese island of Kyushu. I remember how their jovial attitudes suddenly changed when Major Fortner replied, in response to one of their direct questions, that we were bound for South Korea and fifty missions in light bombers, where our constant and customary cargos would be an array of high explosives, fragmentation clusters, and napalm bombs.

As the Golden Gate Bridge and the bright lights of San Francisco faded into the darkness and a low cloud deck behind and below us, I reluctantly turned from the window and was rudely confronted by the imminence of an unknown world and many unknown dangers and uncertainties that lurked within it.

I felt a creeping sensation of apprehension, a strange awareness approaching an unfamiliar sense of fear: fear of the unknown, fear of not being able to perform competently the multiple tasks that I was trained to do, fear of danger, fear of serious injury or a violent death in flight, and the ultimate fear of capture by North Korean peasants and a lingering death by slow torture administered by their fists and feet. And I was suddenly struck by the stark reality that I was, in military speak, "in the pipeline": being relentlessly and rapidly transported to the isolation of combat duty far removed from a civilized country and familiar world. Now there was for me no turning back.

Simply stated, it was my turn to serve. To do otherwise was unthinkable: it was my duty and obligation as a young American male to so serve and perform. So I took the last look back, turning my head and twisting my upper body as far as I could to stare out the small cabin window of the C-54. But the bridge, the city, and my past were gone; only the unknown and menacing future lay ahead.

SLEEPING WITH THE DEAD

I HAD NEVER MET A KOREAN UNTIL MY FIRST DAY IN KO-
rea. And I did not realize until decades later that a major reason for
my respect for and my identification with the plight of the long brutalized people of South Korea, and consequently for my flying and fighting so willingly and earnestly in their defense, was because of my close
daily contact with an innocent seventeen-year-old Korean girl, known
to us simply as Kim, a very common Korean surname for a very uncommon person. Without realizing it, Kim had quickly become for me the
prototype of the silent, oppressed, and ever persevering refugee of the
Korean War: a victim with scant material goods and little future.

I first met Kim when I arrived at the 95th Bomb Squadron, 17th
Bomb Group, at K-9 AFB just a few miles east of the teeming seaport
city of Pusan at an early morning hour and just a few days after Christmas of 1952. I had been assigned to a so-called shack that I would share
over my tour of duty with a succession of company grade B-26 pilots and bombardier/navigators who were continually passing through
K-9 in the process of completing their fifty-mission combat tours. This
crude, roughly constructed dwelling tightly contained eight undefined
rectangular living spaces called "areas," each about ten feet long and six
feet wide. Each of these areas contained a narrow black metal bed frame

covered by a thin mattress, with an olive drab metal footlocker before it, a wooden shelf attached to the rough wall behind and above it, and a horizontal wooden clothes pole hung below it.

The footlocker was for T-shirts, boxer shorts, socks, and other such items of clothing and personal effects. The wooden shelf was for military headgear, baseball caps, windup alarm clocks, personal photographs, whiskey bottles, and assorted souvenirs and personal items. The pole was for hanging first- and second-class uniforms, flight suits, fleece-lined flight jackets, and rarely used civilian clothes.

Kim had been hired by procurement personnel at Wing Headquarters. She was responsible for keeping our clothing clean and in repair, sweeping the shack's rough wooden floor, and washing its inadequate number of small and high windows. Kim kept the oil-burning pot-bellied stove in the center of the shack continually in good operating condition during the long and bitterly cold winter months. I quickly learned that each of us, eight flight officers in number, were to pay Kim five dollars each month for her excellent domestic services. I did not realize until several months later that forty dollars per month had tremendous buying power in the city of Pusan, where she and her younger brother lived quite comfortably upon her earnings. A one thousand won note, a basic unit of South Korean currency at that time, was so reduced in buying power by rampant inflation that it was then worth only sixteen cents in American money. Even so, I always gave her an additional five dollars monthly, even after I learned of its considerable local value. I later learned that most of the other guys were equally or more generous, as we seemed to sense that Kim and her little brother would soon be facing very hard times.

When I first arrived at my assigned shack, Kim was sitting on a footlocker on the left side of the room. She was staring at the bed across from her, where the mattress had been folded back so that half of its springs were exposed. I clumsily opened the door and thrust my heavy and cumbersome duffel bag inside before noticing that she was very quietly weeping. She looked up at me, startled, with tears streaming down her face. She rose to her feet and stepped back. I walked in and lowered the bag upon the top of the footlocker in front of the empty bed. As I stood up, I stared at her. I started to speak, but she rushed by me and fled from the shack.

I looked around at my new home away from home. The seven other areas were neat and orderly in appearance and showed every sign of current occupancy. Each bed was nicely made up and the clothing at each location was neatly arranged and displayed. There being no sheets or blankets in sight, I extended the folded mattress down and across the lower half of the empty bed, laid down, and promptly fell asleep. Having a major sleep deficit from travel and keeping late hours in Tokyo the nights before, I was sound asleep in seconds. I slept until approximately twelve noon, when several flight crewmen walked in and I was awakened by their noisy arrival. Introductions were made and I was invited to join them for lunch. When we got back from the officers club I found that my bed had been made, my duffel bag had been unpacked, and my gear was properly positioned in the foot locker and on the shelf and clothes pole.

Kim was nowhere in sight. My new buddies told me it was her job to do what she had just done. I truly appreciated this unexpected service, as unpacking was a task that I never enjoyed. However, it was a personal service that I had not experienced before, and it disturbed me; I felt that my privacy had somehow been violated. Belatedly, I remembered that I had hidden some money in a sock and wondered if it would still be there. I quickly found all of my socks neatly folded and placed in the top tray of the footlocker. All eight ten-dollar bills were still in one of the socks, just as I had placed them. Kim surely must have felt this paper money as she handled the sock and placed it in the tray. I immediately felt regret and remorse: I had suspected that she might have stolen some or all of it. I can well imagine that she may have been sorely tempted.

Kim did not return to the shack that afternoon, although I learned that each day, six days a week, she generally stayed until 1500 hours, when an open two-and-a-half ton truck pulled up in front of the squadron's operations shack and Kim and other Korean female domestics boarded the truck that took them back to Pusan. When I walked toward the operations shack later that afternoon I saw Kim sitting tall and straight on one of the two long wooden side benches in the back of a truck as it drove away. I wondered where she had been since leaving the shack. She quickly looked away when she noticed that I was staring at her. She was considerably taller than the other house girls as she sat silently among them, chattering noisily around her. And she had fully regained her composure. I suddenly realized that she was one of the most beautiful young women that I had ever seen; she projected an inner tranquility and regal bearing that was truly breathtaking.

The next morning when I awoke at an early hour I discovered how warm and comfortable the shack was. My bed was one of the four beds closest to the old-fashioned potbellied stove, with the other four beds being in the four corners of the shack. It was much colder in the corners of the room and I wondered why no one occupying a bed in a corner had not relocated his personal property and bedding to my new bed when it had first been available.

The stove crackled pleasantly as it sat upon a large enclosed square of clean sand, putting out waves of comforting warmth. Clad only in boxer shorts and a T-shirt, I swung my bare feet to the cold wooden floor and looked around the room. Four beds were occupied by sleeping flight crewmembers. Three were unoccupied, with disarrayed sheets and blankets upon them. With her back toward me, Kim was making up the bed in the furthest corner. I put on my lucky pair of comfortable brown gabardine pants, a heavy and coarse winter flight suit, and clumsy fleece-lined flying boots and headed out the door for a brisk and short walk to the latrine for a shower and a shave.

Because of the primitive nature of the base's human waste removal system, the latrine was one place where one did not linger any longer than necessary, so I quickly returned to our shack. Kim was gone. I wondered what I had done to offend her. I reflected upon my brief contacts with her but could not remember anything offensive about my conduct that would have disturbed her, except that I had not yet spoken to her.

I walked to our rather primitive officers club, ravenously hungry. In fact, I was always hungry. I was then five feet and eleven inches tall and weighed but one hundred and forty pounds. They served a hearty breakfast twenty-four hours a day at the OC. Combat crews were always coming and going, and breakfast to us could never be too early or too late. Two of my new squadron buddies whom I had met the day before were just finishing their breakfasts. I joined them and they introduced me to several other young officers at the long communal table. When these other guys left the table I asked about Kim. I told them that she seemed not to like me and I did not wish to further offend her. They looked at each other for what seemed like thirty seconds. Then one of them, a first lieutenant who was close to finishing his fifty-mission tour, informed me that I shouldn't be disturbed; I should continue to be friendly, cordial, and respectful, and things would improve day by day.

Then he explained: The space that I was now occupying had been that of a first lieutenant, a highly competent and well-respected pilot, with several minor children, who had not returned from his forty-eighth bombing mission over North Korea several nights before and consequently had been duly classified as "missing in action." He added that this pilot had treated Kim with great kindness and gentle humor, almost as if she were one of his own daughters. He further explained that Kim had cried uncontrollably every time she glanced at his empty bed and that I must undoubtedly remind her of the sudden loss of his sincere friendship and compassion.

And then, for the first time, I realized why the choice bed space next to the old potbellied stove had continued to be unoccupied until my arrival: nobody dared sleep on a dead man's bed.

ORPHANS

RAMROD STRAIGHT, AIRMAN FIRST CLASS JERRY DAVIS, my air gunner, and I stood at attention before Colonel Delwin D. Bentley, a command pilot and squadron commander of the 95th Bomb Squadron at K-9 AFB. He sat in silence after returning our salutes, reading from the content of Jerry's 201 File (personnel folder) for what seemed like an hour in the cold, barren operations shack, empty but for the three of us. Still looking down at Jerry's assignment orders, he said, with what seemed more than mild disdain, "Orphans! Not two more orphans!" He fixed his eyes upon Jerry's face and commanded: "Sergeant, get your ass over to the Motor Pool, you're a truck driver until I get you crewed up. With your record you might be useful." With that combination of abrupt order and implied compliment, Jerry saluted, hardly waited for a return salute, and scurried out the door without the slightest glance in my direction. The colonel then focused his attention on the contents of my personnel folder as I continued my stiff "at attention" posture. I suddenly realized that either the intense cold or my apprehension of this large and menacing colonel was causing my legs to tremble uncontrollably and, hopefully, unnoticeably.

I continued to stare fixedly at a spot on the crude wall directly above and behind this dour colonel until he finally looked up at me. He asked: "What the hell are you doing here, lieutenant?" I was startled, being totally unprepared for the question. During my short tenure and limited experience in the USAF, checking into a new base with a new duty assignment had always been a relatively informal and pleasant procedure. My immediate response was the standard and appropriate one, and I answered him in the most steady and strong voice that I could muster: "Reporting for duty, sir!"

His reply, with some slightly concealed measure of impatience and disapproval, was a challenging question: "Isn't that rather obvious, lieutenant?" At this point, my apprehension was escalating rapidly into fear and panic, as I still had no idea which answer he sought. So I weakly responded: "Sir, I don't understand the question, sir."

He leaned back in his battered leather chair, fixed me again with his tired, watery, and piercing gray eyes, and stated in a dull but patient voice: "Let's put it this way. Here you are, in the anus of Asia, checking in for combat duty, and you have no reason to be here. You've got an MBA in accounting from a high-priced university. You could be riding a desk at the Pentagon right now. So why the hell are you here?"

My immediate and unthinking reply: "I always wanted to be here, sir. I can always be an accountant."

He gazed at me for what seemed like five minutes, as if calculating the exact degree of my sincerity and/or sanity. Then he asked: "You see that desk over there?"

My eyes followed his to a small gunmetal gray desk in the corner next to an old vertical metal file cabinet. Without waiting for my response he instructed: "That's your desk, lieutenant, until I can figure out what to do with you. In the meantime, you are my assistant administrative officer. So just get to work. The file cabinet goes with the desk. Get well familiar with its contents."

He then abruptly stood up and walked around his desk as I saluted. Out the door he went, throwing back over his shoulder a declaration to the effect that he needed a haircut and that he would be back within the hour. I was left standing there alone in this barren Quonset hut without even the foggiest idea of what my duties were as the assistant administrative officer to an iron-assed bird colonel.

On the wall behind the colonel's desk was a Table of Organization and Equipment (TO&E) for the 95th Bomb Squadron. I studied it carefully and realized that there was an operations officer designation with a name penciled in below it. There were maintenance officer and armament officer categories followed by names and ranks. There were also several vertical listings of three-member Douglas B-26 combat crews, approximately twenty-five to thirty in number, each naming a pilot (aircraft commander), a bombardier-navigator, and an air gunner. I stood there totally confused, as there was no mention anywhere on that TO&E of an administrative officer for the 95th. So how could I be an assistant administrative officer to a nonexistent administrative officer? I walked to the small battered metal desk and sat on the cold metal folding chair before it, asking myself how I had gotten into this predicament.

Jet-black Douglas B-26 Invaders were landing on the adjacent runway, returning from North Korea with empty wing racks and bomb bays, while I was confined to a small corner of a grubby Quonset hut with a desk, a folding chair, and a file cabinet. I did not volunteer for *this!* Jerry and I had first had the misfortune (or so we then thought) to be crewed with an old, incompetent pilot who upon our arrival in Japan had been withheld from combat because of something called "dangerous flying tendencies." Then I had lost Jerry to the 95th Bomb Squadron's motor pool while I was stuck here! I had lost my pilot, and now I had lost my gunner! I knew how and I knew why. But why me?

As I stared out a dirty window at the returning combat crews, laughing and joking as they passed by in the backs of open trucks on their base perimeter ride to mission debriefing, I was as depressed as I had ever been in my twenty-four-year life. Little did I then realize, or even vaguely appreciate, that this apparently dire situation would present rare opportunities for a myriad of enriching but all too frequently terrifying experiences. Little did I realize the unique opportunities that these apparent setbacks had created for me. In fact, it took me over fifty years to process and fully appreciate the fortuitous combination of perspectives that my being a figurative "orphan" had coincidentally bestowed upon me.

I was soon to experience the brutality and unexpected beauty of air combat in stark form and living color over the next seven months. It would provide me with ever-changing admixtures of activities, experiences, and emotions that were subliminally but indelibly imprinted upon my memory and psyche. It gave me the rare chance to live and feel the thrill of flying and soaring; the tingling anticipation and excitement of the hunt; the anxiety, fear, and sheer terror of the threat of sudden and imminent loss of life; the mind-numbing guilt and remorse in killing, collaterally but necessarily, unknowable numbers of innocent, unseen civilians who were commingled with the attacking hordes of communist foot soldiers; the relief and exhilaration in surviving yet another combat mission; and the sense of doing something really important and truly meaningful as evidenced by the visible appreciation and self-conscious smiles of some of the brave, impoverished, and displaced Korean refugees that I came to know and respect. But of equal or greater value, as I sat at my little gray desk in the corner, I would be able to listen intently, observe closely, and assimilate well the essentials of leadership, the concepts, tactics, and techniques of aerial combat, and the basic principles and practices of human resource management and military logistics that revealed to me how air-to-ground combat in a dark and deadly war was effectively and efficiently waged.

JUST ANOTHER
AIRPLANE DRIVER

JERRY AND I THOUGHT THAT WE WERE THERE TO MEET our new pilot, a fellow named Crow. And there were our names, one after the other (Crow, Capt.; Haarmeyer, 2 Lt.; Davis, A/IC), listed together as a combat crew on the daily Battle Order posted on the front exterior wall of the operations shack. (I well remember being intrigued and puzzled by the title of this notification. The words "Flight Schedule" or "Mission Schedule" seem more appropriate and accurate than "Battle Order." I concluded that Battle Order must be a vestige of earlier wars.) Over the seven months to follow our names would be similarly posted in the same logically descending order of authority and responsibility in the aircraft: as pilot (aircraft commander), bombardier-navigator, and air gunner.

The Battle Order also stated, to our disappointment, that we were scheduled for take-off at 1000 hours, not that morning but the next morning, on a practice bombing and strafing mission. It instructed us to assemble as a crew at the same location at 0800 hours the following day for truck transport to the parachute shack, then to our mission briefing, and finally to our assigned B-26 for pre-flight and take-off.

Since our arrival at K-9 AFB, Jerry had been driving combat crews to and from the 95th Bomb Squadron's area, our flight line and parachute shack, and mission briefings and debriefings at Group HQ on the other side of the runway. I had been typing, editing, copying, and filing an array of standard military documents, such as procurement orders, personnel orders, letters, and memoranda to Group and Wing HQ, and so on. Now, after ten days, Jerry and I were together again, to do what we were trained and strongly motivated to do. So we were eager with anticipation but very curious and anxious about the flying proficiency, personality, and character of Captain Crow.

The next day, at least fifteen minutes before the designated hour, there was a large number of combat crews, engaged in talking, horseplay, smoking, laughing, and generally milling around the operations shack in a friendly and relaxed manner. All of us were dressed basically the same, in various combination of full flight gear, except without parachute harnesses or life preservers.

Jerry and I walked up and stood together on the edge of this melee. We were looking for this guy named Crow and hoping that he was looking for us. We knew absolutely nothing about him, other than his pilot status and rank. While we looked about and waited, we had a chance to renew the easy and close relationship that had started back at Crew Training at Langley AFB in Virginia. Now, we were about to meet the pilot with whom we would be flying all of the fifty missions that then constituted a standard combat tour of duty.

We didn't have long to wait. Within but a few minutes a clear eyed, sun tanned, and sturdily built captain materialized before us and informally and jovially inquired if we were the "two guys looking for an airplane driver." I was impelled to salute him and I probably should have, and I am sure that Jerry would have followed my lead. However, I felt or knew instinctively that this captain would have been made uncomfortable by such a reaction. And from that moment on and throughout the next seven months during which we regularly flew together as a productive and totally compatible B-26 crew, there was never any saluting done among us, nor any semblance of either military status or social differentiation.

There was one exception. Bob Crow had heard that Jerry had earned an extra stripe by qualifying as "top gunner" in his gunnery class. So we would almost always address him as "Sarge," as it seemed to provide this fine and excessively modest young guy with a justifiable sense of pride of accomplishment.

That morning we flew southwest to Mundo Island in the Straits of Japan and just a few miles off the southern coastline of South Korea. There I dropped a series of one-hundred-pound practice bombs by visual Norden bombing techniques on a designated aiming point located at the convergence of two sharply vertical rocky surfaces and precisely at water level, and upon different headings and from different altitudes, ranging between eight to twelve thousand feet. Because the Norden bombsight was most accurate within this range of altitudes, it was most frequently utilized in our combat operations against stationary targets during daylight hours. My calculated CE was pleasantly and surprisingly small that day. Jerry got in some excellent gunnery practice runs. And Bob flew the 26 like it was a natural extension of his body; he was so smooth on the controls that Jerry and I could not determine exactly when the wheels left the runway and when they returned to it. And everything else he did at the controls was accomplished with ease, fluidity, and authority. He was a natural pilot!

For Bob Crow this practice mission was just another routine training flight. However, for Jerry and me it was a most memorable and pleasurable one: Visibility was virtually unlimited. We were riding in a great airplane. All three of us had demonstrated our technical competence. Jerry and I were crewed with a highly proficient and truly likeable pilot, and together we were already a compatible and happy crew. Finally, all was indeed right with the world!

PART III
JOINING THE BATTLE

THE DOUGLAS
B-26 INVADER

FIRST CAME THE TWIN ENGINE DOUGLAS A-20 HAVOC, and then its enlarged, improved, and refined successor, the Douglas A-26 Invader, which began to roll off the Douglas Aircraft Company's production line in Tulsa, Oklahoma, in August of 1943, having made its first test flight just thirteen months earlier. The A-26B and the A-26C were identical except that the B variant had a hard nose equipped with an additional eight .50 caliber Browning machine guns (aligned vertically in two rows of four guns each), whereas the C variant had a soft nose, that is, a Plexiglas-enclosed compartment equipped with the then highly secret Norden bombsight and a small instrument panel that were utilized by a single crew member, a dual-qualified bombardier-navigator. The other two members of the crew were the pilot (there was no co-pilot) in the left seat of the cockpit and an air gunner operating remote-controlled twin .50 caliber Browning machine guns in a cramped dorsal compartment aft of the bomb bay. The right cockpit seat was occupied by the bombardier-navigator when the crew was flying the hardnosed B-26B variant.

The Douglas A-26 Invader began its long and brilliant military career during World War II when it entered combat with the Fifth Air Force in the Southwest Pacific theatre on June 23, 1944, successfully bombing the Japanese-held islands near Manokwari. Just three months later, in September 1944, the A-26 arrived in Europe for permanent assignment to the Ninth Air Force. The B-26 Invader entered combat operations two months later on the 19th of November flying out of the Midlands of England, attacking by day ground targets in both France and Germany.

In the *Pilot Training Manual for A-26,* drafted in 1944 by the flight staff at the 4400th Combat Crew Training Group at Langley AFB, Virginia, it is directly but dramatically stated:

> The Douglas A-26 Invader has been described as a glorified A-20, a new fighter-bomber, and a cross between a B-26 and a B-25. Actually the Invader is a new airplane substantially modified late in its design to meet the pinpoint requirements of the theater commanders. No other medium bomber has the versatility, the speed or the tremendous combination of striking power the A-26 has. At its altitude it's as fast as a fighter, carries more bombs farther and faster than any other medium bomber and packs a nosefull [sic] of strafing firepower and two torrents of protective firepower at the same time.
>
> The combat history of the A-26 is short but brilliant. It has lived up to and surpassed the results that the designers and the AAF theater commanders expected of it. The new A-26 groups had the first opportunity to show their stuff in the fall of 1945 [sic] when the German Army under Von Runstedt made its powerful counter-offensive in the Ardennes and forced the historic Belgian Bulge in the allied lines. The sorties and the withering damage by the A-26 in support of our ground forces was eloquently stated by Von Runstedt when he was taken prisoner. He said: "But for the savage Allied strafing attacks our counter-offensive would have driven on to Paris."

As this book is being written A-26 groups are leaving for the Pacific. You as a new A-26 pilot will soon be a member of one of these groups and it is up to you to write the A-26 history against the Japanese.

Make no mistake about it, the Invader is not a small boy's flying machine. It is a high-speed airplane with a high wing loading. It requires exact procedures, top flying technique, and headwork to exploit its striking power. So use this manual, study it, learn it! It represents the combined experience to date of the factory engineering test pilots, AAF test pilots, and your instructors, who have many hundreds of hours of A-26 know-how upon which to draw.

The Douglas A-26 was driven by two Pratt & Whitney R-2800–27 18-cylinder, double row radial, 2,000 horsepower engines. It had a maximum speed of 376 miles per hour, an operational range of 2,914 miles, and a ceiling of 24,500 feet. It measured 70 feet wing tip to wing tip, and 51 feet from nose to tail. It weighed 22,360 pounds empty and 41,800 pounds fully loaded. It carried a wide array of bombs, napalm tanks, machine guns, and rockets, usually maxing out with 16-to–18 .50 caliber Browning machine guns while hauling over 5,000 pounds of high explosives and/or rockets and full gas tanks.

It should be noted that the Martin Marauder was the first Army Air Corps medium bomber rendered fully operational, designated as the B-26. Years later, and after many delays in modifications and flight testing, the Douglas Invader was finally approved and made fully operational, entering into air combat over Europe in 1944 and later in the South Pacific. To avoid confusion in distinguishing these two aircraft one from the other, the Douglas Invader was formally identified as the Douglas A-26 and continued to be so labeled until 1947, well after the end of World War II.

By the time the Korean War began in June of 1950, the Martin Marauder had been fully retired from military service, and therefore the Douglas A-26 became officially and commonly known as the B-26 Invader. Consequently, in this book when an aircraft is identified as a B-26, or simply as a "26," it will be understood that the aircraft so designated is the Douglas B-26 Invader.

DOLLAR RIDES

THE DAY AFTER JERRY DAVIS AND I WERE "CREWED UP" with Bob Crow to fly a practice bombing and gunnery training mission to Mundo Island, we were separated again. All three of us would fly the first two of our fifty combat missions, our so-called dollar rides, with different, combat-experienced B-26 crews. We rode along simply as passengers—none of us had any substantial functions or duties to perform during the course of either of these actual night bombing missions over North Korea—but we did receive full "credit" for two combat missions anyway. For all practical purposes, we were merely spectators, attentive observers, earning free mission points for observing and learning, or attempting to learn, the established and approved combat operational tactics, techniques, and procedures of the squadron.

It was my good fortune to be scheduled for both of my "dollar ride" missions with Captain George Vioux, a proficient senior pilot from Oklahoma, and Captain Tom Cameron, a skilled bombardier-navigator from West Texas. (It turned out that this was a scheduling error, as it was intended that each "dollar rider," read "rookie," fly with two different crews.)

On my first mission with Vioux and Cameron I sat in the jump seat and learned practically nothing. I did not know it was referred to generally as the "idiot seat" until several days later, when I had the opportunity to share my experiences with another recent arrival from the ZI

(Zone of the Interior, i.e., the United States), who said he had learned practically nothing on his first ride. One reason I learned so little during my first venture over North Korea was that the jump seat was a very, very confined space located directly behind the right seat in the compact B-26 cockpit, and from there my visibility within and beyond the aircraft was very restricted. Furthermore, the range of motion of head, arms, and legs was almost nil, with my movements further reduced by four layers of heavy clothing needed to protect against the rigors of twenty to forty degree below zero temperatures. Adding to my orientation and learning deficit was that throughout the mission I had no intercom connection equipment (a headset with either a throat or boom mike), so I was totally unable to hear what the crewmen were saying in coordinating with each other, nor could I speak to them. Also, the noise level in the uninsulated B-26 while airborne was horrendous, so being without a headset was like being in the middle of a hurricane . . . unprotected ears, a lot of continuous noise, and no communication or intelligence. The cumulative effect of these multiple and negative factors was that I could see little of what was happening outside the aircraft, nor could I understand what was happening inside the aircraft.

Back on the ground, while we were being bounced around in the back of the open crew transport truck and at mission debriefing, I learned something more about what had been accomplished on the mission and how it was accomplished. I also learned, much later, that the reason for my seven-hour confinement in the idiot seat rather than in the right seat was that there was another dollar rider in the nose compartment, much older and of higher military rank than a recently graduated aviation cadet. So Captain Cameron sat in the right seat as navigator that night to enable this older bombardier trainee in the nose to concentrate on finding and hitting, or attempting to find and hit, targets of opportunity.

After landing I immediately gave everybody on board a dollar bill after they got unstrapped and climbed down from that little black bastard (as the B-26 was often so designated, especially if there were any mechanical or electrical malfunctions to register with its crew chief). I even gave a buck to the over-age-in-grade novice bombardier. It was a squadron ritual or tradition that a new, raw crewman was required to "pay for his free ride" by handing a one dollar MPC (military pay certificate) to each member of the host crew. MPCs were instruments of monetary exchange, usually in $1, $5, $10, and $20 denominations, used by the U.S. military to compensate troops while overseas to prevent U.S. currency from falling into the hands of the enemy in the event of death or capture. These units of monetary exchange were generally the size and shape of American currency but visually different in color and general appearance.

I subsequently heard that as the war wore on, these old traditions and rituals were breaking down, and I could see why. In those days, a dollar bill had the purchasing power of ten to fifteen of today's dollar bills, so the frequent sentiment was, "Why give away that much money to a stranger who was not really doing anything other than his military duty?"

My second "dollar ride" mission with pilot George Vioux and bombardier-navigator Tom Cameron was a very different story and a much better experience! I sat next to George in the right seat of the B-26, where I had a well-functioning headset with attached throat mike. And here is where I performed the customary duties of the gunner, keeping a current and accurate strike report as I got the data from Tom in the nose during the course of his bomb runs and strikes against enemy rolling stock on one of the red routes west of the seaport of Wonsan. I also kept a roving eye outside the cockpit for triple A and an eye inside for red warning lights on the complex control panel to detect and report indications of engine or instrument malfunction or irregularity.

George was a great big guy who was reputed to have been an outstanding college football player. He stood well over six feet tall and must have weighed at least 225 pounds. Tom, on the other hand, was no more than five-seven and 135 pounds. Tom was very mild mannered and had a delightful and impish sense of humor. (However, he did display startlingly intense anger and hostility if anyone referred to the pair as "Mutt and Jeff," which did happen at mission debriefing following our second ride.)

These two highly experienced and skillful flight officers were truly a thing of beauty to behold when engaged in air-ground combat. They had a free and easy working relationship that was a sheer delight to observe and admire. They worked amazingly well as a team in identifying, tracking, and bombing rolling stock in the darkness of a cold and cloudy night over a lightly traveled and twisting and turning armed reconnaissance route. If there were supply trucks to be hit, they did a helluva good job in approaching and targeting them. That night there were several low and troublesome cloud decks, but with a near full moon and sufficient frequency of cloud breaks, George and Tom were able to make deep and sudden penetrations down to two hundred to five hundred feet of terrain clearance along the valley floors, when possible and advisable. Thus they could surprise and devastatingly strike small clusters of trucks, whose drivers were undoubtedly well convinced that there would be no threat of air attacks because of the cover of darkness and the thick clouds decks overhead.

I thoroughly enjoyed being an active participant on this free ride: George and Tom made me feel like a member of the team, and I tried very hard to make a genuine contribution. Although there was a lot of light banter, jokes, and ribbing going on during the inbound and outbound legs of the mission, over enemy territory things were serious and intense. These guys were motivated, competent, and competitive: if there were targets, they were out to get them, with no horsing around. This time after climbing down the side of the B-26, I gave George and Tom each a dollar bill with both pleasure and alacrity, not just to honor an established tradition (already becoming uncontrollably for me a superstition) but also to show in a very small way my sincere appreciation for their helpfulness and their friendship.

MAXIMIZING TRAIN
AND ROAD KILL

COLONEL BENTLEY WALKED BRISKLY INTO THE OP-
erations shack early one frigid January morning and informed
me that I would be riding with him and his "regular" flight engineer/
gunner the next night. I later learned that Captain Robert Abelman,
his "regular" bombardier-navigator, was then overstaying an R&R in
Tokyo, to the colonel's mild displeasure. My not totally sincere response
was something quick and immediate, such as, "That's great, colonel,
it will be a pleasure." So later that afternoon, when the ops shack was
empty except for the colonel and me, I got a quick but valuable briefing
on the way the colonel did military business north of the bomb line.

Colonel Bentley was a natural as an instructor, and it was my good
fortune to be one of his students very early in my tour of duty with the
squadron. It seemed that he had a well-conceived SOP (standard operational procedure) for just about everything, including his battle-honed
strategies and tactics in maximizing train and road kill. A reasonably
accurate paraphrase of his instructions that afternoon is as follows:

Start gradual descent from assigned inbound altitude after crossing the front line and bomb line, "ghosting in" by gliding down with
reduced power settings to three thousand feet at entry point into the assigned MSR (main supply route) of the enemy and at a reduced airspeed

of 180 knots. Enter the MSR at or near its mid-point, turning either up or down the targeted valley depending upon the comparative values (the "richness or poorness") of the observed targets. Hit the "best target" first, giving top priority to *any* locomotive regardless of the number of railcars it is hauling or its direction of movement. The second priority is the longest truck convoy heading south (almost always fully loaded with cargo or foot soldiers). The third priority is the longest truck convoy heading north. The fourth priority is the bombardier-navigator's judgment call.

Approach targets from their back ends and over-fly the locomotive or the lead truck. Drop the first wing bomb (outer left) on the track or road at the lowest safe altitude an eighth of a mile ahead of the lead vehicle to induce the engineer or lead driver to panic and stop and abandon his train or truck. If either target is close to a tunnel mouth, select the tunnel mouth as the aiming point and concentrate on target alignment. Then, even if your strike is "short," or "under," the result will be a rail- or road-cut; if "long," or "over," it could cause a blockage of the tunnel with a rockslide from above the tunnel mouth.

Perform a racetrack pattern and drop the second five-hundred-pound bomb just short of the train's last railcar, or just behind the last truck in the convoy, in order to seal off possible escape.

Then go back and forth over the train or convoy but approach successive bomb runs at slightly different angles to make small arms fire and triple A fire less accurate, dropping usually two bombs at close intervals by use of the reflex sight affixed to the top of the bombsight housing. Fly lower (fifty to one hundred feet of terrain clearance) consistent with safety and limitations of visibility when splashing napalm bombs, and at a minimum of five hundred feet of terrain clearance when dropping five-hundred pound GPs (general purpose bombs) to avoid shrapnel damage to the aircraft from the cumulative effects of bomb bursts in close sequence and released from low altitudes. If hit by searchlights the pilot will go "balls to the wall," by quickly advancing the knobs of the two throttle levers full forward to the firewall while turning sharply in a steep climb, and head out to sea to enable the crew to attempt to recover night vision. The right seat guy (usually the gunner) keeps his head and shoulders down and his eyes inside the cockpit at all times while leaning close to the instrument panel to continually check for red (warning) lights in order to alert the pilot of any malfunction.

Fully empty the bomb bay before the pilot starts making multiple machine gun passes. He should "stitch the tracks" with short bursts (to prevent overheating and weapon jamming) of .50 caliber Browning machine gun fire to suppress small arms and automatic weapons fire.

Stay over the MSR, consistent with preserving adequate fuel reserves, to destroy and/or damage other vehicles coming down the line behind a stopped train or convoy. If you can't destroy or damage, then harass and delay movement. Extend time over target to practical limit. Expend all .50 caliber rounds even if target sightings are marginal.

Before leaving the strike zone the bombardier-navigator will verify exact location of strike(s) to assist the pilot in providing target data to Ground Control for transmission to the next B-26 coming into the area, to enable him to do further damage to rolling stock or for this data to be passed on to daylight strike forces for further combat action or for acquisition of photography of the destruction and damage caused.

SUSTAINED AND RELENTLESS

"They know we're coming. We know they'll be waiting."

—Colonel Delwin D. Bentley,

USAF, January 1953

OUR AIR-GROUND OPERATIONS IN THAT LAST YEAR of combat in Korea could be described as an entrepreneurial war, given the character of our primary mission: Most of us flew alone, we flew mostly at night, and we flew frequently without defensive weapons and almost always without the protective cover of fighter-interceptors. We bombed and strafed both stationary and moving targets on the ground and within an assigned but somewhat discretionary geographic area, at very low altitudes, and under all types of weather conditions, for an undesignated period of three to five hours over targeted areas for which we had sole responsibility and total accountability. We most often sought, identified, fixated, and attacked targets of opportunity without benefit of sonar, radar, or other electronic equipment or assistance. We conceived and implemented our own plans of attack and evasion. I visually selected and bombed our targets by use of the most basic bombing equipment and techniques, manually, and frequently dropping old and unstable World War II ordnance, with Colonel Bentley or Captain Crow then finishing them off visually and most effectively and efficiently with old six-inch-long rounds fired from World War II vintage .50 caliber Browning machine guns.

We performed these hazardous and solitary night missions, then generally and euphemistically referred to as "armed reconnaissance missions," by patrolling our assigned target areas back and forth and then back again. These areas varied in size and configuration but were almost always along stretches, 80 to 140 nautical miles in length, of enemy main supply routes. These so-called MSRs were generally long, rectangular segments of steep, rugged mountainous terrain located along and on both sides of rivers flowing down deep valleys that almost always intersected with strategically and tactically vital railroad tracks and/or roadways. These transportation lines were punctuated by numerous viaducts, bridges, and tunnels and also contained railway spurs and secondary roads and trails that fed into them. We exercised almost total decision-making authority and discretion as to the targets we were authorized or permitted to select and destroy if possible, or at least damage or disable if total destruction was not possible. We had a wide range of categories of additional targets to consider for bomb and machine gun attacks, such as munitions and/or fuel dumps, shoreline shipping facilities, anti-aircraft artillery emplacements and/or radar sites, machine gun nests, communications facilities, docks and warehouse structures, coastal freighters, and even long columns of coolies with large wooden A-frames strapped to their backs and upon which huge amounts of weapons, fuel, and supplies would be carried for long distances. And surprisingly, we occasionally happened upon a mule or camel train during hours of first or last light.

Interspersed among the relatively few rail lines and major, well-surfaced roads in North Korea were mazes of interconnecting, supporting, and poorly constructed and maintained roads, trails, and cart and footpaths that carried a large proportion of the men and materiel of warfare from Russia, Manchuria, and China by way of small trucks, wagons, carts, oxen, and A-frame carriers. So when our nightly bombing and strafing raids caused rail and road cuts, started rockslides that blocked tunnel mouths, and knocked down bridges interrupting rail and road operations, these mazes of secondary roads, trails, and footpaths assumed the major burden of keeping the reinforcements and supplies flowing relentlessly to the communists' front lines.

Indeed, one of the major and direct consequences of our sustained and relentless interdiction of MSRs and ancillary and secondary roads, trails, and cart and footpaths was the use by communist forces of staggering numbers of men, women, children, oxen, etc. As beasts of burden, they were forced to carry heavy, and frequently extremely heavy, loads of food, weapons, ammunition, heating oil, clothing, and fuel, literally on their backs for long distances over winding and mountainous trails and foot paths in remote country far removed from major roads, railroads, and sleeping facilities.

Despite all of our efforts, the combined air force, marine, and naval air operations did not and could not stop the flow of men and materiel to communist frontline forces: we simply did not have enough aircrews, aircraft, and logistical structure and support to achieve that result. But we did have enough to prevent our communist enemies from assembling sufficient ground forces and accumulating sufficient equipment, ammunition, and supplies to enable them to support and sustain major and successful offensive operations and deep penetrations into South Korea.

It cannot be emphasized too strongly that our collective United Nations Command (UNC) efforts, comprised of well-coordinated but limited air, land, and sea forces, were effective only as a holding action, as none of the political decision-makers of the major powers involved, on either side, wanted to see the war expanded to the extent that World War III would or could be triggered off accidentally. Thus, the operative and maddening "rules of engagement" prevented us and other UNC air forces from bombing the sources of troop reinforcements and re-supply of the materiel of warfare, located along or close to the northern border of North Korea within Russia, China, and Manchuria and, concomitantly, prevented the combined North Korean, Chinese, and Russian communist air forces from penetrating our air space south of the front lines. Therefore, in this last phase of the war North Korea was essentially a chessboard of tactical air-to-air and air-to-ground combat, with our F-86F Sabre pilots maintaining almost total superiority over the Russian-built and Russian, Chinese, and North Korean piloted MiG-15s, thereby enabling us in slow-flying 26s to do our part of the work.

Another major consequence of our ceaseless interdiction of transportation lines was that it forced the communist side to commit, on a permanent basis, very large numbers of work crews (together with large quantities of construction equipment and materials) to live and work next to or close by their many lines of transportation. This proximity was required so workers could quickly replace the destroyed rail lines, roads, bridges, and tunnels, or repair those that were continually being destroyed or bomb damaged. In fact, the communists set up hundreds of work camps, closely spaced and at permanently established points, usually three to five kilometers apart and along MSRs, to achieve fast and effective replacement, reconstruction, or repair of these vital transportation lines and ancillary facilities. As a result, we continued to the end of hostilities to attack and destroy the work camps whenever and wherever located. These construction workers' camps, as well as related fuel and supply dumps, were often located near secondary roads and trails, so we attacked them whenever and wherever we could find them.

Other enemy encampments, hidden short distances off the MSRs, were primitive housing facilities permanently provided as rest stops for communist foot soldiers, who were often forced to march from the Yalu River, the natural boundary that separates North Korea from China and Manchuria, all the way to the front lines close to the 38th Parallel, a distance ranging from approximately one hundred miles to over three hundred miles. That arbitrary boundary had originally divided Korea into North and South at the end of World War II with the surrender of Japan—an expedient political compromise between the Soviet Union and the United States that resulted in equal political dissatisfaction and firmly planted the seeds for the Korean War, the first hot war of the long Cold War.

During one early evening raid in late January or early February of 1953, I luckily saw the glow of campfires up a side canyon about a quarter of a mile north of the MSR that we were then patrolling. This was the first, or possibly the second, of the few missions that I flew with the colonel while his regular bombardier-navigator, Captain Robert Abelman, was in Tokyo on a well-deserved R&R. For about two hours we had been prowling one of the purple routes along the eastern coastline of North Korea, well northeast of Hamhung and Hungnam, but we had found nothing to bomb or shoot. There had been intermittent but thin layers of low clouds and ground fog in the valleys below.

Assuming it was an encampment of communist soldiers on their way to the front, I alerted the colonel to their presence, and he quickly aligned the B-26 for a straight-ahead bomb run. As we approached, heading upwind, there was a break in the clouds and I could see that the encampment appeared to contain about ten to twelve fires in a close cluster. We were at a safe three thousand feet of altitude with a full and rising moon. There was a low but still thin layer of ground fog. I quickly and inaccurately calculated wind speed and direction to be a quartering one off the nose from the north but at minimal velocity.

I dropped all four five-hundred-pound GPs off the wing racks. The first two were off line and well to the right of the campfires, but the third and fourth, also off-line but in sequence, surprisingly touched off several large explosions that triggered a series of secondary explosions of somewhat equal or lesser sizes, brilliantly illuminating the close by snow-covered mountainsides. The colonel then declared, "Let's do that again from 750 feet."

So he circled widely to the right and flew out over the Sea of Japan, descending steadily to 750 feet of terrain clearance upon passing over the shoreline. I toggled open the bomb bay doors while sighting, on almost the original heading up the side road, on the largest sustained fire. The well-delineated mountains rose up on both sides of us as we turned and headed into this narrow and confining target area. On alignment with the largest fire, still burning brightly, I punched out three five-hundred-pounders "early" and three "late." Again we scored major hits, resulting in both brilliant secondary explosions and sustained fires in alignment with our bomb impacts. I reached back to close the bomb bay doors but before I could lean forward again to gaze downward and backward to make a more comprehensive visual bomb damage assessment, a single stream of green tracers passed closely by us, off the right wing tip and from a higher firing point up the mountainside, and from the right and behind us. The colonel saw the tracers before I did. He sharply increased power settings and executed a steep climbing turn to the right to cut off the firing angle of this weapon, which apparently had been fired from some flat area on or in a tunnel recessed into the mountainside. We got out of there very quickly!

We had obviously stumbled upon, and had totally obliterated, a major fuel dump, and I thought that we were through for the night. I was about to give the colonel an initial heading back to base when he announced on intercom, "Let's try to locate that artillery piece and take it out."

I was shocked: To me, this decision was a dangerous one, as the passage up that valley was just too narrow for the aircraft to be maneuvered in the time we'd have to locate the weapon, achieve a good angle shot against it, fire off a short burst from our six machine guns, which were built into the leading edges of the wings and could be fired only in the direction that the plane was heading, and then somehow avoid hitting the mountainside! I was speechless, and horrified. But how could I possibly tell an aircraft commander, who just happened to be a full colonel and my squadron commander, when he should or should not conduct a machine gun attack?

Fortunately, the colonel's gunner, an older crew chief who regularly flew with the colonel and who acted like he had known the colonel all his life, said to him words that I will never forget: "Colonel, don't you think we should quit while we're ahead?"

There was a long silence on intercom, and then Colonel Bentley chuckled and replied, "Donnie (or Ronnie, I'm still reasonably sure it was one or the other), I think you're getting too old for this game."

I was in silent but total agreement with the old gunner. Quite by luck, we had happened upon a small encampment of enemy troops. And solely because of my miscalculation of wind speed and direction, we had taken out a major supply depot that that mountainside gun was intended to protect. So why go back in again? There could be two, three, or four other gun placements with trigger-happy gunners spoiling for revenge. So I made a quick mental calculation, took a wild guess at the correct heading, clicked on intercom, and gave the colonel an initial heading home (my recollection is that it was 210 degrees of magnetic compass heading) without being asked. The colonel chuckled again and said, "Well, I guess I'm outvoted two to one."

He promptly turned steeply to that heading and we winged out to sea. I don't remember anything else about that mission or the debriefing that followed, so I guess the rest of it was uneventful. But I have often wondered during recent years whether the colonel was testing the old gunner and me, or if he really intended to go after that artillery piece well concealed in the rocky surface up that narrow mountain passage. We will never know. But knowing how fearless and determined he was, the probability is that if he had not been "outvoted," the colonel would have gone right back in.

DOWN AND OUT!

MY HEAVY FLIGHT BOOTS CRUNCHED THROUGH the deep, wet snow on a miserably cold and windy January morning in 1953.

"Two crews down and out." That was all Colonel Bentley said, glancing at me as I entered the operations shack. He quickly lowered his head and appeared to be concentrating on the content of the documents before him.

Two crews down and out. "Who were they, sir?" This was my hesitant and belated question as I recovered from the shock as if it were a breath-taking body blow to the solar plexus. The loss of two crews on the same night had not happened since I had joined the squadron just after Christmas of '52. I had heard that if we lost aircraft it was always one at a time. My question elicited no response from the colonel.

I walked slowly to my grey metal desk in the corner of the drab work area that we alone occupied at this early hour. I sat down and looked at the unfinished writing project he had assigned to me. I tried to concentrate, but it was impossible. I just sat there, numb and immobile. It seemed ten minutes had passed before he finally replied, "They weren't ours. One was with the 37th and the other was from the 3rd Bomb Group." It was still early in my tour of duty and I did not even know that the 3rd Bomb Group existed, much less where it was stationed. Not wanting to display my ignorance, I asked no further questions. I learned later that day that the 3rd Bomb Group flew its missions out of K-8 AFB near Kunsan near the west coast of South Korea. Like the three squadrons in our 17th Bomb Group, each of its three squadrons was permanently supplied with sixteen twin-engine B-26 light bombers. These six squadrons constituted the totality of night-time bombing and strafing capability for the UNC operations throughout the thirty-seven months of the Korean War.

What I did know, however, was that if the two aircraft were B-26s then six men had probably experienced violent deaths within the past twelve hours. I was greatly relieved that I did not know any of them. I suddenly realized that I did not know any of the flight crewmen of the 34th Bomb Squadron or the 37th Bomb Squadron, quartered on the other side of the runway. I did not even know very many of the approximately ninety crewmembers of my own squadron. I had been "stuck" from my first day in Korea, at a day job as assistant administrative officer, six days a week, when not flying missions or engaged in preparing for or recovering from them. (Upon reflection, "clerk-typist" could aptly be substituted for the job title that the colonel had given me).

To this day, whenever I hear that phrase "down and out," a metaphor that luckily is not used very often anymore, I experience a near total and startlingly accurate flashback to those few moments when the colonel and I briefly discussed the fate of the six downed airmen, men I never knew and probably would never have known. That ignorance was, in retrospect, probably a good thing: it is much more painful to mourn the loss of someone you knew personally and with whom you have shared a ride, a laugh, or a drink, than the sudden death of a total stranger.

I learned something else from the colonel that day. Something that I was then eager to learn but now wish I had never learned. "Down and out," the colonel explained, meant not only dead, but unrecoverable. I don't know, with any degree of accuracy, the casualty statistics from the Korean War, but practically every B-26 crewman from the 95th Bomb Squadron shot down over North Korea never got out of North Korea, either dead or alive. I became well aware of this brutal reality when I still foolishly believed that it was always the "other guy" who would "buy the farm" because it certainly could not be me.

I do not remember the colonel's exact words, but his message was clear. It was intended to be helpful, almost fatherly advice: calculated risks were worth taking in most combat situations but excessive risks were to be strictly avoided. I was learning that drawing the line between acceptable risk and excessive risk was very hard to do in the heat and confusion of combat. He then set forth a hypothetical. If you stopped an enemy troop train with two well-placed five-hundred-pound bombs dropped on or near the railroad tracks an eighth to a quarter mile ahead of its steam engine, it is likely that dozens or hundreds of North Korean and Chinese foot soldiers would pour out of the slowing boxcars behind the braking locomotive. They would open fire with small arms and automatic weapons from along the sides of the tracks. It would then be an excellent idea to hit the intercom button and call for a reciprocal heading (a reversal of direction) to sweep over the entire length of the train at minimum safe altitude to release two more bombs at closely spaced intervals. Of course, if you were dropping napalm bombs you could go in very low, as low as fifty to one hundred feet above ground level under perfect conditions. With 260-pound fragmentation bombs, the bomb run could be as low as two hundred to three hundred feet of terrain clearance, because of the smaller bomb size and reduced concussive power that would enable the B-26 to avoid blast effect and bomb fragments.

Upon rolling out after another reversal of course, you would come out of the turn straight and level on target and utilize the burn areas as reference points. Then you would toggle open the bomb bay doors and punch out two or four more bombs in rapid succession as the plane closed on target at three miles a minute, aiming for the engine if it had not yet exploded, or the troop, munitions, or freight cars trailing behind it. The last two or four bombs shackled in the bomb bay would be released consistent with the opportunities and dangers of the moment. A call for another reciprocal heading for the pilot's first strafing run might be justified by the visual sightings of any or all three crewmen as to the nature, extent, and location of damage inflicted. We were always looking for secondary explosions and sustained fires. If anti-aircraft, automatic weapon, and small arms fire was not too intensive or accurate, three or more strafing runs could well be warranted and quickly accomplished. Quite often, with his limited range of visibility, the pilot was simply unable to see and fully appreciate the location(s) and intensity of enemy ground fire streaming up from below while these operations were being conducted. Therefore, it was the gunner's duty to scan the target area to his right and my job to concentrate on blast areas and targets to the left and nose of the aircraft.

Sometimes the locomotive engineer would panic and cut his steam locomotive free from the twenty, thirty, or forty trailing boxcars and make a frantic run for a nearby railway tunnel. In that case, we would execute another 180-degree turn and pursue the locomotive, a prized target, and drop either two or four bombs in rapid succession in front of and upon it as the engineer fled in terror to the safety of the tunnel mouth.

It must be acknowledged that too many bombardier-navigators succumbed to "target greed." The explanation for this dangerous mistake was simple. When pressing an attack upon a choice target, such as a stopped or slowly moving troop train, we had an almost uncontrollable urge to extend the attack to cause maximum destruction and damage with "just one more" bomb run down the tracks and over the steam locomotive and its trailing, troop-laden boxcars. The lethal downside of this compulsion was the brutal reality that by this time there was progressively more intensive enemy ground fire. And by the fourth or fifth bomb run, literally dozens or hundreds of North Korean or Chinese riflemen would be in full prone position, firing at will as they lay upon their bellies along the tracks and sighted their weapons up or down the railroad tracks. And if it was a dawn patrol mission, these riflemen could accurately sight in on the distinct image of the approaching black B-26 sharply defined against the backdrop of an ever-brightening pre-dawn sky.

This dangerous situation could develop easily and suddenly. It was then that our pilots, as aircraft commanders, would exercise their appropriate authority, banking and climbing sharply out over the Sea of Japan and toward the possibility of air-sea rescue, if necessary. Regrettably, many bombardier-navigators forgot or ignored the simple fact that a train kill could be completed in daylight by our F-84 fighter-bombers, or navy or marine pilots coming in off Task Force 77 carriers in the Sea of Japan, which usually operated less than one hundred miles off the east coast of North Korea. Although these nearby fighter-bombers had much smaller bomb loads, they could be highly effective, as they had the benefit of numbers, full daylight, and much higher airspeeds.

In a calm and utterly impersonal manner, the colonel then described the stark realities of survival in night combat over North Korea. First, if a B-26 lost an engine or if the cockpit or a wing or an elevator or rudder control was demolished by enemy fire while flying at low level down a deep valley in North Korea, it was unlikely that any crewmember would survive either the hit itself or the impact of the aircraft upon the valley floor or against a mountainside. If a crewmember did made it through these hazards, he was not likely to survive the subsequent fire caused by flaming gasoline pouring from the ruptured wing tanks and/or the main tank after crash landing. And, if the crewman survived enemy fire, the crash, and burning high octane gasoline (as well as exploding machine gun rounds) and extricated himself from the aircraft (highly unlikely for the bombardier-navigator in the nose), it was a near certainty that he would be captured quickly by communist North Korean soldiers who patrolled the roads and tracks along the valley floors. Or he would be captured by vengeful Korean peasants who farmed the valleys and lower mountain slopes and who had been bombed night after night, month after month, year after year, by B-26s such as his own aircraft. Therefore, the colonel reasoned that capture, irrespective of the identity of the captors, would be followed by brutal torture and a slow and painful death. The only exception might be if the crewman were fortunate enough to be captured by Chinese forces. In that case his chances of survival could well be increased substantially, as he might be considered more valuable alive than dead for communist propaganda and/or intelligence purposes.

As a direct consequence of the colonel's cold-blooded analysis, I became very practical, even fatalistic. On my next mission with my own crew I left behind my Smith & Wesson Police Special .38 pistol and the heavy leather shoulder harness that secured it in place. The colonel had convinced me that a handgun would be of little value if I were shot down. A few missions later, after takeoff and attaining altitude, I began to remove my large and bulky plastic P-1 helmet and replace it with my blue baseball cap, which was much lighter and provided a much greater range of visibility.

I had been wearing a self-contained parachute rig, the backpack variety that would allow a quicker bailout than the chest pack type. The latter required locating the parachute pack within the dark nose compartment of the aircraft, grabbing it with both hands by its thick braided handles at both ends, and attaching it across the chest by clamping its two metal rings onto the sturdy and heavy parachute harness hooks projecting forward from the parachute harness.

I soon realized that if ground fire hit our aircraft, it was highly unlikely that we would be at sufficient altitude for me to bail out, with a gain of needed altitude being unlikely. So after takeoff (always the most hazardous phase of any mission with a full bomb load, full gas tanks, and ten fully loaded .50 caliber machine guns), climbing to altitude, and crossing into enemy territory, I began removing my chest pack harness as well. This gave me even greater mobility, more comfort and ease of motion, and therefore less weight and fatigue.

However, I continued to wear my inflatable life preserver at all times in flight. This life preserver was generally called a "Mae West" in recognition of the impressive measurements of a bosomy, blonde Hollywood entertainer of the 1930s. It was very light in weight, and there always was a possibility, although remote, that if we actually reached the frigid waters of the Sea of Japan and ditched the aircraft, I might have a chance to exit the aircraft head first via the drop-down hatch upon which I knelt during bomb runs. And it was even possible, though even more unlikely, that I would be able to exit the aircraft by crawling through the narrow tunnel leading back and up into the cockpit. If I chose this narrow passageway, I knew that I would have a better chance of getting through it quickly and safely because I had discarded so much other heavy clothing and equipment, which collectively was a major impediment when wiggling through on my belly.

By "losing" my parachute and harness, my pistol and holster, and my clumsy helmet, I was able to observe and react more quickly, more easily, and with much less fatigue over the course of a physically exhausting and emotionally draining five- to seven-hour mission. Because my duties as bombardier-navigator required me to have my head and torso continually "on a swivel," I could now see better in every direction, more quickly detect incoming ground fire, and better advise my pilot on evasive action. I could also better assist him in maneuvering the aircraft toward targets. In contrast, my pilot and gunner, positioned side by side, were strapped into their seats before takeoff and remained so restrained until the plane came to a dead stop on the tarmac after landing. They had no need for freedom and ease of movement within the plane as I did.

I knew that I was breaking a number of USAF regulations and directives in stripping down for battle, but I readily assumed that risk. Perhaps intending to do so, Colonel Bentley had convinced me that in the event of being shot down at low altitude over North Korea, the protective gear I wore would make little difference in my chances for survival. If anything, my lightened load would make me more agile, perceptive, and combat-effective and thereby increase our crew's collective potential for survival. I would have shorter reaction time when under enemy fire. I could locate and destroy targets more quickly and better navigate back across North Korea, where total darkness and scarcity of identifiable cultural and natural land features and other navigational aids made accurate navigation extremely difficult.

But should I inform my regular crew of my decision to pile my gear in a corner of the nose compartment while we were over enemy territory? I quickly decided not to tell them anything, for two reasons. First, if I told them of the colonel's conclusions as to the remote possibility of survival if shot down, it might diminish their self-confidence, high level of morale, and prospects for elevated levels of combat performance. Second, if they survived and I did not, one or both of them, out of a feeling of remorse and regret, might feel compelled to inform responsible authorities that I was not properly outfitted for combat survival, and that they had, implicitly, acquiesced in my multiple violations of these air safety regulations. And such disclosures might possibly compromise their military careers.

So I never told anyone what the colonel had candidly and forcefully informed me, and I never said anything to anyone about my decision to strip deep down for action. Luckily, our crew completed its tour of duty together, without any major physical injuries, and with relatively minor to moderate structural damage to several of the various B-26s we flew. However, not until the end of our last mission, when the wheels of the B-26 squeaked pleasantly upon soft impact with the black asphalt of runway 33 at K-9 Air Force Base, did the nagging concerns about being "down and out" ever stray far from the back of my mind.

GIRDING FOR BATTLE

WE FLIGHT CREWMEMBERS HAD THESE LITTLE ME-chanical wind-up alarm clocks that stood just about four inches high. After getting my government-issued wristwatch synchronized at the Mission Briefing the morning before a mission, I would return to our primitive shack on the east side of the runway and immediately set this simple mechanism by hand to the exact minute and second as established by the presumably precise time displayed on my wristwatch. I would then set the alarm to ring exactly two hours before our scheduled takeoff time for the next night's bombing and strafing raid into North Korea. If our crew had an early evening departure I would strip down to boxer shorts and a T-shirt and climb into bed right after an early dinner that night.

For all of us, almost without exception, the most undesirable take-off times were the last of the night, with start of takeoff roll scheduled between 0200 hours and 0300 hours (2 AM or 3 AM). These late departures generally resulted in being over enemy territory during the hours and minutes just before dawn. Some of our number referred to these missions as the "deadly dawn patrols," as most of our crew losses seemed to occur during the predawn hours. The most probable reason for these disproportionate losses is that crews tended to press attacks upon truck convoys and troop trains much too long. Thus, our black painted B-26s became very clear silhouettes against the brightening eastern horizon during the fifteen to twenty minutes just before the sunrise, making them clear targets for triple A, automatic weapons, and small arms fire.

I should mention that we all slept in boxer shorts and T-shirts. I don't think it was required (i.e., "regulation") but we all tended to unconsciously conform in this way. I remember a new replacement, a bombardier-navigator who had just arrived from the ZI. He donned a set of blue silk pajamas his first night with us. We just stared in disbelief as he was tying the drawstring around his waist. Three or four of us signaled our agreed intentions by hand and finger gestures, after concurring upon our course of action by pointing to him and then to the door. Upon the count of three, we rushed him, threw him out the door, and locked it behind him. We left him out there for five or ten long minutes, shivering in the intense cold as he shifted his weight from one bare, wet, and cold foot to the other. Needless to say, we never saw those blue silk pajamas again!

By deliberate restraint, the dinner we consumed the evening before every night mission was sparse and lightly seasoned. It was also combined with little liquid intake. Of course, alcoholic beverages would never be consumed during the day of a scheduled night combat mission. The intake of very small quantities of food and beverage throughout the day of a flight night was a practical necessity, as voiding and defecating while encased in a heavy flight suit, over multiple layers of clothing, was practically impossible.

On one well-remembered mission I experienced the uncontrollable urge (a need approaching physical pain might be more accurate) to void while on the return leg of an unusually long night flight. I had finally been able to extend my appendage somewhat into the metal funnel at the end of the flexible "relief tube" only to startlingly experience an unpleasant phenomenon known as "blowback," whereby a stream of atomized, frozen urine was suddenly propelled back upon me and throughout the nose compartment. (We were then outbound at approximately seven thousand feet and the temperature in the nose was close to thirty-five degrees below zero.) This was an unforgettable learning experience, most unpleasant and very uncomfortable. Of course, to my crew it was hilarious.

If anyone in our shack was flying on any given night, which was usually the case, the glaring, unshaded, and high wattage light bulb hanging from the middle of the ceiling would be left unlit and the only illumination throughout the night would come from small bedside lamps that were adjustable to cast directional lighting within a very limited range at each bedside.

Sound and refreshing sleep on flight nights would not come easily, if at all. I would lie flat on my back with my eyes closed and concentrate upon blocking out every thought and emotion. Rarely did I succeed. I then would attempt to focus my mind upon the creation of a black void in time and space, but this effort rarely worked either. I would reach out and turn the clock face, and its white luminescent numbers would tell me that just five or six minutes had transpired since the last time I had looked at it. I would again verify that the wake-up arrow was properly positioned. It always was, but I checked anyway. If our takeoff roll was scheduled to begin at 2000 hours our crew would be picked up at 1900 hours in front of our squadron's operations shack. My clock would accordingly be set for 1800 hours to allow adequate time for a last trip to the latrine and ample time for dressing for combat operations, a long process jokingly but accurately referred to in our shack as "girding for battle."

The preflight dressing process was not a simple or quick one. In fact, it was rather complex, thoroughly planned, and quite time-consuming. This process was also, for most of us, unthinkingly but essentially ritualistic. And for more than a few of us, it involved a strong element of unrecognized superstition, as it constituted a final and significant element in the long process of psychologically and physically gearing up for and going off to do battle over the frozen and menacing Korean peninsula. Battle involved flying into a brutally cold and dark night with no guarantees that there would be a return trip. It was for all of us a relentless continuum that began the morning of the day before, when we learned of the posting of our crew upon that day's Battle Order.

For me, the final phase of this process began by reaching out to grab my alarm clock, depressing the alarm button with the forefinger of the same hand, and reluctantly throwing back the warm top sheet and multiple blankets while simultaneously swinging my bare feet to the chilling coldness of the coarse wooden floor. I would then quickly extract from beneath my pillow my lucky brown gabardine pants, which I had folded neatly and placed there just before trying to begin my night of fitful sleep. After stepping into these soft and comfortable silk-lined pants I would pull on a pair of white knee-length cotton socks and pull them up and over the folded-over cuffless legs of the gabardine pants. I would stretch the socks as far up my calves as possible, vigorously massaging my legs as I did so. I next pulled over my head a long cotton sweatshirt that I tucked into the waistband of the gabardine pants. Now my body was substantially protected against the bitter coldness of the fireless shack. I then put on a pair of knee-length woolen socks. I would then step into the heavy black boon dockers that had been issued to me at the start of Basic Airman Training back at Sheppard AFB, for a quick dash to and from the latrine for necessary last-minute plumbing operations.

Donning the two-piece "electric flight suit" was the next phase of the girding-for-battle process. The bottom component was configured like a thick, padded pair of overalls, and I would step into them as I would a conventional pair of overalls. These, however, included vertical zippers that extended from hip level to just under the arm on both sides of the body. These would be zipped up as far as possible. I would then don a similar upper-body electrified component that had full-length sleeves, zipping it up from waist level to just under the chin. By way of a short length of electrical cord, about one foot long, I would connect the bottom segment of the electric suit to its top segment. Later, upon entering the nose compartment of the aircraft, by way of an additional six feet of electric cord, I would actually plug myself into its electrical system, a convenient socket being located just below the bombardier's control panel on the left side of the nose compartment. What made the suit electrically heated were rows of insulated wires, spaced one inch apart, that coursed through the entirety of both of the connected upper and lower suit components. Heat emanated from the wires to supplement one's natural body heat.

The electric suit functioned very much like a bread toaster—that is, of course, when it functioned properly. Next to the socket into which the electric suit was plugged was a rheostat that presumably enabled the wearer to vary the intensity of heat provided by simply rotating a control knob. However, there were occasions when the rheostat did not function properly. That problem could be solved in flight by simply "pulling the plug" when it got too hot and reinserting the plug when it got too cold. The frequent pulling of the plug and then reinserting it was a distinct nuisance, but I felt that I was lucky to have an electric suit, even a defective one, particularly at altitude where the temperature ranged between twenty degrees and forty degrees below zero in an unheated, uninsulated, and unpressurized B-26 from December 1952 when I arrived until well into April.

Over the electric flying suit I wore the traditional woolen winter flight suit that was zipped up from crotch to neck. Next would come the high-topped, fleece-lined heavy flight boots. Over the flight suit would be added a fleece-lined flight jacket. This battle garb was then topped off with the standard baseball cap, dark blue for those of us in the 95th Bomb Squadron, irrespective of the little warmth that it provided. Later, in the parachute shack, this cap would be exchanged for a P-1 helmet, a large semi-hemispheric hard plastic protective headgear that weighed more than it was actually worth. Next from the parachute bag would come a leather shoulder harness for a personal weapon, in my case a never-fired Smith-Wesson Military Police Special .38 caliber revolver that I bought at a gun shop back near Langley Field, Virginia, during crew training. As I've explained, the .38 was regularly left behind in my parachute bag.

The next item of apparel to be secured in place was a canary yellow inflatable life preserver, usually dirty. Although the life preserver added some additional weight and reduced mobility it did offer a small chance of crash survival and rescue. (That is, one might survive if the plane ditched successfully into the Sea of Japan and the water temperature was not so low that freezing to death would occur before an improbable pick-up by a ship in the U.S. Navy's Task Force 77, which patrolled and controlled the coastal waters off the east coast of North Korea.)

The final article of apparel encasing and encumbering the body was an entire parachute (if it was the backpack type) or only a heavy parachute harness (if it was of the chest pack variety). Again, I had learned that a parachute, of either variety, would be next to useless in the event of an emergency. So I selected the backpack version and generally went through the motions of securing it in place upon my heavily ladened torso. I would climb into the plane with the parachute in place, but I removed it later after we had attained inbound altitude, as I had far greater mobility in combat operations without it.

We bombardiers also wore thin and tight-fitting silk-like gloves that afforded some minimal protection against the bitter cold while on the bomb run. Far more importantly, they gave us the required delicacy of touch in adjusting the controls of the sensitive and immediately responsive Norden bombsight. When not on the bomb run, we wore heavy, padded half-forearm-length mittens over these gloves for greater warmth. The mittens were always removed during the bomb run, but none of us dared to remove the thin bombing gloves during flight as even the slightest moisture upon the skin caused immediate and painful adherence to any brutally cold metal surface.

Before heading out to the operations shack, I removed my battered, brown leather government issue navigator's briefcase from under my bed and sat on my footlocker to examine, once again, its contents: the large and small scale maps of Korea, the E6-B computing device needed in determining wind speed and direction as well as plotting course headings and ETAs (estimated times of arrivals). Of course, I knew that every item needed to navigate and bomb was already there and in its assigned and familiar position, but irresistibly I was compelled to check it out again and again.

By this point in preflight preparation, I usually had ten to fifteen minutes left before walking out into the frigid night air. Now, after completing this ritualistic process of preparing for combat, deliberately done in precisely the same manner and in precisely the same sequence before each and every combat mission, I would sit on my footlocker in the near total darkness and consider, in my mind's eye, the visualizations of my selected checkpoints up the Korean peninsula and into that night's assigned target area. And then, with knees spread and my elbows upon my knees, I would lean back, extend my right arm outward, and spread the fingers of that hand in a rigid horizontal plane, palm down, and carefully observe the tremor that seemed to expand almost imperceptibly with each flight flown. Then I would sit there quietly and ask myself that constant, ultimate, and unanswerable question: "How long can I keep on doing this before my luck runs out or my nerves give way?" This worrying question would almost always be followed by a few moments of silent and desperate prayer. I would then lean forward, rise slowly, grab the worn handle of my briefcase, and head for the door, plodding into the chilling darkness beyond.

Then came my labored climb up and into the back of an open truck for a bumpy, cold, and windy ride to our assigned Douglas B-26 bomber, standing silently somewhere down the weathered tarmac that glittered in the reflected moonlight. I strained multiple muscles in climbing into the nose compartment of the B-26, as I was then carrying upon my bony frame between forty and fifty pounds of dead and, most probably, totally useless weight.

The fear, anxiety, and apprehension of nightly air-to-ground combat was always with us. It was with us as it built to a crescendo at take-off, as we gained enough speed and altitude to avoid crashing into the icy waters of Suyong Bay, as we entered North Korean airspace, as we descended to our assigned target area, and as we completed our bombing and strafing runs. It began to dissipate slowly as we headed homeward and out of North Korea.

But there were, inevitably, the countervailing and substantial benefits of these raw emotions issuing from the unknowable and impending life-threatening dangers that seemed to always hover over us. These treasured benefits were measurably enhanced physical strength and endurance, augmented nervous energy, and sharpened sensory perceptions (particularly sight and sound) that naturally flowed from the strong adrenalin rush that every crewmember was experiencing. But for these wondrous physiological and psychological consequences of fear, occasionally approaching sheer terror, I know that I would have reached near-total exhaustion just from the process of girding for battle and entering into the dark and cramped nose compartment of that cold and silently waiting instrument of effective and efficient destruction.

PULLING THE PINS

ONE BY ONE, HEAVILY CLOTHED, WE JUMPED CLUM-
sily down from the bed of the rough-riding open truck that took
us from the parachute shack to the flight line. Our B-26 Invaders stood
in black silence, almost wing tip to wing tip but still separated by rude
revetments constructed of two tiers of sand-filled fifty-five gallon oil
drums. We stood in silence for a few moments, adjusting our eyes to
the near-total darkness of the Korean night. The truck rumbled away
across the muddied hardstand, with the waste oils that permeated it
reflecting the moonlight's cast. Bob Crow would then say: "It looks like
an airplane." Jerry and I would then instantly respond in unison, with
the same silly refrain, "Well, it better be, or we're in deep shit!"

Then, Bob, followed by Jerry, began to visually examine the B-26
in a thorough and routine preflight check, with the slight illumination from their hooded flashlights marking their deliberate movement
around the airplane in the customary counter-clockwise direction. Simultaneously, I walked to the aircraft's left wing just outboard of the
huge engine nacelle, where two five-hundred-pound GP (general purpose) bombs were racked and hanging below the wing. I moved to the
trailing edge of the wing and directed the beam of my flashlight upon
the tail fin assembly of the outboard bomb, quickly locating the soft,
pliable, grey metal "safety pin" that disabled the bomb shackle release so
that the bomb could not be inadvertently dropped while the plane was

still on the ground. The safety pin was in the same configuration as a hairpin but was somewhat larger and thicker, with the ends bent back to secure the unit in place.

I would then carefully bend the tips of the safety pin back together so that they were straight and parallel and the appearance of the pin was that of an ordinary hairpin. Then, slowly and deliberately, I would pull the pin straight out and away from the bomb release shackle with thumb and forefinger. The second item on the SOP was to check that the arming wire was correctly secured to the shackle. The third, final check was to ensure that the other end of the arming wire was correctly secured in the fusing mechanism. That sequence completed, the bomb was still in an unarmed status. The bomb become fully armed only in flight when the bombardier-navigator activated the arming switch and the bomb was subsequently triggered off by the automated functioning of the Norden bombsight or was "punched out" manually by the bombardier-navigator's left thumb when bombing at low level.

I repeated this basic preflight process on the left inboard bomb and then the front-end fusing mechanisms on both bombs. Still wearing my white, hard plastic P-1 helmet to prevent head injuries that could easily be caused by the multiple sharp edges on the fin assemblies of these large five-hundred-pound bombs, I would duck down and cautiously enter the bomb bay and remove the safety pins from both the front and rear-end fusing mechanisms of all six bombs racked one above the other, three on each side. I then would walk to the two five-hundred-pounders racked under the right wing of the aircraft and duplicate the safety pin removal procedure upon them.

This required SOP was always an uneventful and relatively simple process for a bombardier-navigator, as it required no more than five or ten minutes of my time. But it was a task that I felt quite reluctant and nervous about performing despite the fact that the bomb loaders invariably did their jobs thoroughly and accurately. I simply did not enjoy being around live ordnance. All of our bombs were left over from World War II and were deemed "unstable" by several ordnance specialists of my acquaintance, and there was a worrisome chemical deterioration factor to be considered. The five-hundred-pound GP bombs that we carried into North Korea were filled with TNT and were identified as being highly explosive by being painted olive drab, with three closely spaced, mustard colored rings painted around both their noses and tails. I was particularly cautious with the five-hundred-pound GPs that were further identified by the addition of the word "TRITONAL" in large black letters near their tail fin assemblies. Tritonal is a mixture of 80 percent TNT and 20 percent aluminum powder. The aluminum increases the speed at which the bomb develops its maximum bursting power. A tritonal bomb is 18 to 20 percent more powerful than an ordinary TNT bomb.

I would always join Bob and Jerry just right of the nose of the B-26 after we had completed our respective preflight duties. I would then place in Bob's open hands, one by one, all of the twenty safety pins that I had just extracted from the bombs' fusing mechanisms by counting aloud the number of each pin as I transferred it to him. I cannot remember if this procedure was a requirement or simply a ritual unique to our crew. It did serve a definite purpose either way, as I wanted him to have real and tangible proof in his own hands that we would not be bringing home any of the bombs that we had hauled all the way to and beyond the front line.

In long-deferred retrospection, I now realize that there was for me a definite psychological benefit in transferring physical possession of the safety pins to Bob. The careful and deliberate dropping of the twenty safety pins into his open palms seemed to free my conscience and mind from all responsibility for the awesome and awful destruction and death that we were about to unleash, thereby enabling me to concentrate my thoughts upon the mechanics and techniques of the navigational and bombing efforts that lay ahead. I never knew what Bob did with those safety pins. And I never asked.

After completing our respective preflight routines, we would walk off, usually in different directions, and void against the base of the revetments on either side of the aircraft. We would then converge at the nose of the aircraft and Bob would always say, "Let's strap our butts to this black bitch and get the hell out of here." Jerry and I would shout in unison, "Hey, hey, hey!" We would then eagerly scramble into the silently waiting B-26, relieved, even pleased, to be again following our familiar, reassuring, and ritualistic routine, however deadly it might be.

A TOLERANCE
FOR KILLING

IN ORDER TO KEEP ON FLYING AND KILLING OVER THE approximately seven or eight months necessarily involved in completing a fifty-mission tour of duty in Korea, it became an absolute necessity for my emotional integrity to quickly become totally desensitized and detached from the brutality and horror of our nocturnal combat actions and experiences. Simply stated, as a bombardier-navigator I had to visually observe on the ground below me, as well as through the magnifying lenses of the Norden bombsight, not other human beings, whether on foot or on vehicles, but instead merely miniaturized and moving targets, dispassionately viewed as APs (aiming points). I fixated these targets and kept them manually in the crosshairs until they were eliminated from view by bomb bursts within seconds after a quick jab of my left thumb upon a little red button. I could not give even the slightest, the most fleeting thought to the death and destruction of human life that I was deliberately causing if I was to continue to be a proficient survivor in the seemingly endless months of our predominately low-level, low-speed bombing and strafing operations over North Korea.

Substantial physical distance from our chosen targets was another vital factor in psychological survival, a survival that was based entirely upon total denial of reality. Although it is difficult to admit, even today and just to myself alone, I strongly believe that if I had to be face-to-face with the enemy in close hand-to-hand combat, as my older brother had as a seventeen-year-old Marine grunt upon many occasions on such distant island battlegrounds as Tarawa, Saipan, and Okinawa during World War II, I could not have been as ruthlessly and as unhesitatingly proficient. Distance from the enemy, even as little as fifty to one hundred feet of terrain clearance, mercifully provided objectivity and dispassionate immunity from regret, remorse, and guilt. This enabled me to deceive myself and to function effectively and relentlessly upon a cold and impersonal plane of destruction and immolation. And I can surmise from our conversations that for Robert Crow and Colonel Bentley, this need to kill or to be killed necessitated for them basically the same individual reactions and psychological accommodations that I achieved.

We well knew, and fairly often were verbally reminded at preflight mission briefings, that our combined UNC ground forces were severely and generally outnumbered by the seemingly endless hordes of expendable North Korean and Chinese foot soldiers who continued to flow relentlessly and crazily across the killing fields of Korea. Only the air supremacy of the UNC voluntary air forces, provided almost totally by closely coordinated efforts of the USAF by night and the US Navy and Marines by day and facilitated by our superior military technology and techniques, could keep the front lines reasonably stable and secure and the general military situation under uncertain control.

The targets that I focused on were either magnified by the Norden bombsight, when at high altitudes, or viewed with the naked eye at low altitudes. When magnified, everything looked miniaturized and generalized in configuration, color, and texture; with the naked eye there was an overabundance of confusing detail, and the minutiae were all too readily perceived. In either case, I had to select my target, fix my total attention upon it, and strike it as accurately and with as much controlled, detached concentration as I could muster. I was always striving for the perfect strike, whether it was upon a troop train, a railroad bridge, a truck convoy, or the mouth of a road or railroad tunnel. Enemy foot soldiers, truck drivers, and locomotive engineers were not, nor could they be, viewed as human beings; I had to see them simply as moving targets to be rendered immobile.

In retrospect, I believe I treated the bombsight as a modern-day computer game, one that both awed and fascinated me with its precision. If this deadly game was played with great care and concern, it captured totally my every competitive urge, the innate desire to win in order to survive. I did not, and in fact could not, consider the massive and horrific pain and suffering that I was administering by my thumb's quick depression and release of the little red button at the end of a contoured black handle—this handle connected to a black cord that instantaneously transmitted an electrical impulse that activated a bomb release mechanism. Usually the first triggered bomb drop was quickly followed by a second thumb "punch" so that two five-hundred-pound demolition bombs (or two somewhat less streamlined five-hundred-pound napalm bombs) were released in rapid succession to closely "bracket" the target and at the same time serve to equalize wing loading and minimize instability of flight.

A choice target of opportunity might be a steam locomotive pulling a long string of boxcars coming directly toward us down a valley as we were flying up that valley. In this situation, I would punch out four bombs at close and evenly spaced intervals to ensure the greatest degree of on-target impact. And if we were extremely lucky on that dark night—with good visibility and considerable illumination being delivered by the eerie light emanating from a three-quarter to full moon and with the target being identified by a telltale white/gray plume of smoke rising from the stack of the coal- or wood-burning locomotive and laid back and over the railcars behind it—those four bombs would be released from the wing racks in pairs (in the order of outer left and right and then inner left and right) to maintain equal wing loading. I would then request my pilot to assume a reciprocal heading so that, within thirty seconds and upon completion of these even and steeply banked turning maneuvers, our aircraft would be heading directly back and down the railroad tracks. At this point, I would quickly flip the toggle switch for the bomb bay doors to the down or "open" position to facilitate an almost immediate and sequenced release of two or four of the remaining six bombs upon the fleeing locomotive (that is, if I missed it on the first drop). If the loco was already destroyed or substantially damaged, I would concentrate my attention and efforts upon the freight cars behind it, which frequently contained troops, ammunition, fuel oil, or some other combustible cargo that might trigger off multiple secondary explosions and/or sustained fires that could be easily recorded and confirmed by both our belly camera and the visual sightings by our crew. Unfortunately, such choice targets did not that often present themselves despite the application of guile, patience, and diligent effort; much more often we had to search for and take what we could find and target.

If the trains and/or trucks were carrying troop reinforcements to the front line, as generally was the case, these foot soldiers would jump out as the boxcars that carried them were coming slowly to a full stop, and they would attempt to scatter and take up firing positions with small arms, such as machine guns, tommy guns, rifles, and pistols. Whether our payload was comprised of high explosives, napalm bombs, or especially deadly miniaturized anti-personnel (fragmentation) bombs, my major responsibility and top priority was to hit the trains or trucks to cause rail or road "cuts" that would stop or impede the flow of subsequent trains and truck convoys coming down that night from Russia or Manchuria. We generally carried ten five-hundred-pound GP bombs when our assigned priority targets were either trains or trucks.

A single five-hundred-pound GP bomb could create a crater roughly fifteen to thirty-five feet in diameter that could be from five to fifteen feet deep at its center, depending upon the hardness of the ground and the season of the year. Even if we were somewhat off target, left or right of the rail tracks or the center of the road, there often would be sufficient damage to totally disrupt the flow of traffic that night.

We would continue our bomb runs until the bomb bay was empty. Then our pilot would take over, raking the target area with streams of .50 caliber Browning machine-gun fire by "walking" the plane up and down the railroad track or roadway, alternately applying pressure to the left and right rudder pedals while simultaneously triggering off short bursts from the six machine guns located along the leading edges of the wings. When he had completed the machine-gunning phase of the mission (all too often cut short by triple A fire, small arms fire, and/or blinding searchlights) and I had computed and given him an initial heading for the trip to base, our jobs had then been substantially completed. I would then attempt, but rarely fully achieve, an accurate recordation of a complete BDA (bomb damage assessment) via inter-com with our gunner in the right seat, for both my bombing phase of the attacks and our pilot's second and final gunnery phase. This task also required keeping my head and upper body continuously moving through a full range of motion, searching for and recording any obser-vation, happening, or condition when over enemy territory that might conceivably have intelligence value at mission debriefing. For example, identifying, confirming, and recording the specific location of flak traps and searchlight clusters was a team effort, often started in flight but completed during mission debriefing. The result of this extra effort was important as it enabled later crews, assigned to the same armed reconnaissance route, to be fully alerted to such hazards to be avoided or destroyed. The inexperienced and/or timid crews would detour around them, but the experienced and/or aggressive crews would deliberately attempt to destroy them.

Calculating strike statistics by estimating property damage and body count was the final, least accurate, and most tedious aspect of night combat operations. Combat crews referred to BDA calculations as "bookkeeping by approximation." Frequently, intelligence-debriefing officers openly expressed their skepticism about our claims, as they considered visual sightings of combat crews to be of only secondary reliability.

We were told that "the camera tells the tale," as photography is not vulnerable to the overactive imaginations of crewmen who may be inclined to over-report their visual sightings of death, destruction, and damage inflicted. But we rarely bothered to contest these cynical Group HQ assumptions. We all knew that our low-level, low-speed raids caused much more devastation than any light-sensitive belly-mounted cameras could record.

KIM

IRRESPECTIVE OF THEIR AGES, THEY WERE SIMPLY RE-
ferred to as "house girls." Most of them were not girls at all but
weathered, wrinkled, and stoic middle-aged Korean women who regrettably appeared much older than their chronological ages. They were
mostly poor and war-displaced peasants working as domestics. They
had been hired by wing headquarters procurement staff to wash our
clothing, keep primitive oil- or wood-burning stoves operating, and
perform housekeeping services for officer personnel stationed at K-9
AFB during the war. Nor did these air force officers, mostly Douglas
B-26 combat crewmen, live in houses, but in crude and cold eight-man
"shacks" that only remotely resembled their houses back home.

Kim was a very quiet, responsible, and physically attractive sixteen-
or seventeen- year-old house girl. I asked her several times what her first
name was, but she simply shook her head, either not able to understand
my question or reluctant to disclose it to me. So I knew her only as Kim
throughout the full term of my combat tour at K-9, "Kim" being a very
common surname throughout South Korea.

One early afternoon during the dark, short, and snowy days of February 1953 I was aimlessly walking through the drab and almost totally
deserted officers club when I heard feminine voices coming through the
closed door of a small side room generally used by members for poker
games, chess games, and the like. I approached the door silently and

identified the voices as those of five or six Korean women interspersed with the voice of a solitary male American. I felt guilty about eavesdropping on their conversation but was curious about the nature of this unusual event. I recognized the deeper American voice but could not put a name and face to it. I soon realized that the American was giving these Korean women a lesson in basic conversational English and that he was frequently and effectively interjecting humor into the discussion, bringing peals of laughter and joy from the Korean women. After some moments, I realized that the women were some of our squadron's house girls, that one of them was Kim, and that the American was Captain Ken Doolittle, with whom I shared living quarters.

I knew immediately that Kim was in the group as she had a distinctive and delightful laugh that I would recognize anywhere. Although she had initially been quiet and uncommunicative in my presence when I first arrived at K-9, we had gradually developed a relaxed and cordial relationship. The "icebreaker" occurred when she had needed to bring her six- or seven-year-old brother to work with her one day. So I bought a checker set from the PX and taught him how to play checkers. I called him Kim-Kim, which for some reason simply delighted him. And when he was permitted to keep the checkers and board our three-way relationship was firmly established.

I was genuinely amazed and pleasantly impressed by the strong rapport and positive and informal relationship that Doolittle had evidently established with these women, who appeared generally to me to be sullen, sad, and silent. Of course, I well knew that they were fully entitled to their "flat" and unemotional demeanor, as they were displaced and struggling refugees with little in their lives to be joyous about.

I was suddenly confronted by a dilemma: I wanted to listen longer to Doolittle's English lesson and enjoy vicariously the enlightenment and gleeful pleasure of his apt students (as he was an excellent instructor) and his obvious joy and gratification in teaching them, but I did not want to be revealed as a violator of their privacy. So I reluctantly but quietly moved away from the door within a matter of but several minutes. Two or three weeks later I had occasion to share a late breakfast with Doolittle and I reluctantly admitted to him that I had overheard part of one of his group presentations. He initially appeared to be hesitant, even embarrassed, about discussing his English classes for the Korean house girls. But when I informed him that I wished that I could get to know the Koreans better and learn more about their culture he opened up and readily described how "the class" had come to pass.

It seems that Doolittle had received a photograph from home of his wife and several of his children, one daughter being about Kim's age, and he had shown this photo to her. An ensuing discussion of his family had been the beginning of an ongoing "father and daughter" type of relationship, with Doolittle giving progressively more instruction to Kim in the proper usage of conversational English. It seems that Kim had an older cousin, also a house girl on base, who had assisted Kim in getting her job with our squadron. This cousin wanted desperately to learn the English language, so she joined Kim in attending the English lessons in our shack. Before long, several other aspiring English speakers among the house girls had also joined the group. Captain Doolittle was soon forced to move their sessions to the officers club as they interfered with the sleep requirements of other combat crewmembers during the afternoons prior to night flights over North Korea. These group English lessons had continued for several weeks before I had happened upon one in progress.

I then informed Doolittle about the awkwardness involved in my initial and minimal relationship with Kim, whom I had met four or five weeks before. I informed him of her reluctance or inability to reciprocate even the slightest display of friendship. He advised me that young, single men were very threatening to Kim, probably because of recent and vivid memories of experiences that she could not easily share with anyone. To explain her conduct, he then proceeded to relate her story to me, which her cousin had painfully and haltingly revealed to him in small bits and pieces over a period of time.

On the day after the invasion of South Korea, when the armies of North Korean soldiers poured across the border into South Korea to start the brutal regional war that was to extend over the following thirty-seven months, Kim had been returning home with her younger brother. Kim was fourteen or fifteen at the time and it was her daily chore to escort her brother to and from his primary school, a quarter mile from their home in a small town near Seoul, the capital of South Korea. Fortunately for them, they were met by some neighbors who were fleeing to the south as refugees with little more than the clothes on their backs. These well-meaning neighbors informed Kim that she could not return to her home as a small contingent of the North Korean political police force had invaded Kim's home and had taken her father and mother away as political prisoners.

Their house had been ransacked and gutted by a fire deliberately set as an example to their neighbors. The political police wanted to demonstrate the high price that was to be paid by those who resisted acceptance of communist doctrines. Kim later learned that her older sister, a democratically active university student, had been raped repeatedly and left with her throat slashed. Kim also learned that her father, a much-respected high school teacher with strong democratic beliefs, and her mother had been taken by force to North Korea and placed in a communist indoctrination center that was in fact a prison. When they both persisted in their opposition to communist indoctrination they were relocated to a labor camp farther north, where they were most probably worked, beaten, and starved to death.

This was the deep and pervasive psychological scar tissue that Kim carried with her to our K-9 AFB and to our squadron, comprised of primarily young and naive American combat crewmen who simply had no experience whatsoever of such brutality and inhumanity. After learning about Kim's terrifying experiences, I flew and fought with special purpose and determination. I had become fully convinced that the horrors of communism could eventually reach the shores of our country should we not vigorously resist both its viciously direct and often insidious advances. And I thought of Kim and her brutalized family every night when our heavily bomb-laden B-26 Invader entered the cold and hostile night skies over North Korea. This intense and vicious war had most certainly become for me a very personal one.

WONSAN BRIDGE

O N A GLARINGLY BRIGHT BUT FRIGID WINTER MORN-ing in the initial phase of my combat experience, I was kneeling in the nose of a B-26 light bomber, peering into the eyepiece of its Norden bombsight and staring at a massive steel-reinforced concrete bridge that extended across a wide river just west of the almost totally devastated industrial sector of Wonsan, North Korea's major seaport on the Sea of Japan. Amazingly, the weather data that we had received during preflight briefing was extremely accurate as to both wind speed and direction. Therefore, the precise settings and adjustments that I set into the bombsight caused the target to "ride" dead center, in the middle of the small space centered by the crosshairs (bouncing ever so slightly every now and then), and almost without perceptible drift in any direction or magnitude.

We were flying straight and level at exactly twelve thousand feet with unlimited visibility. Our airspeed was exactly 180 knots, slightly over three miles per minute. Since our first flight with Bob Crow, our pilot, Jerry Davis and I had been totally convinced that he was the best bomber pilot in the 95th Bomb Squadron, if not the entire 17th Bomb Group. Now it was his primary function to "nail" the two critical factors of speed and altitude during the bomb run by maintaining them exactly on the numbers despite moderate to heavy turbulence, and so he was doing once again with amazing consistency and accuracy.

Now if I could keep the center of the bridge in the center of the crosshairs by way of fine manual adjustments of the rate and drift knobs on the right side of the bombsight, our payload of ten five-hundred-pound GP bombs would be triggered off automatically by the bombsight at exactly the right point in time and airspace and a vital North Korean supply route would be seriously, if not permanently, disrupted. Anti-aircraft fire, generally referred to simply as "flak," varied from light to light-to-moderate. This was surprising, given the fact that three other jet-black Douglas B-26 bombers were tucked in closely behind us in a diamond configuration, with their bombardier-navigators awaiting my verbal "bombs away" command for the immediate release of their full bomb loads.

We had been assured during mission briefing that we would have adequate "top cover" over the target, delivered by Australian fighter-interceptor pilots flying Great Britain's first operational jet fighter, the Gloster F.8 Meteor. I never saw Meteors cycling overhead but most probably they were there at over forty thousand feet of altitude. Our major concern was that there might not be enough of them because highly proficient Russian "instructor" pilots, well experienced from fighting Germany's best Luftwaffe pilots during World War II, were at the time flying their own Russian manufactured MiG-15 jets displaying North Korean markings. If the MiGs were in fact there, far from MiG Alley where they generally operated, they would come screeching down out of the sun from fifty thousand feet or more at airspeeds over seven hundred knots. That meant that we would be sitting ducks in our vulnerable light bombers, flying straight and level for four painfully long minutes, with the Norden bombsight "locked in" and controlling the heading of the aircraft as we tracked down the bomb line.

I will never forget the sudden jarring of that bomb load's release: My large and clumsy P-1 helmet struck the sloping Plexiglas overhead as the aircraft rose abruptly upon the sudden loss of five thousand pounds of dead weight. Bob instinctively reacted by shoving the yoke forward to regain straight and level flight so that our bomb bursts could be accurately photographed by the camera, mounted in the underside of the fuselage. Momentarily dazed by the impact, I quickly recovered to stare downward and backward, leaning as far forward over the bombsight as the sloping Plexiglas nose would permit.

Being at medium altitude enabled me to see, with 100 percent visibility, the awesome impact of forty five-hundred-pounders on and around this major strategic target. Our formation took down four long steel-reinforced concrete sections of that massive bridge that day, and in so doing we cut off a substantial part of the heavy flow of men and materiel to the communist front line, then located just fifty miles to the south.

At debriefing we celebrated our success, drinking some really bad debriefing whiskey diluted with warm soda pop. There we acquired multiple crew sightings of substantial damage done as well as clear photography establishing its nature and extent. An intelligence officer gave me a black and white printout of the bomb strike. It was the most beautiful photograph that I had ever seen. But the purity of its beauty would be blurred and dulled with time and the confusing events that marked its passage.

I brought the photograph home with me upon completion of my tour of duty in Korea. Parenthetically, in 1954, while attending the Air Command and Staff School at Maxwell AFB in Montgomery, Alabama, I happened upon its reproduction in an official USAF Air University magazine. Somehow, somewhere, I lost both that aerial photograph and the USAF magazine where it was displayed, along with every other tangible reminder of my exciting, exhilarating, and yet terrifying and emotionally disturbing experiences in Korea.

Approximately a year after the Wonsan Bridge mission, I was at the Pentagon on official Air Force business. I happened to encounter a 95th Bomb Squadron bombardier-navigator who was at K-9 when I was there. We exchanged references to events, names, and months of service in Korea. Within a few minutes, he was telling me that he was "riding in the slot" directly behind our 26 on that memorable bomb run. As we both had appointments to keep we promptly ended out conversation but agreed to meet later that day for a few drinks. Continuing our discussion during a late afternoon session at a bar on K Street, we inquired about possible mutual friends in the squadron. We quickly established that there were few in number, as he had been finishing his tour of duty just as I was starting mine. He did not know Bob Crow and I did not know his pilot. He knew Colonel Bentley only officially as the new commanding officer of the 95th Bomb Squadron. Our conversation returned to the Wonsan Bridge daylight formation mission, which stood out in his mind, as it was the only one that he had participated in.

He volunteered that he had "shadowed [me] down the bomb run" through his bombsight and had observed a school bus on the bridge, relentlessly approaching my aiming point in the middle of it. He told me that he had often wondered if I had been aware of the school bus. I replied that my total concentration was upon the center section of the bridge and in keeping it in the absolute center of the crosshairs, and that I was totally unaware of the presence of a school bus, then and to the present day. He asked me what I would have done if I had seen the school bus on the bridge. I replied without hesitation: The bridge was a major strategic target and I would have proceeded to destroy it to the best of my abilities. After a few awkward moments, he stated that he did not think he could have done so had he had the responsibilities of lead bombardier. I assured him that he would have performed exactly as I had, but he remained quietly unconvinced.

He just sat in silence and stared at me. His statements, attitude, and conduct baffled and irritated me. So I asked him why he volunteered for service in the air force and why he later volunteered for training as a bombardier-navigator. His belated and unsatisfying response was something to the effect that he did not know what he was getting into when he enlisted and volunteered. Our session ended within a few minutes with each of us professing to have a prior commitment. No attempt was made by either of us to get the other's address or telephone number. To this day I cannot remember his name. And to this day I remain unconvinced that there was a school bus on the bridge at the time of our bomb run. Furthermore, if there had been a school bus on the bridge it is highly likely that it had been seized by the North Korean Army for use for troop transport.

To the date of this final manuscript submission, I have not diligently attempted, for some inexplicable reason, to contact any of the other B-26 crewmembers, about twelve in number, who participated in that successful four-ship daylight-bombing mission during January of 1953. Nor have I attempted to pursue a search of official USAF records to locate the air force periodical that contained the black and white strike photograph of the Wonsan Bridge taken all those years ago. I surmise that a psychiatrist could well conclude that the psychological block that has prevented me from delving into such distant and potentially disturbing memories is the consequence of some combination of unremitting guilt, remorse, and denial.

COMPARATIVE RISK

URING THE LAST SIX MONTHS OF THE KOREAN WAR the front line zigzagged across the middle of the Korean peninsula, with UNC forces well entrenched along the southern edge of the sporadically shifting no-man's land and overwhelming hordes of North Korean and Chinese communist forces aligned along the northern edge. This 150-mile strip of bomb-scarred battlefields shifted here and there and from time to time, but it rarely moved any substantial distance. Every major ground offensive, almost always initiated by the communist side, was met immediately, and usually quite effectively, by massive opposition and heavy retaliation by both UNC land forces and close air support.

On most of the approximately forty-five night missions that I flew in Douglas B-26s back and forth over this front line to bomb and strafe targets in North Korea, I had many excellent opportunities to gaze down from seven or eight thousand feet at the frequent and awesome exchanges of artillery, machine gun, and small arms fire that would suddenly erupt and then dwindle and die, frequently within just thirty seconds to three or four minutes. As a B-26 bombardier-navigator, I was in an ideal position to make these observations, as I could easily lean forward over the bombsight and use this perfect vantage point to look straight down through clear Plexiglas at truly impressive displays of firepower. Being in a situation of comparatively little risk, at least during these brief intervals when anti-aircraft fire was only infrequently directed toward our B-26, I was able to give these surreal battlefield sightings my rapt and undivided attention.

The primary reason for this unique opportunity to view these horrific but totally fascinating ground-to-ground combat operations was that the threat of an attack upon us by Russian-built MiG-15 fighter-interceptors was minimal. Although often flown by highly skilled and World War II combat-experienced Russian pilots, the MiGs could and would be driven off by our two squadrons of F-86F fighter-interceptors stationed at K-14 AFB, Kimpo, in close proximity to the front line. Another major reason for my sense of personal security and safety was that our small twin-engine bombers were painted jet black so that we were virtually invisible in the vast darkness of the Korean sky. Also, our enemies, strangely, did not seem to have the types of anti-aircraft artillery that had any high degree of accuracy, as we were rarely fired upon in entering or departing North Korean airspace at these mid-level altitudes.

Although a significant number of disturbing visual images of these ground-to-ground battles have become somewhat blurred in my recurring bad dreams over the years, I recall clearly one particularly significant incident. It occurred during one of our late night B-26 penetrations into North Korean airspace during the initial phase of my on-the-job training as a combat bombardier-navigator, probably on the ninth or tenth mission of my tour of duty.

Bob Crow had extinguished our running lights five minutes south of the front line in accordance with SOP. A brilliant chalk-white full moon was shining directly overhead, and everything below was cast in blackness or in one of many shades of silver or gray, except for the hot colors of sporadic and random exchanges of ground fire up and down the front lines.

Suddenly, directly below and before me, a long burst of machine gun fire erupted from the south side of the Punch Bowl. This half of this easily recognized and ancient volcanic crater, about five miles across and rimmed by peaks ranging from one to two thousand feet high, was then occupied by American troops, and the machine gun fire came from a position that seemed to be well forward of our line of resistance. This stream of red tracers swept quite rapidly back and forth, as if its small crew, probably just three or four men in number, were attempting to slow or suppress an advancing charge by communist foot soldiers attacking from the north. It appeared to me that the North Korean or Chinese forces had succeeded in crawling much too close before they began a crazed charge in massive numbers, and that this UNC machine gun team was firing rapidly and almost continuously to avoid being overrun. In any event, in just moments four communist machine guns, well spaced and firing from positions of varying but higher elevations, one quickly after another, had honed in on that single machine gun team and relentlessly poured round after round into it. All of these communist machine guns were consecutively vectoring their streams of fire upon that single gun placement, but for some inexplicable reason there was no responding cross fire, no visible retaliation whatsoever coming from other UNC gun positions nearby!

I was aghast: I simply could not understand the total lack of fire support. And it seemed to me that the incoming streams of fire continued for several long and painful minutes, although it was probably no more than thirty seconds before a small yellow-white explosion suddenly appeared where that isolated machine gun crew was located. For several minutes the communist machine gunners continued to pour in needless rounds of green tracered fire. Then these guns fell silent, one quickly after the other.

I continued to stare downward in total disbelief as I knelt in an appropriate posture of prayer above and behind the bombsight: I was quite certain that I had just witnessed three or four young American lives brutally extinguished in a matter of seconds or minutes. Although I could not see their mangled and bloodied bodies I knew that they were there, bleeding out in the snow, wind, and darkness. But then I also knew that there could and should be little time to mourn their deaths.

But now I must acknowledge, with some substantial measure of guilt and shame, that the exchanges of deadly front line ground fire on our inbound approach to assigned North Korean targets prepared me for the bombing and strafing runs that awaited us in the deep darkness of North Korea. Witnessing these intense but short battles always sharpened my vision and quickened my reflexes. But on our outbound leg several hours later, I would almost always shudder uncontrollably with a sense of dread and sadness as we passed slowly over the front lines at a relatively safe altitude into the totally safe airspace over South Korea. It was there and then that I was irresistibly impelled to stare fixedly downward at the killing fields receding behind us while vicariously feeling the pain and loneliness of the foot soldiers below.

I would then inevitably visualize all too clearly the cold and miserable American soldiers and marines living and dying in that primitively brutal environment beneath us, with little or no hope or expectation of escaping from it. In sharp contrast, we were, with little comparative risk, fleeing to safety and personal comfort, being just a few hours away from warm and clean beds and the deep sleep of total exhaustion, as well as relief, at least for another two or three days and nights, from the anxiety, tension, and raw fear that always lurked subliminally and never really ever left us.

ONE POINT FOR THE HOME TEAM!

THE DOUGLAS B-26 HAD TWO POWERFUL PRATT-
Whitney R-2800 rotary engines, each generating two thousand
horses of raw power. It could stay airborne for quite a distance and for
quite a while with only one engine churning. The major exception was
during takeoff roll, liftoff, and the initial climb toward outbound altitude, when very heavy wing loading from the aggregation of maximum
bomb loads, full fuel tanks, fully loaded machine guns, and full combat
crews made the start of every combat mission an exciting, precarious,
and gut-wrenching experience. Bob, Jerry, and I were always acutely
aware and concerned about this initial and most dangerous phase of
the mission: the takeoff roll and liftoff and the struggle for airspeed and
altitude when full power from both engines was vitally needed.

I remember remarkably well the start of a typical combat mission
when we were irreversibly committed to the first phase of that adventure. I was strapped in for takeoff on runway 15 in the noisy and unheated Plexiglas nose of a bone-chillingly cold B-26C. We were first in
line, with our engines idling near the end of the taxiway. Bob and Jerry
were behind and above me, also ready and eager for our departure. We
were waiting for voice clearance from the control tower to begin trundling onto the asphalt runway for departure on its south-southeasterly

heading of 150 degrees. Upon receiving clearance, Bob taxied the aircraft to the very edge of the overrun on the north end of the runway, reaching for every extra foot of level surface, to give proper respect to the significance of maximum weight combined with a short bumpy six thousand foot runway that was only five feet above sea level and thirty yards from the frigid waters of Suyong Bay.

Figuratively "standing on the brake pedals," Bob steadily and progressively added power evenly to both engines ("balls to the wall") and, with maximum power settings of 52" of manifold pressure and 2,700 revolutions per minute, eased off the brakes to begin a hurtling rush down and between the two rows of white runway lights. The B-26 bounced roughly on the oleo struts and lurched forward, slowly and then steadily gaining speed. The one-thousand-foot markers on the sides of the runway rushed past us with ever shortening time intervals between them. By the time Bob attained the critical minimum take-off speed of 135 knots (nautical miles per hour) we were almost at the end of runway 15. He gently pulled the steering column toward him and eased the 26 into the air. Looking straight down, it seemed to me that we were no more than five feet off the ground as the base perimeter road, and then the wide sandy beach, zipped beneath us. Still with maximum power settings, Bob held the nose down, flying dangerously low and close to the white-capped, murky yellowish brown waters of Suyong Bay to gain, slowly but steadily, additional airspeed and then to lift almost imperceptibly into the dark Asian sky. Finally, with a margin of safety attained, he gradually turned the 26 back to the left and north toward the darker winter skies of North Korea.

We could not take off in the logical upwind (northerly) direction to gain quicker liftoff because of the excessive weight of our fully loaded aircraft and resultant risk of not having sufficient airspeed and altitude to clear the coastal mountains that closely contained K-9 AFB on three sides: west, north, and east. We were carrying that night a maximum bomb load of ten napalm bombs, each weighing five hundred pounds, with two of them racked under each wing and the other six in the bomb bay. The ammo cans were fully loaded with five hundred rounds for each of our ten .50 caliber Browning machine guns, with three machine guns embedded in the leading edge of each wing and two machine guns in the top turret and two in the bottom turret. We also carried a topped-off main tank of high-octane aviation fuel and full wing and auxiliary fuel tanks, as our primary target was a recently rebuilt and strategically critical railroad bridge and viaduct located in the far northeastern quadrant of North Korea close to the coastline and only seventy-five miles southwest of North Korea's common boundary with Russia.

By happenstance, from our first night combat mission deep into North Korea, our crew had begun developing and repeating almost ritualistic pre-flight and in-flight procedures and practices that we continued through the end of our tour of duty. We did not realize these rigidly structured behavioral patterns were based upon superstition, but they most assuredly were! I am sure that we all believed that unknown and unknowable dangers or disasters would befall us should we not fully and assiduously comply with each and every one of our rituals.

The first ritual that comes to mind was our clumsy and seemingly whimsical manner of keeping track of the running total of our combat missions flown. During the final stages of the Korean War, every Douglas B-26 crewmember was required by Fifth Air Force directive to fly only fifty missions over enemy territory to qualify for a free ride back to the United States, usually on a chartered commercial airline. Our crews were fortunate, as the B-26 bomber crews before us (i.e., during 1950 and 1951 when fully qualified B-26 flight crews were in critically short supply) had been required to fly from fifty-five to eighty missions for their tour of duty to be deemed to have been completed.

To gain "credit" for a combat mission flown, a crew had to have made penetration into enemy territory, combined with some type of substantial combat activity, such as dropping bombs upon enemy targets and/or being exposed to hostile enemy action by way of taking fire from enemy aircraft or ground weapons (e.g., triple A batteries, automatic weapons, small arms). For some unremembered reason, our crew counted each qualifying mission as 2 percent of the total, or two points, upon the premise that 50 missions times two equals 100 percent of the required tour and qualification for the return ticket home.

Thus, when the coincidence of attained safe speed and altitude occurred, Bob, Jerry, and I simultaneously double-clicked our mike buttons. Immediately and together, we shouted out the score: "One point for the home team!" In retrospect, it seems now to have been rather silly or childish, and even more embarrassing in the telling, but at that instant this ritual confirmed for us that this mission had reached the half-way point in terms of dangers and difficulties to be encountered and that we were on a downhill glide, when in stark reality, the combat mission had hardly begun.

To several other combat crewmen of the 95th, our crew's method of tallying missions flown simply made no sense at all, and they did not hesitate to express their disdain or amusement. But to us, it made perfectly good sense. So we relentlessly continued the practice straight through our last mission in late July of 1953. And we had a simple and valid reason: it was our unique way of continually recognizing and respecting the brutal reality that the most hazardous phase of every B-26 bombing mission started with the takeoff roll at the far north end of runway 15 and ended when we had achieved sufficient altitude and airspeed to be able to start a gradual climbing turn back to the north for our final ascent to the assigned inbound altitude of eight thousand feet en route to North Korea.

Upon completion of the mission and just as the B-26's three huge rubber-tired wheels squeaked upon first impact with the runway, hours later back at K-9, we would again shout out in unison, this time uttering just two words, "two points," and without the customary double-click. For quite a while I could not remember why we did it differently upon touchdown. Now I believe it was because Bob's hands were then strongly gripping the yoke at the top of the steering column, at the three o'clock and nine o'clock positions, in aiming the plane straight down the center of the runway and against any prevailing crosswind. And Bob was off the intercom channel at that precise moment when the wheels seemed to be feeling for the runway in the darkness, and the B-26 was no longer a beautiful bird in flight but suddenly a land-bound projectile streaking and decelerating up runway 33 as Bob pumped the brakes and brought the plane under control on its tricycle landing gear.

Another memorable crew ritual was manifested in collective and instantaneous response to the enemy's blinding and terrifying searchlight beams. It seems that when we least expected it, we would get caught in the glare of high-powered searchlights that reached vertically to thirty thousand plus feet and were well coordinated in operation with radar-controlled batteries of triple A weapons. Searchlights shattered night vision for five to ten minutes and necessitated pulling off targets until full vision was restored.

Being usually at low altitude, we would enter and depart the narrow beam of light quickly and leave it behind us. Then, the colonel or Bob Crow, as the case might be, would accelerate to the maximum by shoving "the balls to the wall" and sharply banking and climbing out of the valley, not to return to that area again that night. When Bob was flying the airplane, Jerry and I would shout in unison, "Turn off the fucking light!" I don't remember Bob saying anything when a searchlight hit us: I guess he was just too busy avoiding vertigo and flying the airplane. That shout of defiance and outrage always had a positive effect upon me, although I realized it was an exercise in hostility, futility, and stupidity. But Jerry and I still did it each of the several times a searchlight blinded us.

There were a number of other combat rituals, or habits or practices if you will, that Bob, Jerry, and I consciously or unconsciously pursued or adhered to. For example, when the squadron's transport truck stopped to pick us up, Bob would always climb aboard first, then me, and then Jerry. Whether I was then a first or second lieutenant, Bob always outranked me and I felt that I had no choice but to defer to his higher military status. And Jerry would do likewise for me. In fact, I remember three or four times when I held the door open for Jerry but he absolutely refused to enter before me. Each time I finally relented and entered ahead of him, saying "thank you" as I did so. I have often wondered if Jerry was acting out of respect for higher rank or was unthinkingly adhering to a ritual in fear of our sustaining the deadly consequence of the failure to honor the mystic powers of an entrenched superstition.

THE TUNNEL

A SHORT, NARROW, AND SLOPING CRAWLWAY ON THE right side of the Douglas B-26C Invader connects its cockpit with the bombardier-navigator's nose compartment. Everybody seemed to refer to it as "the tunnel." The actual length of this confining passageway is between five and seven feet, depending upon who measures it and how it is measured. But until just recently, I firmly believed that it was at least nine to eleven feet long because of certain unpleasant memories of the tunnel that I have carried over many decades. Often I've dreamt about and remembered, with disturbing clarity, the stressful experience of crawling downward at a sharp angle and in total darkness, from the right seat in the cockpit to get into the nose of the aircraft.

I was introduced to the Douglas B-26C and its Plexiglas nose compartment on my arrival at Langley AFB in Virginia in the autumn of 1952 for crew orientation and training. At the start of every training mission, or subsequent combat mission in Korea, I entered the nose directly by way of three "steps" recessed into the interior surface of a drop-down rectangular door cut into the bottom of the bombardier-navigator's compartment or via the clamshell canopy of the B-26C and then through the tunnel from the right seat. I consistently preferred to be in the nose before the aircraft took off and to continue to be there throughout the entire mission, until finally exiting down through the same door to the PSP (pierced steel planking) hardstand below.

However, our standard operation procedures changed drastically in late January 1953 after several tragic B-26C crashes occurred just before and after I arrived on base.

On December 10, 1952, a 34th Bomb Squadron bombardier-navigator was killed while in the nose compartment on takeoff of a B-26C when the nose wheel collapsed near the end of runway. His pilot, SHORAN operator, and gunner/flight engineer were injured when the aircraft crashed close to the shoreline of Suyong Bay. That accident occurred at K-1 AFB, on the west side of the city of Pusan, where our 17th Bomb Group was operating temporarily while the worn out PSP runway at K-9 was being replaced by asphalt.

On January 13, 1953, a second B-26C crash occurred back at K-9 after the 17th Bomb Group had returned upon the completion of runway reconstruction. In this accident, a B-26C assigned to the 37th Bomb Squadron crashed into Suyong Bay, and all three crewmembers were killed just two miles after liftoff from runway 15.

A third crash had occurred earlier, on August 5, 1952, when a 95th Bomb Squadron Douglas B-26C ran off the end of runway 15, veered sharply to the left, and finally came to a dead stop near the water's edge. Either this B-26C lost power in both engines as it hurtled down the runway or the pilot pulled the throttles back and ground looped it on the beach. The pilot, James Timossi; the bombardier-navigator, Edwin West; and the gunner-flight engineer, Wayne Knowles, all escaped without serious injuries.

As the direct consequence of these and similar mishaps on B-26C takeoffs and landings in-theatre, a directive came down from Far East Air Force (FEAF) Headquarters in Tokyo that specifically prohibited the bombardier-navigator from being in the nose compartment during takeoffs and landings. Instead, he was to remain in the tunnel for the duration. I did not readily embrace this edict. In fact, I attempted to resist it by ignoring it. Initially, I was unsuccessful. And my pilot was instructed to instruct me to cease and desist further resistance to the directive.

Immediately upon delivery of this generally unpopular directive from Tokyo, a crude but effective harness was devised and installed half way down the tunnel by our creative aircraft maintenance personnel. "Jerry-rigged" was the term used in describing the installation process. By use of this new torture device, the bombardier-navigator entered the tunnel from either end and, with considerable turning, twisting, tugging, and cursing, connected heavy straps around his upper legs and across his chest while lying back upon the "floor" of the tunnel. The other ends of these short, confining straps were rudely attached to the rough and irregular metal surfaces of both sides of the tunnel. But the bombardier-navigator had no intercom connection in this confined space during subsequent takeoff and landing if he happened to forget to bring with him an extension cord for his intercom connection. Furthermore, because of multiple layers of heavy winter flight clothing, parachute harness, life preserver, and so on, it was much too easy for him to get "hung up" in the tunnel due to the many sharp-edged and protruding metal flanges, ribs, and rough surfaces.

As I remember all too well, the first time I was secured in the tunnel for takeoff I could not extricate myself without the assistance of Jerry Davis, who had to reach down into the tunnel and struggle mightily in lifting and tugging me back toward the cockpit. It is very embarrassing to admit, even now, but I quickly became claustrophobic in that cold, noisy, and confining space before I was pulled free. Then I had to hurriedly repeat the tunnel entry process from the cockpit side, get again secured in the clumsy harness rig, extricate myself from it after we attained altitude, and then wiggle through the rest of the tunnel to enter the nose of the B-26C to belatedly begin my navigating and bombing chores.

As it did not get any easier on the next two or three missions, I began to take off and land in the right seat, with Jerry occupying the jump seat, directly behind the right seat. After the aircraft climbed safely to inbound altitude, I entered and slid and wiggled through the tunnel as Jerry climbed into right seat, where he remained until I returned to the cockpit before the start of letdown, upon returning to and approaching runway 33 from the south at K-9.

After two or three more missions and without consent from Captain Crow or any expressed agreement among us, I began to enter the nose compartment through the nose hatch and remain in the nose compartment throughout the entire approach and landing process. Upon returning to base, I then exited the aircraft as I had before the FEAF directive went into effect, by the simple process of lifting the partial, hinged metal panel upon which I knelt while performing Norden bombing operations, then reaching down and turning the metal exterior door handle ninety degrees to the left, and pushing that exit door downward and backward. I would then take three steps down to the ground below. In the event of an emergency bailout of the Douglas B-26, whether the B or C variant, this exterior exit door would be swung down and back and it would be immediately torn from the aircraft by the force of our 180 mph slipstream. I would then be able to safely, quickly, and easily exit the aircraft headfirst while facing downward and toward the tail of the B-26.

After another mission or two, I climbed directly into the nose compartment prior to takeoff. And Jerry climbed directly into the right seat for takeoff. Nobody said a word about this final step in our gradual transition back to our original positions within the B-26 prior to takeoff. And I recall vividly a great feeling of elation and relief when we roared past the control tower in reaching for takeoff speed. Although I am quite sure that my white P-1 helmet could not be seen by anyone in the control tower as we hurtled past it on takeoff roll and liftoff, I nonetheless leaned far back against the bulkhead to prevent visual detection by anyone who might be in a position to report my willful violation of that obnoxious directive.

Shortly after my return to the nose compartment for the entire combat mission when with my own crew, I was designated by Colonel Bentley to ride with him on another mission. Again, but with false confidence, I climbed directly into the nose compartment after my removal of the safety pins from our bomb load. The colonel never said a word about it.

My decision to willfully and repeatedly disregard the FEAF directive may sound crazy to some, but I then considered the risks of death or injury in being positioned in the nose of the B-26C during takeoffs and landings as minimal and therefore acceptable. The logical reasons were just two in number, but they were overwhelmingly persuasive to me: I was flying with one or the other of the two best B-26 pilots in the air force, and the Douglas B-26 at that time was the most powerful and sturdy light bomber ever designed and constructed.

Not to be minimized is the fact that experiencing the deafening roar of the B-26's huge engines while seeing and feeling the maximum acceleration quickly attained as we rushed down that short six-thousand-foot runway were for me among the high points of my entire tour of combat duty. The combined elements of danger, excitement, expectation, and adventure were simply indescribable. And as the thousand-foot markers along the side of the runway flashed by at successively shorter intervals on takeoff roll, a sensation of sheer exhilaration charged my body with levels of elation, energy, and exuberance that were truly electrifying.

LOOKING FOR TROUBLE

WHILE WE WERE LITTLE CHILDREN GROWING UP IN Chicago during the privations of the thirties, my older sister and brother and I would become bored during the frequent winter storms. We could not play outside and there was little to do inside, and little to do it with. Television was yet to be discovered, radio was limited and not directed to small children, and toys and books were few in number and ours had but little unused entertainment value. Inevitably, the teasing sessions that ensued would quickly escalate to finger jabs, punches to the upper arms, and other minor assaults and batteries, one upon the others. Our mother would then suddenly appear and sternly inquire as to who was "looking for trouble?" Although she was very patient, gentle, and persevering, we all knew that she could and would resort to corporal punishment if and when sufficiently provoked, and we would, collectively, often provide more than adequate provocation. We would then, in vocal unison, assure her that none of us was looking for trouble, and we would quickly improvise and discover useful things to constructively engage us.

Years later, while involved in a single ship B-26 armed reconnaissance mission along the eastern shoreline of North Korea in the dead of a bitter cold winter night, I might find little if any vehicular traffic moving down the roads or railroad tracks from Manchuria or Russia. On such occasions I would hear Bob Crow's static-ladened voice come into my headset with an occasional question, generally phrased as "Art, what are you doing down there?" My customary and immediate response was simply, "Just looking for trouble, Bob." And that was in fact my primary military duty at that time and place. There really was nothing more to say, so generally I said nothing more. Some B-26 combat aircrews were very "chatty" over enemy territory, there being an almost endless stream of talk of little value between pilot, bombardier-navigator, and gunner via intercom. But on our aircraft we spoke to each other only when reasonably necessary. We knew that Bob's multiple contact frequencies with K-9 Tower, Ground Control Stations, Forward Air Controllers, and other UNC aircraft were wired separately from our B-26's intercom circuitry, but I saw no sense in taking chances with electrical devices that were always capable of malfunctioning.

We kept almost total radio silence because of the obviously serious nature of our situation. We all liked and respected each other but found little need or value in aimless or comedic conversation. Furthermore, total silence seemed to help us in concentrating our attention and efforts upon seeing and responding quickly to the streams of anti-aircraft fire that could come our way at any time. We were all too well aware that at three thousand feet or less, the sudden and simply terrifying triple A tracers and/or searchlights could be upon us before we could either see or react to them.

Working daily in the 95th Squadron's operations shack and overhearing Colonel Bentley in conversation, I had learned that there were a significant number of mobile radar-controlled anti-aircraft gun batteries, commonly referred to as "flak traps," often positioned well north of the front line and capably manned by highly trained and skilled Russian gunnery crews. These enemy triple A crews were comprised of World War II combat veterans who were highly seasoned during

Russia's extensive ground defense operations against German aircraft, and they had performed together for years with accuracy, consistency, and determination. They were distanced well behind the front line for the additional purpose of providing training for North Korean ground personnel in the use of Russia's advanced and highly technical radar tracking systems in areas where there were frequent overflights of enemy targets, such as our tactical group's intensive and nightly B-26 low-level, low-speed bombing and strafing raids. Furthermore, by being positioned a safe and secure distance north of the front line, these Russian flak traps faced minimum risk of being overrun and captured by UNC ground forces. Of course, such a capture of combat personnel would be a major embarrassment to both the Russian and North Korean governments as it would again be revealed to the whole world that Russian military forces were actively engaged in what North Korea still claimed was its own "civil war" upon its own peninsula.

I was sorely tempted to share this interesting but worrisome intelligence with my own crew, but as they did not have the "need to know" I withheld it. Another good reason for not divulging it to them was that it would be an additional cause for fear and anxiety that Bob and Jerry did most certainly not need. Besides, what could they do with this information if they had it? But I myself was glad to know about the flak traps, as this knowledge served to increase my vigilance and resolve.

Over enemy territory I was continually on my knees, simulating the appearance of a praying mantis, leaning forward and looking down over the Norden bombsight. In this position I would either stare fixedly at the rarely straight and frequently intertwining road and railroad tracks below us or range my eyes, by quick and frequent movements of my head and upper body, left and right and then left again. By moonlight, Bob could quite often see the darkened roadway and/or railroad bed almost as well as I could, and he would make heading corrections without the need of instruction. But when it appeared that he had lost or was losing sight of the road and/or tracks, I would call to him with approximate heading changes, such as "ten [degrees] left" or "fifteen [degrees] right." When he was again approaching on-track alignment I would simply say "on course" or, much more frequently, I would simply give him a quick double click of the intercom button continually held firmly in my left hand.

I had, and still have to a somewhat lesser extent, superior night vision. However, I did not then appreciate the considerable value of this capability: it frequently enabled me to see and cause quick and positive responses to ground targets during hours of darkness well before they were seen by others with equal opportunity. But this visual acuity had both upside and downside consequences; I learned early into my combat tour that this advantage in achieving fast target identification and fast reaction was a major reason why Colonel Bentley drafted me to fly with him after Captain Bob Abelman, his regular bombardier-navigator, had completed his fifty mission tour and had departed K-9 AFB.

This capability, which both my assigned pilot and the colonel were apparently quite willing to rely upon, enabled us to fly deeper into the valleys of North Korea and to gain a greater degree of target accuracy, particularly under frequently adverse weather conditions. Ours were mostly moving targets, and the lower we could get, the shorter the bombs' trajectory and the greater the probability of more direct hits, or at least near misses. The latter were frequently as destructive as direct hits because even a single, small, and jagged bomb fragment could penetrate the firebox of a steam engine or the gas tank or fuel cargo of a truck and cause total destruction.

These target sightings gave rise to many hard decisions for me as a bombardier. In fact, a typical night bombing mission, particularly during winter months of heavy cloud cover when trains and trucks were more likely to be on the move, was an almost endless series of difficult decisions that had to be made quickly and accurately before the multiple options they presented were suddenly gone. For example, I might sight three or four trucks in close proximity to each other that were moving with headlights activated. Would this closely clustered target justify release of two five-hundred-pound GP bombs when I could look further up the road and see larger clusters of trucks, also in close proximity one to the others, which were a better application of our ordnance?

Of necessity, as bombardier, I usually had sole discretion on each mission as to the time, place, and number of bombs on each release of bomb load, totaling either ten five-hundred-pound demolition bombs or ten five-hundred-pound napalm bombs. I was always well aware that I needed to make every bomb count, and each of these critical decisions involved the careful but quick consideration of numerous factors of ever-varying weight.

But with gained experience and confidence came the judgment and decisiveness required. And sometimes prodigious and truly awesome results were achieved. One night two locomotives, hitched in tandem, exploded, and their trailing and heavily loaded box cars plowed into them and they, in turn, exploded in sequence like a short string of firecrackers. This sort of outcome was exactly why "looking for trouble" was worth all of the efforts made, the physical and emotional energy expended, and the substantial risks willingly but sometimes stupidly or even recklessly assumed.

ACCIDENTAL HEROES

ONE NIGHT IN EARLY MARCH OF THE LONG AND SE-
vere winter of 1952–53, our three-man Douglas B-26 crew was
working over the truck convoys coming down the rugged east coast of
North Korea from Russia. The multi-deck cloud cover was moderate to
heavy. But the big winds sweeping down from Manchuria provided us
with numerous openings and frequent visual sightings of heavy truck
movements toward the front line. We were assigned to patrol and bomb
targets of opportunity on one of the enemy's critical main supply routes,
a winding MSR almost at water level that extended about one hundred
miles from Hungnam northeast to the seaport city of Kimch'aek (previously known as Songjin), which was a coastal city just another one
hundred and fifty miles south of the Russian border. Another seventy
miles further northeast of the border was Russia's major seaport of Vladivostok, from which high numbers of truck convoys and freight trains
departed, carrying weapons, munitions, and supplies that continually
poured into North Korea, despite our persistent attacks.

We had been more lucky than skillful that night. With only the
slightest changes in headings, I had been able to drop two five-hundred-
pound GPs in rapid sequence on each of four widely spaced moving
target clusters comprised of small segments of truck convoys. We caused
secondary explosions and/or sustained fires at three of the four drop-
sites without receiving any significant triple A or small arms fire. We

had been benefited by strong head winds, ranging from forty to fifty knots directly on the nose, giving me ample time to carefully line up each target on all four runs on generally northeasterly headings. We were cruising at approximately three thousand feet and just clearing the peaks of the ancient and worn eastern mountain ranges of North Korea. Whenever I could see a string of headlights of convoyed southbound supply trucks, when coming to a break in the clouds or through a thin shroud of ground fog, I requested a fairly steep dive, rounding out at seven hundred to eight hundred feet of terrain clearance for each bomb run, initiated almost immediately upon level out to preserve the element of surprise. Right after each bomb run Bob would apply full power while climbing sharply out over the Sea of Japan. For the next run he would execute a racetrack pattern back over land in what would again be an upwind direction heading northeasterly along the coastline.

Just five months before, I had been thoroughly trained as an aviation cadet at Mather AFB to operate the Norden bombsight, generally from bombing altitudes ranging from eight thousand feet to twelve thousand feet. However, that training was almost totally useless as we were forced to attack targets of opportunity in North Korea at night at much lower levels necessitated by brutal winter weather, limited visibility, and the movement of targets. Fortunately, we did receive adequate on-the-job training at K-9 in the proper use of a simplistic optical device referred to as the reflex sight. I used this primitive but effective appendage to the Norden bombsight on over forty of my fifty combat missions in Korea.

The reflex sight was a small and simple optical mechanism that was securely attached to the top of the black metal frame housing of the Norden bombsight, which was then locked permanently in a straight-ahead alignment. The Norden contained a well-functioning gyroscope that ensured that the bombsight was level throughout the bomb run, despite the rocking and rolling of the aircraft due to turbulence. The reflex sight did not require use of this stabilizing feature of the Norden: it was simply not needed at such low altitudes due to the short time span of the trajectory of the bomb. The reflex sight's targeting component was simply manipulated by the bombardier's right hand in "leading" the selected target as it appeared visually to move toward and below the aircraft. The bombardier used the end joint of his left thumb to manually "punch out" the bomb, as the target appeared to pass under the reflex sight's horizontal crosshair.

In normal operation at altitude, the Norden bombsight automatically adjusted for the speed and direction of the then prevailing wind. So when it was "locked in" to the pilot's autopilot and controlling electronically the heading of the aircraft down the bomb line, the bomber pilot was responsible only for maintaining precise airspeed and altitude as the Norden was continually directing the plane's heading into the wind by way of the bombardier's continuous and minute adjustments of its rate knob and drift knob to and through the point of automatic bomb release. In contrast, when the bombardier was using the reflex sight alone at low altitudes, he would just "call out" on intercom the desired heading corrections, such as "seven degrees right, three more right, one left," to his pilot to enable him to manually make appropriate and timely course corrections throughout the bomb run. At such low altitudes, at but three nautical miles per minute, direct hits were not essential or in fact that often achieved. The objective was to "bracket" the AP (aiming point), that is, the specific pair of truck headlights or the plume of steam from a streaking locomotive, selected for target sighting, with one bomb being released "early" and the second bomb released "late" along the railroad track ahead of the moving target.

In the periods of heavy truck traffic that most frequently occurred at night, and especially during bad weather conditions, the trucks in convoy often ran with only every third or fourth truck being driven with its headlights on so that what appeared to be a five-truck convoy was in fact often a fifteen- to twenty-truck convoy. In such "target rich" situations, precision bombing was always sought but not essential, with wide-ranging bomb fragments doing their deadly work. Nor was precision often possible, due to the simple, primitive nature of the manual reflex bombing system and the varying speeds of the trucks along almost continually winding roadways through rough mountainous terrain.

After our fourth bomb run, with just two five-hundred-pound GP bombs still hanging in the bomb bay, we decided to head back down the coast. We had spread out our attacks over considerable time and distance for maximum efficiency and desired TOT (time over target), and we still had a long trip home without too wide a margin of safety as to fuel left in the tanks. Nonetheless, I suggested we make one last run at the wharf-side cargo unloading and warehousing facilities at Hungnam. Bob hesitated but reluctantly agreed.

Carried away by overconfidence, I felt that we were "on a roll" and that four out of five productive bomb runs would indeed make it a most satisfying night. However, just as we entered the industrial and warehousing sector of the city, five or six streams of fiery green tracers zipped vertically past us, terrifyingly close, and suddenly lighting up the sky on all sides. So without aiming at any target whatsoever, I punched out the last two five-hundred-pounders and flicked the bomb bay toggle switch upward to the "doors closed" position, while screaming "Break left!" into the intercom and ducking back and away from the exposed Plexiglas nose of the aircraft, as if this would provide any more protection.

Bob shoved the "balls to the wall," banking sharply to the left and heading over the shoreline and out to sea. He kept the nose low to gain speed, and the plane crossed close to Yodo Island while we were still below five hundred feet. He then began a gradual but steady climb to our customary outbound altitude of seven thousand feet.

I apologized to Bob and Jerry about eight or ten times on our way back to base, as I realized that I had foolishly been much too "target greedy." In fact, during the last hour of flight hardly anyone spoke on intercom as we had just experienced another episode of sudden fear and chilling terror and, for me alone, there was the additional psychological burden of both embarrassment and guilt for an exercise of very poor judgment: I had simply pushed our luck too far and too hard and all three of us had almost paid the ultimate price.

After landing uneventfully and, amazingly, without detecting damage of any kind to the aircraft, we circled the runway in the back of an open truck and entered the debriefing shack. There we gave a detailed strike report and all three of us confirmed the bomb damage assessment. By that time I was totally drained, physically and emotionally, and did not even consider stopping at the mess for a cup of canned fruit juice and greasy bacon and eggs.

The next afternoon, as I sat alone in the latrine, Jerry Davis poked his head in the outer door and shouted that our crew had been ordered to report to the debriefing shack immediately. He inquired as to Bob's location. I informed him that I had no idea. He said he would continue looking for Bob and that a truck was waiting for us in front of the operations shack. We quickly gathered at the truck and rode in total silence back along the perimeter road, each of us wondering anxiously what could have gone wrong. Upon entering the 17th Bomb Group's debriefing shack we were confronted by two silent intelligence officers, a lieutenant colonel and a major, neither of whom we had ever seen before. No one else was in the room. There was total silence. We were alone, as all other crews who had flown the night before had long since come and gone after their debriefings.

Before we had always been debriefed by one or two of four or five familiar and friendly captains and/or first lieutenants. These two unfamiliar field grade officers, seated side by side, were quite solemn, and we hesitated before we sat down across from them. I was about to salute them but stopped just in time, as such was not the accepted military protocol in a combat area. The major shoved a black and white photograph toward me and I looked at it. Nothing registered. I passed it to Bob, who studied it carefully. He then passed it to Jerry. We looked at each other and Jerry passed it back to the major. None of us had recognized anything in the photograph. Nobody spoke. Each of us just continued to look at the other four at the table and no one said anything. At least a minute crept by. Total silence.

The major finally smiled and said, "Well, it comes from the belly camera in your aircraft." So each of us scrutinized the photograph; again, nothing looked familiar. We passed the photo back across the table again. "Look more closely, gentlemen," the major instructed. And he continued, "The slightly curving lines on both sides of the print appear to be the sides of a fully loaded coastal freighter. Lieutenant, your first bomb impact is right there, landing just aft of the main smoke stack, and the second hit near the bow of the ship. You must have released them in a very rapid sequence." All of us stared at the photo. Near the bottom was a large bomb burst and near the top of the photo was a smaller burst, but of a darker color against an almost white background. I acknowledged that I did "quick release" our last two bombs without any target in sight because "golf balls" had suddenly begun to stream past us, arching upward from both sides. I explained that I had not wanted to waste ordnance and that we then had to make a hurried departure.

To our considerable relief and surprise, both the lieutenant colonel and the major then commended us upon the success of our mission and shook the hand of each of us in turn. After a few minutes of small talk and forced laughter, Bob, Jerry, and I came to the obvious conclusion that nothing was left to be said. Our crew rose in unison, saluted needlessly, departed the building, and returned to our squadron area via the waiting open truck. We laughed excessively on the way back, totally relieved from the anxiety and apprehension that we had felt earlier. Apparently each of us quickly forgot the entire incident afterwards. I know that I did. In fact, I don't think that I mentioned the accidental sinking of a coastal freighter to anyone else in the squadron.

Over the next three or four days it snowed heavily and almost continuously so all squadrons "stood down." On the morning after the snowstorm we went to crew briefing at the customary early morning hour, as the skies had fully cleared and our crew had been on the posted Battle Order the previous day. Upon our arrival, we walked up the crude wooden steps and into the group's briefing shack. Several steps inside the door was an interior and partial wall upon which miscellaneous notices and bomb photos were posted periodically for general informational purposes. To my surprise there was prominently displayed at eye level an enlarged version of our errant bomb strike upon the enemy coastal freighter. Right beside it was another photograph of the freighter that appeared to have been taken in broad daylight and from a much higher altitude.

This second photo, probably taken by an air force or navy reconnaissance aircraft the next day, showed the front third of the freighter under water and revealed considerable damage to its fore deck. This photo was aligned to parallel our line of flight, from stern to bow, just as we had happened upon the unseen freighter that night before. It showed the entire vessel and the adjacent dockage facilities parallel to it. Across the top of the photographs were officially and carefully printed the laudatory words "A Mission Well Done!" But across the bottom, on coarse white scrap paper, were the scribbled and clumsily added words "Crow, Haarmeyer, and Davis—Accidental Heroes!!!" These words were added, I am quite sure, by one of our playful mates in the 95th Bomb Squadron who had learned the true story of our inadvertent sinking of the freighter and felt compelled to reveal it to the entire bomb group.

As other crews from all three squadrons tumbled in around us and as we all sat and waited for the briefing to begin, our crew became the center of attention, amusement, and raucous humor. We began to be called the "Lucky Strikes," the name of a popular brand of cigarettes of that era. Other names for our crew were offered, with most not being printable. These labels were soon forgotten. The name that did survive was "Accidental Heroes." So during the remainder of my three-year contract term of service as a company grade officer I would infrequently run into some other USAF flight officer with whom our crew had served in Korea, and the all too hearty greetings and subsequent introductions to others present occasionally called forth those two words. A brief and oftentimes inaccurate recollection and retelling of the ship-sinking incident would follow, with readily shared hilarity, amazement, and, sometimes, some appreciated measure of friendship and camaraderie.

Before I departed K-9 Air Base, a staff sergeant at 17th Bomb Group HQ gave me a print of the photograph of our accidental sinking of the coastal freighter. At some point later I lost and/or misplaced all of my military clothing, flight gear, personal handgun, personnel records, and memorabilia accumulated during my Korean tour of duty, including this aerial photograph. But I am sure that I would recognize in an instant the black, white, and shades of gray content of that lucky bomb drop, anywhere and any time, even after the passage of over sixty years. In fact, I am quite sure that the original photograph, or a true copy of it, lies somewhere in the vast archives of the United States Air Force.

STOP THE
FUCKING BUGLES!

B OB CROW AND I WERE ON A RARE THREE-DAY R&R TO
Miho AFB near the southern end of the main Japanese Island of
Honshu, where our Douglas B-26 bombers were sent for flak damage
repair and/or major engine overhaul. Miho had been a major Japanese
fighter-interceptor base during World War II, and the USAF had enlarged and converted it into our primary rear-echelon maintenance and
repair facility after the start of the Korean War.

We had just flown across the narrow Sea of Japan in a slightly battered B-26 that had engines almost past due for inspection and repair.
After signing off the plane we grabbed a motorized rickshaw and proceeded to the nearby city of Oshinozu, where we would remain until
informed that the plane was ready for return flight to our base at K-9.

By early afternoon, we were sitting at the bar of the famous (some
would say infamous) Golden Bear Club off Oshinozu's main drag, sip-
ping 7&7s, when another USAF combat team entered and walked
directly toward Bob and me as we turned to face them. The bar was
nearly empty at the time, and meeting another flight crew on a rest
and recuperation junket was always pleasurable. We immediately recognized them as combat crewmen from Korea by the imprinted silver
"wings" upon their blue flight jackets and their squadron's "color," so

we waved them over as though we knew them well. Their color was red, and their red nattily knotted scarves, made from smooth silk parachute canopy material, were augmented by red baseball caps, with the silver bars of their rank centered vertically above the peaks of their caps. By the double silver bars they were easily identifiable as captains from quite a distance. To this day I cannot remember their names or even if they were from one of the two other B-26 squadrons stationed at K-9. In fact, they could have been from K-8, a USAF B-26 air base located near the Yellow Sea at Kunsan, South Korea. It really did not make any difference to us at the time. We were just happy to have someone to talk with, to have a chance to have a few laughs, toss down a few drinks, and swap a few combat stories.

Just as we were introducing ourselves to the new arrivals a young army second lieutenant walked toward us from the back end of the shadowy bar. We hadn't noticed him, but he had been sitting there silently since our arrival at the bar ten or fifteen minutes earlier. He stopped five or six feet away and waited quietly until our introductions had been completed. He stood perfectly still, staring at the pilot whom we had just met, until the pilot finally turned toward him and suddenly recognized him. They grabbed each other roughly and began to pound each other's back and shoulders, laughing and wrestling each other around in an awkward manner, almost losing their balance and falling.

The new arrival turned out to be the younger brother of the USAF captain, although he was at least four inches taller and outweighed the pilot by thirty to forty pounds. The army second lieutenant had indirectly informed his older brother that he would meet him at that place and at that time, but neither seemed to have expected it to happen. After this boisterous family reunion ended, all five of us moved to one of the many empty tables. We proceeded, as our Aussie cohorts would say, to "knock back" a few. In truth, we ingested more than a few, as we were still there when a ten- to twelve-piece Japanese band, dressed impressively in tuxedos and sounding very much like Glenn Miller, started its first set at 1800 and the club began to get quite busy and noisy.

It soon became evident that the three captains had a surprising number of mutual friends from World War II training and combat days, with many inquiries being made, back and forth, and stories told about people I did not know. Quite frankly, the young army lieutenant and I lost interest in their raucous conversation and I quickly found myself listening intently to him. He seemed to have a need to talk, and I was eager to listen.

He stated that he had been "on the line" continuously for the past four months, frequently leading a small contingent of highly trained snipers on what seemed to be extremely hazardous patrols behind enemy lines. He was returning to his special operations unit the next day. Just twenty-three years old, he looked much older. There was strain and tension in his face, with deep and dark hollows under his eyes. In fact, his eyes had a haunted aspect to them that was disturbing, hypnotizing, even scary.

I was very curious about what he did, but initially he was very reluctant to give me any specifics. I knew he had some interesting stories to tell and I sensed that he really wanted to share them with me. In retrospect, I think he was also very annoyed and offended that his older brother had apparently preferred to talk with other air force officers than with him. I also gleaned from several oblique remarks that he resented the many advantages that we, as air force flight officer personnel, had over most army and marine combatants of comparable rank and responsibility. He had referred to us as "flyboys," a word that we consistently interpreted as being one of scorn and derision, and he had referred to his older brother, somewhat sarcastically, as a "hotshot pilot." But I could well understand his resentment: we had much better clothing, wearing comfortable gabardine dress uniforms and fleece-lined flight jackets; we received more pay for our services, advancing in rank more rapidly; and we returned from combat engagements to shots of whisky, steaming coffee (no tea), hot and wholesome meals, hot and frequent showers, and warm and clean beds.

I could tell from the lieutenant's accent that he was a mid-west-erner. I asked him where he was from and he mentioned a little town, sounding like Cedarville, somewhere in Iowa. I was born and raised in Chicago, but I stated that I was from northern Illinois. Upon further inquiries it was established that each of us had graduated from close-by universities. He had a four-year degree in business management and I had an MBA in accounting and finance. I volunteered that I had enlisted as a basic trainee in the air force to protect my status as a pro-spective aviation cadet. He had enlisted in an army ROTC program in college and received a commission upon graduation.

Upon further inquiry, he stated that he had then completed a spe-cial "night missions program" involving intensive hand-to-hand combat training. I mentioned that en route to our assigned target areas, our B-26 bombers were occasionally and abruptly "diverted" by Ground Control to a specific target area along the front line for the express pur-pose of dropping strings of ten five-hundred-pound GP bombs or ten large napalm bombs on communist forces attacking in force and during hours of darkness.

He asked why I seemed to resent such diversions. To me it was obvious. We had to fly straight and level on an extended bomb run at eight to ten thousand feet. There we were vulnerable to radar-controlled anti-aircraft artillery fire as well as Russian-manufactured searchlights that reached to over thirty thousand feet and totally de-stroyed our night vision for five to ten minutes. Also, we were always flying parallel to the front line, and any of a number of miscalculations could result in our dropping ordnance upon friendly forces; at these altitudes it was extremely difficult to determine the nature and extent of bomb damage achieved. There was always the possibility, although remote, that we would be attacked by Russian MiG-15s, which had powerful cannons that could take us out with a single shot. Furthermore, we had been instructed and we reasonably believed that we could do much more damage to the Chinese and North Korean forces by bombing and strafing their troop trains and truck convoys, by striking them from low levels with a higher probability of accuracy, and by staying over their MSRs for sustained periods of time to destroy, damage, stop, or slow the heavy, nocturnal flow of men and materiel to the front line. I told him that we had been frequently informed at intelligence briefings that the communist gun placements were well protected in secured revetments and mountainside caves and tunnels, making them poor target prospects for our air attacks and, furthermore, that masses of communist foot soldiers were quartered deep in mountain caverns and tunnels near their frontline and that they were vulnerable to our bombing and strafing runs only when they were in the open and on the move.

It was obvious that my contentions fell upon deaf ears as this intense young man slowly and solemnly shook his head as I spoke. He responded angrily when I stopped for breath. "You don't understand. We are outnumbered ten, maybe fifteen, to one. When their bugles start blasting suddenly in the middle of the night and they launch a massive attack across the valley floor separating our positions, the noise level is unbearable. They may have only forty or fifty bugles, but it sounds like there are hundreds, with the waves of bugle blasts bouncing off the mountainsides. And they keep resounding, minute after minute, hour after hour. The endless repetitions of those fucking bugle blasts are simply maddening, psychologically debilitating to my troops."

A crazed look came over his face as he glared at me. Then he suddenly stopped talking. My belated and hesitant reaction to his prolonged silence was a weak statement to the effect that we were simply following orders: we were certainly not the decision-makers. If we were ordered by Ground Control to divert to a front line target area we did so immediately and as accurately as instructed, although admittedly without enthusiasm. What I did not tell him was that we lived in apprehension and dread of dropping on our own troops. We did not totally trust the input data (i.e., target latitude and longitude coordinates) that Ground Control gave us, or our ability to fixate them and release bombs accurately enough upon them.

At this point, an air force jeep driver from the base came into the Golden Bear and told my pilot he was wanted back at the base. I got up to leave with him. As we finished shaking hands all around the young lieutenant held my hand in a long and vise-like grip. As I turned to leave but before he released my hand, he pulled me toward him, leaned into me, and fiercely whispered four simple words: "Stop the fucking bugles!" I still shudder whenever I remember looking into those fearsome eyes, being again confirmed in my conviction that I had made the right decision in enlisting in the air force.

The next day Bob flight-tested another of our squadron's B-26s and we were rescheduled to take that aircraft back to K-9 that afternoon, rather than the one we brought over from K-9 the day before. So we headed to the Miho AFB Officers Club for a noonday meal before our return flight to Korea. There was a large table in the middle of the dining room where "transient" officers dined together. This table presented a choice opportunity to meet other crews from air bases near and far and to inquire about mutual friends, weather conditions, and other items of current interest. Generally, soon after exchanging greetings and shaking hands, the first question would be: "Where are you stationed?"

There were ten or twelve other company-grade officers at the table; a couple of navy guys, several army, and the rest air force. After the first upbeat and laughter-filled remarks dwindled down, within five or ten minutes, there were suddenly a few moments of total silence, such as frequently occur where there is a gathering of total strangers. Into this silence was injected an unusual question by one of the two navy pilots. It was directed to the army officers at the table, and these inquiring words I will never forget:

"Did any of you guys know the army second lieutenant who blew off the top of his head behind the Golden Bear Club last night?"

The others gathered at the table looked around while slowly shaking their heads. But I could not move, and I could not speak. I am as sure now as I was then: I had met that young army lieutenant just the day before, and I was one of the last people on earth ever to talk with him before his tragic death.

ONE MIGHT ASK WHETHER AFTER THIS EXPERIENCE I FELT any less apprehension, or actual fear, of flying night SHORAN missions or engaging in any other type of close support bombing operations along the front line, day or night. I don't believe there was any reduction in my aversion to dropping bombs close to friendly forces, and I am convinced that this aversion extended throughout the squadron. There were simply too many unforeseeable and uncontrollable variables for me, and for most of the other bombardier-navigators I knew, to willingly assume such dreaded and awesome responsibilities. However, a mission order was an order, an implied but direct command, and these missions, like any other, had to be flown.

LIVE BY THE SWORD . . .

WE HAD JUST COMPLETED A DETAILED INTELLI-gence debriefing at 17th Bomb Group HQ. Our mission had been a long and relatively unproductive armed reconnaissance raid over an MSR that was just a little too close for comfort to Pyongyang, the heavily fortified and defended capital city of North Korea. Although we did not know it at the time, this was the beginning of the last massive buildup of both men and materiel by the communist forces for their last major offensive before the signing of the July 1953 armistice. A treaty would never come.

Our mission had been interesting, but frustrating. We flew at three thousand feet over heavy streams of trucks heading south toward the front line, but we could not get down to them because of heavy ground fog and low level cloud decks over the entirety of the narrow valley through which the convoys were passing. This valley was continually winding and twisting, and our MSR was winding and twisting with it. And there were crosswinds of high velocities that varied in direction as well. As night-time visual bombing is very difficult at best, with moving targets traveling at varying speeds and in varying directions, the cumulative effect of these multiple and adverse conditions made accuracy strictly a matter of random chance.

We had a drop of two five-hundred-pound GP bombs that completely missed the convoy segment that I was targeting but hit another cluster of vehicles further up the road, much to my joy and amazement. We got two sustained fires from that "miss." But Jerry and I observed, and duly reported at debriefing, that the trucks coming up behind these fires merely detoured around the burning wreckage and continued on down the road without even extinguishing their running lights. Considering all the targets I had centered in the crosshairs of the Norden's simplistic reflex sight, it was a bad night, to say the least. However, the intelligence guys were much interested to learn about the sudden and substantial increase in road traffic and the fact that an attack bomber flying comparatively low overhead, and releasing heavy ordnance as well, did not seem to be any deterrent whatsoever to the flow of vehicle traffic, as it ordinarily would have been. Generally, before this night, if I dropped a single five-hundred-pounder that missed the road, the explosion would scatter the trucks, causing them to turn wildly left and right off the surface of the road. It seems that the drivers, sometimes very young and inexperienced, would often panic and drive their trucks off the roadway and into an adjacent river or ravine, or into each other. This chaos could result in significant disruption of the flow of men and materiel to the front for several days. But not on this night. They just kept coming and coming! And we kept missing and missing! Or, more correctly, *I* kept missing and missing, in total defiance of the laws of probability and those of compensating errors.

Bob, Jerry, and I collected our scattered flight gear and were just passing out the door of the debriefing shack when we heard the loud and long wails of multiple sirens. We rushed down the narrow flight of unpainted wooden steps to one of our transport trucks standing by with a driver at the wheel but without passengers. A second transport truck arrived almost immediately with another crew from our 95th Bomb Squadron. This crew reported that a B-26C (the version with a Plexiglas nose) had lost power on take-off with full bomb and fuel loading and that it had skidded across the perimeter road and smashed on the sandy beach just beyond but short of the edge of Suyong Bay. Luckily it had not yet exploded. We inquired about casualties but they had no information as the Air Police had waved them past the wreckage.

Bob instructed the waiting truck driver to either get out of the truck or move over into the passenger seat. When the bewildered driver did neither, Bob moved close to him and quietly but firmly ordered him to move to the right seat, which he hastily did without protest or comment. Bob waved Jerry and me into the back of the truck as he took the wheel. We started rolling onto and down the perimeter road almost before our tails hit the long side seats. It was a wild, bumpy, and crazy half-mile ride to the scene of the crash. Three fire trucks, two ambulances, and several jeeps were already parked there or just approaching. The officer of the day, an unrecognized captain, suddenly appeared on foot before us. He waved Bob to a stop about a hundred yards short of the severally damaged soft-nosed B-26. He informed us that we could not come any closer to the wreckage as there was nothing that we could do that was not being done. And he abruptly insisted that we depart the area without delay. Bob quickly became agitated and argumentative. The aircraft might contain injured crewmen, and he was eager to assist in their removal from the aircraft, which could easily burst into flames at any moment, with the heavy bomb load possibly exploding with disastrous consequences. Bob inquired about casualties.

The Officer of the Day replied that both the pilot and the gunner in the right seat were slightly injured but they had been safely removed from the aircraft just minutes before.

Bob's next question: "What about the guy in the nose?"

The shocking and horrifying answer: "He never had a chance. He was impaled by his own bombsight."

"LIEUTENANT, GET YOURSELF A CUP OF TEA"

I GREW UP IN CHICAGO, WHERE FROM JULY UNTIL THE first frost later each year, hay fever caused by ragweed was a very real medical problem for many residents. My vague recollection is that hay fever and related asthmatic issues began for me at about the age of five or six. I would often sneeze twenty to thirty times in rapid succession, leaving me physically exhausted and emotionally drained. And these symptoms were frequently combined with major episodes of uncontrollable coughing and wheezing. Particularly late at night, my difficulty in breathing could become so terrifying at times that I believed I was actually suffocating to death. So at that early age, my mother took me to Children's Hospital for diagnosis and treatment. I remember distinctly the scratch tests that were administered by a young medical technician. She created a rectangular pattern of closely spaced scratches in the outer layer of the skin of my upper arms. She then applied concentrates of various foods and other substances upon these abraded areas. Within a short time the specific allergies that afflicted me were revealed by red, swollen, and itchy blotches that appeared where these concentrates had been inserted, with my upper arms now a veritable checkerboard of allergies exhibiting varying degrees of intensity.

In this way I learned that my allergies were many, with some severe, such as to coffee and citrus fruit. I was told that my body was strongly reactive to chocolate, milk, cheese, beans, and many other foods and substances, such as wool, dust, and windblown weed and tree pollen.

For obvious reasons, I did not happen to disclose to the USAF, at the time of my voluntary enlistment in 1951 in its Aviation Cadet Program, that hay fever and asthma continued to present breathing and related medical problems for me. My father fought in France during World War I. My older brother fought with the Second Marine Division in multiple island invasions in the South Pacific during World War II. Now it was my turn; the Korean War would be my war. I never gave it conscious thought: I was unthinkingly programmed for combat duty, allergies or no allergies.

When the Korean War erupted in June of 1950 I was six months away from receiving an MBA in accounting and finance from a leading mid-western university. I am reasonably sure that I could have received a direct commission as a lieutenant in the USAF and functioned as an accounting or finance officer upon graduation, but I never seriously considered that option. Instead, I made a contractual commitment to enter the Aviation Cadet Program and to fulfill a three-year contract commitment thereafter. Due to a long waiting list, I was compelled to enlist as a basic trainee to protect my potential flight status.

Of course, I never mentioned my medical issues to anyone at K-9 AFB, either. This minor oversight applied particularly to Colonel Bentley.

The colonel was a truly big man in every sense of the word. He stood over six feet four inches tall and had the physique of a former professional football player. I did not learn until several years ago that he worked his way through a western university as a cowboy and bull rider, which fully explained his broad shoulders and huge hands. He had piercing grey eyes and a commanding presence. And he wore hand-tooled leather cowboy boots just about everywhere. The rumor was he slept in them!

He was a command pilot as well as being five levels above me in rank and responsibility. And the informed opinions around the squadron indicated that he had amassed a truly awesome combat record in flying low-level bombing and strafing missions in Martin B-26 Marauders against the Germans before and beyond Normandy during 1944 and 1945, and that he had earned and received numerous and significant awards and decorations for outstanding combat performance and superior leadership qualities. We rarely wore Class A or Class B uniforms on base, usually wearing just some combination of flight gear. Therefore, no one in our squadron ever wore combat awards or decorations, so nobody knew, by outward appearance, the nature and extent of the military achievements of others in the squadron. But to say that Colonel Bentley was both impressive and intimidating to this newly commissioned and insecure twenty-four-year-old bombardier-navigator is a gross understatement. Frankly, this bird colonel scared the hell out of me!

As an assistant administrative officer I sat just eight or ten feet from Colonel Bentley in the operations shack, so I saw much of what he did and heard much of what he said. His knowledge of piloting, command and control, air combat, weapon systems, aircraft maintenance, ordnance, materiel, personnel motivation, management, and so on was truly encyclopedic. Until quite recently I did not appreciate, to the extent that I most certainly should have, the unique qualities of leadership that the colonel provided each and every day of his command. For example, he flew as lead pilot on a number of the daylight formation-bombing missions that our squadron was occasionally assigned. But he would take a secondary position in the formation when there was a pilot in the 95th Bomb Squadron whom he considered to have command potential and whose career could benefit from such leadership experience.

I was particularly impressed by the way he continually evaluated the performance of crews in his squadron and how he scheduled and motivated them to perform to their realistic combat potentials. Of particular significance to me was the way he established and implemented multiple criteria of combat effectiveness and efficiency by continually evaluating each combat crew's efforts.

His first and most obvious criterion was bomb strike photography. A camera was located in the underbelly of the B-26's fuselage. It was automatically triggered by way of a time-delay mechanism adjusting for altitude, providing highly reliable photographic documentation and the best evidence of daytime bombing accuracy or inaccuracy. Night photos of bomb impacts were acquired by light-sensitive photographic equipment and were often as accurate in determining targeting proficiency as those acquired during daylight raids. If the photos did not show bomb damage, the colonel would be unhappy.

Another basic criterion utilized by the colonel was the amount of fuel consumed during the course of the combat mission being evaluated. Although our night missions were referred to as "armed reconnaissance missions," actually they were primarily "search, find, and destroy" missions, with reconnaissance being a secondary function. Each combat crew was charged with primary responsibility for destroying or damaging as many steam locomotives, bridges, boxcars, trucks, tanks, coastal freighters, ammo dumps, and other moving or stationary military targets as possible while still bringing the aircraft safely back to base. In the unusual event of the complete absence of such targets, or the inability to target them due to bad weather, equipment malfunction, and the like, our primary duty was to patrol our assigned MSR at minimum safe altitude, usually by flying back and forth over a segment of 80 to 140 miles of track and/or roadway for maximum time periods to order to "menace and delay" the flow of military traffic to the front line. On slow targeting nights we were obligated to maximize TOT (time over target) by flying up and down the assigned MSR at minimum speeds while still not jeopardizing our fuel reserves for the long return flight to base. If the fuel tanks were too full upon return to base, the colonel would not be reluctant to express his displeasure.

Another of the colonel's criteria of crew performance was the number of .50 caliber rounds remaining in the ammunition canisters after each combat mission. After the four wing bombs and the six bomb bay bombs had been dropped by the bombardier-navigator, it was then the pilot's function, weather and degree of intensity of ground fire permitting, to fly up and down roadways and/or railroad tracks at minimum safe altitude and strafe the locomotives, freight cars, trucks, tanks, foot soldiers, and other such observed targets of opportunity. This major responsibility of a B-26 pilot was especially critical if an enemy train or truck convoy was long and heavily laden with troops destined for the combat zone. If a B-26 returned to base with no or relatively few .50 caliber rounds expended and if there had been target opportunities that night, facilitated by good vision and good weather, Colonel Bentley would not be a happy man the next day when he learned of such lost targeting opportunities by an underperforming crew. It was the colonel's conviction, frequently expressed, that "the emptier the cans, the more successful the pilot."

When the colonel decided that a particular crew was not performing up to his high standards, he would turn toward me and say, "Lieutenant, get yourself a cup of tea." Of course, I soon realized that this suggestion was a somewhat subtle direct command. So I would respond with an immediate "Yes, sir," quickly depart the operations shack, and walk to my nearby living quarters. As I walked away I would frequently observe the colonel's vehicle being driven away by its driver, who had been quite apparently instructed by the colonel to locate and bring back to our operations shack that particular underperforming pilot and bombardier-navigator team for a critical and thorough review and evaluation of their recent combat performance.

I always had a distinctively labeled box of Lipton's tea bags, a large bottle of water, and a small teapot under my bed, so I would prepare a pot of tea on the top of the old potbellied stove occupying the center of our communal sleeping area. Then I would sit on my footlocker and sip steaming hot tea until I thought that the summoned crew's "review and evaluation" was completed and it had departed our operations shack. When I returned to operations the colonel would appear to be relieved and pleased that the crew's chastisement was over. He would occasionally make a joke or comment about my penchant for drinking tea, as I was to my knowledge the only flight officer in the squadron who did not drink coffee, with many of our number seeming to have a strong, even overpowering, addiction to it. Of course, the colonel did not know of my allergic reactions to coffee.

I remember how he would playfully elevate his huge right hand as if he were holding a small teacup delicately between the tips of his thumb and forefinger, his little finger pointed vertically into the air. "And did you enjoy your cup of tea, lieutenant?" I would generally respond in kind by saying with feigned sincerity: "Yes, sir, and thank you, sir, I thoroughly relaxed during those few pleasant moments."

SUPERSTITION

FOR FOUR MONTHS I LIVED WITH THEM, FLEW WITH them, ate with them, and drank with them. But I did not die with them.

I never really knew their first names. To all of us in the 95th Bomb Squadron, they were simply "Doolittle and Hall." Both of them were reserve USAF officers, a captain and a first lieutenant, who had served as B-26 pilot and B-26 bombardier-navigator, respectively, during World War II and had been recalled involuntarily to serve again in Korea. I don't believe they flew together during the "Big One" but instead had met each other while serving later in the Air Force Reserve. There they probably flew together on weekends and during their annual summer two-week tour of active duty while completing their college educations and otherwise living normal civilian lives. I recall vaguely that Bob Crow said that Doolittle had been a professor or instructor at a college or university somewhere back east and that Hall had been working as a statistician when the Korean War erupted in 1950.

They had been abruptly recalled to active duty, as such was their responsibility for accepting basic compensation and flight pay for part-time reserve military service. Both were provided additional training in the many hazards and pleasures of flying, bombing, navigating, and strafing in the Douglas B-26 Invader. They had then spent ten rough days in living through the rigors of Survival Training northwest of Reno, Nevada, struggling through the deep snows of the Sierra Nevada Mountains. Their crew was then summarily transported via chartered commercial airliner to Tokyo, Japan, into K-9 AFB, Pusan, South Korea, via military air transport, in the same way that I had arrived, at the beginning of the very severe winter of 1952–1953, but several months before my arrival.

Doolittle appeared to be about thirty-five years old. He was of slight to medium build, average height, with a thin pointed nose that was not unattractive. He was quite articulate without being talkative, with a kind and impish sense of humor. He was obviously very bright but did not readily display his intelligence. He was sensitive and perceptive. He was a gentleman and a truly gentle man. My guess is that if you met him on the street dressed in civilian clothes you would never have thought that he was a combat pilot and a very good one. He was also superstitious, being impelled to wear a battered orange baseball cap on his way to the flight line before every combat mission.

Hall was a different type of person and personality, an unlikely prospect for the field of statistics, stereotypically populated by the sober, serious, and analytical. Hall was the stocky and muscular type: he looked like a linebacker in early retirement. He was also loud and temperamental. He talked to anyone and everyone, whether they were listening or not. He was outspoken, boisterous, and opinionated. Unfortunately, he annoyed others without being aware that he was doing so.

Hall frequently postulated that it was statistically impossible to get shot down over North Korea if reasonable precautions and common sense were invoked. He had no superstitions and continually tried, but without success, to convince Doolittle that statistical probability, and not superstition, would carry the day. Occasionally he would verbalize obscure statistical formulae that allegedly proved his theory.

In summary, Doolittle and Hall were a very improbable pairing, but there they were, functioning very well night after night by bombing and strafing assigned tactical targets as well as varied targets of opportunity in North Korea. Surprisingly, they got along extremely well, possibly because they were both what Colonel Bentley called "pussycats."

Among those flying B-26 bombing missions over North Korea, there were three kinds of flight crews, according to Squadron Commander Delwin Bentley's simplistic classification: tigers, tomcats, and pussycats. He posited that, almost always, a new crew fell quickly into one of these three categories within its first five or six missions flown, and it rarely changed its attitude and combat performance enough to justify a change in his informal classification. In other words, once a pussycat, always a pussycat. And the Doolittle and Hall crew was so identified by Colonel Bentley and remained so regarded through their 39th combat mission.

It should be emphasized that it was no dishonor to be so considered, as such a crew was almost always competent, conscientious, and generally accomplished its mission objective. However, once tagged as pussycats such crews were generally assigned shorter penetrations into North Korea and given less dangerous mission and target assignments, such as night-time SHORAN (electronically triggered short range radar navigation) bomb drops that involved close front line support but at safer (higher) altitudes and at substantially lesser risk.

Of course, Colonel Bentley was most discreet as to his informal classification of combat crews under his command so it was not generally known beyond the walls of our 95th BS operations shack. It simply was useful to him in evaluating crews and determining target priorities and crew assignments. My pilot and I often wondered how Colonel Bentley classified our crew. We hopefully concluded that he probably considered us to be tomcats, but with occasional tiger tendencies, as we frequently were given more challenging armed reconnaissance missions involving deeper penetrations along the heavily trafficked North Korean coastline. The colonel also observed that most combat crews, irrespective of his useful classification system, become noticeably more cautious after they had flown forty missions, when these "short timers" began to think and talk more about their families and going "back to the world." And I also observed that they became progressively more apprehensive, particularly if they were married men who had experienced heavy World War II air combat action.

On the late-April night of Doolittle and Hall's fortieth combat mission, the completion of which would fully qualify them for the official scheduling of their return to the United States, they went through their normal preflight routine. And they understood that they would be required by FEAF directive to fly their final ten missions within the following thirty days.

Our crew happened to meet them and their gunner in front of our operations shack. We rode with them to the parachute shack on the narrow wooden side benches in the back of a cold, windblown, and open truck, the truck having arrived over fifteen minutes late, to the not-so-quiet irritation of everyone aboard. As the Doolittle crew was scheduled to take off fifteen minutes before us, they entered the parachute shack first and walked to the wooden counter that separated flight crews from the squadron's secured storage room where crewmembers stored their large parachute bags under the sole control of a grumpy old supply sergeant. Apparently Doolittle had opened his parachute bag at the counter and checked to be sure it contained his parachute and harness, a canary yellow Mae West life preserver, his sidearm, heavy flight gloves, and so on.

Presumably being satisfied that all of their required flight gear had been removed from their bags, Doolittle and his crew returned their parachute bags to the supply sergeant and hurriedly climbed back on the empty truck. They then raced down the perimeter road to the hardstand where their assigned hardnosed B-26B, tail-numbered #449, was regularly parked and serviced, with Crew Chief Gordon Cooper then standing by with a fire bottle, ready for takeoff. Tactical takeoffs meant that each crew took off on the exact minute and second assigned, and I am quite sure that Doolittle had no intention of being "written up" for a late takeoff.

Our crew went into the parachute shack right after the Doolittle crew's late arrival and quick departure for the flight line. I recall that I was still carrying my heavy brown leather government-issue navigator's briefcase and that Jerry Davis held the door open for both Bob and me. As I was crossing the narrow space in front of the counter I noticed that Bob was attempting to hang an old orange cap from a tenpenny nail that had been pounded into a rough wooden panel directly above the counter. Bob swung the back of the soft cloth cap, held just by its peak, at the nail several times before it finally caught the nail's head and held in place. It was Doolittle's cap, which had apparently fallen out of his parachute bag after he had taken his P-1 helmet from the bag. Preoccupied by our impending mission, we didn't give any thought to the ownership of the cap, nor did it seem significant to us at that time that the cap had been carelessly dropped on the floor and forgotten by some crewman who had entered the parachute shack before us.

We flew a deep, long, and unremarkable mission that night. We then went through the customary mission debriefing, drank a shot or two of poor quality debriefing whiskey bearing the label of "Old Methuselah," and then Bob and I returned to our shack, which we shared with Doolittle and Hall, along with four other flight officers.

Bob and I woke up six hours later with the sun glaring in our eyes. We were immediately aware that Doolittle and Hall were not there. We also noticed that their beds had not been slept in. The other two crews were still asleep. As Kim had just arrived from Pusan, she could provide us little information. However, she sensed that something was seriously wrong and became anxious and agitated. Bob and I dressed quickly and hurried over to the operations shack, where our duty officer and armament officer confirmed our worst suspicion: Doolittle and his crew had not returned from their mission, nor did anyone, anywhere within or off the coasts of South Korea, have any information about their status. Since their fuel supply would have run out hours earlier, they had already been officially classified as "missing in action." Nor did their MIA status ever change thereafter.

Two nights later we were again on the flight schedule for early evening departure for North Korea. When we walked into the parachute shack the old orange cap was still hanging from the tenpenny nail above the counter. Apparently we were the first crew to appreciate the significance of Doolittle's good luck charm, which had carried him safely through thirty-nine combat missions. The silent presence of the orange cap, coincident with his MIA status, spread through the 95th Bomb Squadron and then to the crews of the 34th and the 37th Bomb Squadrons housed on the other side of the runway. To the best of my knowledge, no one touched the orange cap, at least not until after I had completed my tour of duty and had departed K-9 Air Base. So the orange cap just hung there collecting dust, visibly and relentlessly reminding each and every crewmember that it simply was not a good idea to tempt fate by deliberately or accidentally failing to heed the mystical imperatives of a habit mechanism that could mean, at least to us, the difference between life and death. As a result, every time thereafter that I entered the parachute shack while preparing for a combat mission, my eyes were drawn magnetically to that grimy and dusty orange cap. Immediately and uncontrollably, I would unzip my outer, heavy, and coarse flight suit and covertly reach in and grasp between thumb and forefinger the waistband of a pair of soft, sweat-stained, and rather fragrant pair of gabardine pants that I had worn on each and every mission that I flew in Korea.

I would tightly compress the fabric of the gabardine pants between the tips of my thumb and forefinger while gazing fixedly at the old orange cap to reassure myself once again that they were still there, and therefore good luck was still riding with me. When not flying a mission I had always secured these pants in my footlocker protected by a heavy combination lock. And I had never allowed Kim to either wash or have them cleaned for fear that they could be lost while out of my sight and control. I might add that every other crewmember in the 95th that I observed entering that parachute shack made a similar grab for his selected good luck charm, whether it was a rabbit's foot, a lucky coin, a wife's or girlfriend's photograph, an old pipe, whatever.

The bottom line? Let's simply say that the superstitions of men in war die hard, but literally dying hard is a far more permanent and terrifying alternative.

A small portion of the hundreds of various types and sizes of bombs that were simply spread out on the ground, row after row, over the K-9 AFB bomb dump, which approximated the size of a football field. A bomb loading crew is shown utilizing a heavy truck and a hoist in lifting bombs weighing as much as 1,000 pounds for delivery to the flight lines of K-9, a mile away. Photo by Paul Geidel.

Shot of an unidentified 95th Bomb Squadron bomb loader leaning on a truckload of MIA2 clustered fragmentation bombs, which were simply and accurately referred to as "deadly little fuckers."

95th Bomb Squadron gunner Paul Geidel displaying a standard metallic link belt that contained 500 armor-piercing incendiary (API) rounds of 50-caliber Browning machine gun ammunition. The Douglas B-26 usually carried two 50-caliber Browning machine guns in the gunner's upper turret and two more in his lower turret that he fired by remote control.

A highly proficient Douglas B-26 combat crew (95th Bomb Squadron, 17th Bomb Group) before its departure from K-9 AFB on a daylight mission in the summer of 1953. Right to left: gunner A/3C Clarence (Pat) Daily, bombardier-navigator 1st Lt. Dick Uyehara, and pilot Captain John Wright.

Lead 95th Bomb Squadron Douglas B-26C, just before take-off on a four-ship-formation bombing mission against the major steel-reinforced concrete bridge in Wonsan, the largest North Korean sea port on the Sea of Japan.

This photo of the lead B-26C, taken by gunner Paul Geidel in the right seat of the number #3 B-26C, shows the lead's bomb bay doors opened by its bombardier-navigator on final approach to his AP (aiming point) minutes before his "bombs away" call.

Photo of the lead B-26C, again taken by Geidel, displaying a much tighter formation as the lead aircraft's first bombs are dropping from its outer wing racks at the same moment in time as the following B-26Cs in formation.

View from the right seat in the cockpit of the B-26, in daylight over typical topography of the eastern half of North Korea, vividly illustrating the unlikely chance of finding an emergency landing site and living to survive the landing.

An aerial overview of K-9 AFB looking northward along runway 33. The flight line of the 95th Bomb Squadron lies to the immediate right of that dark-colored 6,000-foot runway, with the flight lines of the 34th and 37th Bomb Squadrons to its immediate left. Photograph courtesy of gunner Antonio Fucci of the 37th Bomb Squadron, 17th Bomb Group.

A B-26 returning in daylight to K-9 after completing a night armed reconnaissance mission over North Korea. On final approach, the B-26 is lining up with runway 33 just before touchdown after passing over the edge of Suyong Bay and the beach at the south end of the runway.

Left to right: Captains George Vioux (pilot), and Tom Cameron (bombardier-navigator), with AIC Paul Geidel (gunner), of the 95th Bomb Squadron, after Vioux and Cameron flew their fiftieth and last combat mission.

The 95th Bomb Squadron's flight line on the east side of K-9's only runway (15/33) looking northward toward the snow-covered coastal mountains that crowd in from the west, north, and east. On April 27, 1953, the B-26 closest to the camera (with #322449 on its tail) took pilot Capt. Kenneth L. Doolittle and crew on a night mission along the east coast of North Korea. The B-26 encountered heavy triple A, was lost over the target area, and never returned. After three days, search by F-84s was abandoned.

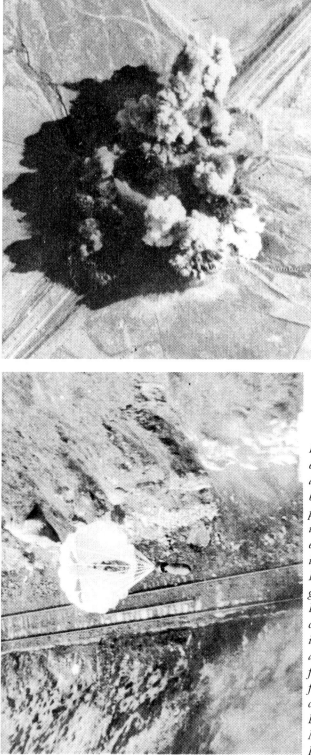

Shot from a dangerously low altitude, this photograph dramatically displays the accuracy of the air crew of a 452nd Bomb Wing Douglas B-26 bomber in scoring a direct hit with its full load of ten 500-pound tritonal bombs upon a railroad bridge in North Korea in the spring of 1952. Photograph courtesy of the Jimmie Doolittle Air & Space Museum, Travis AFB, Fairfield, California.

Released at an extremely low altitude, a 500-pound tritonal bomb is slowed by a parachute attached to its tail as it is about to enter a railroad tunnel in northeastern North Korea. This technique gave the 452nd Bomb Wing's B-26C crew that dropped it adequate distance and time to escape from its fragmentation field. Photograph courtesy of the Jimmie Doolittle Air & Space Museum, Travis AFB, Fairfield, California.

At K-9 AFB, Pusan, South Korea. Right to left: Captain James Boyd (pilot), 2nd Lt. Robert Tanner (SHORAN operator), 1st Lt. William Chatfield (bombardier/navigator), and A/2C Ted Baker (gunner and later P-51 pilot). This weary B-26 crew (730th Bomb Squadron, 452nd Bomb Wing) had flown its fifty-fifth and last mission over North Korea the night before, on March 16, 1952. Photograph courtesy of William Chatfield of the 95th Bomb Squadron.

This plexiglas-nosed B-26C, losing take-off power from K-9 AFB, slid on the ice-covered runway, plowing into the snow-covered beach at the edge of Suyong Bay, in January 1953. The bombardier-navigator in the nose was instantly killed.

GHOSTWRITER

I DON'T KNOW WHAT COLONEL BENTLEY ULTIMATELY did with them. I had drafted and redrafted them as concisely and flawlessly as I could on my ancient and malfunctioning manual Royal typewriter, using the low quality, letter sized, plain white paper that was all that was available to me while working as an assistant administrative officer in the 95th Bomb Squadron's operations shack. I recall distinctly that I finalized three letters at the same time, with the only difference in their content being the rank and name of the downed crewmember and his correct designation and responsibilities as pilot or bombardier-navigator or air gunner. Upon their completion I stacked them on the corner of Colonel Bentley's desk. One of them read as follows:

It is with deep and heartfelt sorrow that I direct this letter to you. Your husband, Captain Kenneth L. Doolittle, and his crew flew north on the night of April 25, 1953, and did not return from their assigned mission. We have yet to receive information regarding the reason or reasons for their inability to return to base. However, if they crash landed in North Korea there is high probability that they will be recovered incident to a scheduled prisoner exchange. You will be advised by appropriate authority as more is known.

I have been your husband's commanding officer for five months and I know him well. He is a highly proficient pilot and a fine officer known for both professional competence and strong moral values. He is very well liked and respected by his crew and all who know him by way of their daily or frequent contact with him. I hope and trust that you feel both pride and gratification knowing that he has and will continue to serve his country and the oppressed people of the new and evolving democracy of South Korea to the best of his abilities.

Very respectfully yours,

Colonel Delwin D. Bentley

I was already pounding away on my battered old typewriter late the next morning when Colonel Bentley entered the operations shack. He walked slowly to his desk and sat down behind it. He did not say a word, nor did I say anything to him. Out of the corner of my eye I could see that he had noticed the three letters in the upper right-hand corner of his desk. He picked them up and placed them squarely before him in the center of the desk. He uncapped a thick-barreled black Parker pen and held it over the top letter, directed to Ken Doolittle's wife, for what seemed like an eternity. Then he began to read what I had written.

I glanced at my watch and noticed with considerable relief that it was 1200 hours straight up, my normal departure time for the officers club and another uninteresting midday meal. After a few awkward moments, I rose and walked slowly to the door of our Quonset hut. The colonel never looked up or said a word. So I deliberately walked away without knowing whether he approved of the content of the letters or not. And I never learned the answer to that question, as neither of us ever spoke of Captain Doolittle or his bombardier-navigator or his gunner again.

AS OF THE DATE OF THIS BOOK'S PUBLICATION, CAPTAIN Ken Doolittle and his crew were still listed as missing in action, along with over eight thousand other American military MIAs who continue to be mysteriously unaccounted for ever since July 27, 1953, when the Korean cease-fire agreement became effective. Related to the foregoing statistic is the infrequently understood, and more infrequently expressed, reality that, to the present date, there are more known UNC MIAs resulting from the thirty-seven months of the "Korean Conflict" of 1950–53 than there are KIAs resulting from both of the declared wars in Afghanistan and Iraq, since they were initiated years ago by formal congressional legislation.

"THE ONLY WAR
WE'VE GOT"

I WAS SITTING ON THE SIDE OF MY NARROW COT ONE dark and depressing Sunday morning during a late April snowstorm, polishing a pair of low-cut military dress shoes. These black shoes were rarely worn in a combat zone, as frequent snowy and muddy conditions would necessitate their being cleaned and shined after every time they were worn. Instead, we almost always wore our high-topped, heavy duty "shit kickers" under fleece-lined flight boots, as that combination provided both warmth and comfort.

I was alone in our shack with a shoe brush and a round tin of black shoe polish, applying successive layers of polish with an old sock, spitting on the shoe where and after the polish had been applied, and then vigorously brushing the polish into the soft black leather, repeating this sequence again and again to bring each shoe to a high shine.

The door to our shack opened and Major Brown briskly walked in. No one ever knocked on our door before entering. I shared this shack with seven other company-grade officers and knocking seemed to all of us to be a needless act. However, I was somewhat startled by this sudden and forceful entry as I was alone and deeply lost in thought while meticulously shining every square inch of each shoe's sparkling surface.

The major was looking for my pilot, Bob Crow, who had recently been given the additional responsibilities of assistant operations officer for the squadron. Major Brown asked where he could find him. Bob was probably on the flight line at the time and so I related that educated guess to the major. It was snowing heavily, and Major Brown hesitated, apparently reluctant to trudge such a considerable distance to locate Bob under hostile weather conditions. He then realized that I was just sitting alone in semi-darkness, simply shining shoes. Apparently displacing his displeasure in not being able to locate Bob immediately, the major scornfully inquired: "Lieutenant, what the hell are you doing shining your own shoes? That's what we have house girls for."

I replied that I had been shining my shoes as far back as I could remember and still enjoyed doing it. At the start of basic training I learned the Air Force way of "spit-shining" shoes. Thereafter I occasionally and thoroughly enjoyed the simple pleasure of that small measure of physical exertion, resulting in a pair of shoes that literally glistened in bright sunlight. It was in essence a simple repetitive process that brought disproportionate pleasure and satisfaction to me, as I believed that I was being productive in a very basic manner. It enabled me to see the direct and immediate result of my efforts, there being many occasions when there was little if any tangible evidence of productivity while being integrated into the military.

The major was becoming progressively more annoyed. So I volunteered that Bob should be returning to the shack very soon as he had gone out to the flight line directly after our morning mission briefing three hours earlier that morning. The major then sat down upon a nearby footlocker to wait for him. At that time I hardly knew the major and was uncomfortable sitting alone with him. He outranked me by two full pay grade levels, had graduated from West Point, was "career"

Air Force, had attained the status of senior pilot, and was rumored to have achieved impressive combat records in both World War II and Korea. In contrast, I was a temporary and lowly first lieutenant, a three-year-term contract officer, a very recent graduate of bombardier-navigator training, and had but a small fraction of the combat experience that the major had. Simply stated, he knew my military record, and I knew his. We had relatively little in common; we were both flight crewmen flying B-26s and by happenstance had been assigned to the same Tactical Air Command squadron stationed at K-9 AFB.

After an awkward period of total silence and as I kept active with my shoe brush, Major Brown asked: "Well, what do you think about our little war?"

This unexpected question perplexed me and I had no immediate answer. I finally stammered something, such as: "I really don't have enough combat experience to have a well-formed opinion. It's challenging, exciting, and I enjoy flying with Captain Crow."

This answer did not satisfy the major as evidenced by his flat facial expression. He then stated in direct and immediate reply: "Well, it's not much of a war, but it's the only war we've got."

I had no response to that strikingly cynical statement, but luckily Bob walked in the door at that moment and I was spared the need to respond. They both walked out the door and headed toward the operations shack where, I later learned, Colonel Bentley had been waiting impatiently for them.

After Bob and Major Brown departed, I just sat there alone and continued to polish my shoes, mulling over the major's words. To me it was a helluva big war, and a very challenging one. Regularly planning and executing low-level, low-speed bombing and strafing missions during hours of darkness and extremely cold weather over rugged mountainous terrain was new and different in the history of air warfare, and not a skill one could easily prepare for in training. Indeed, back in the United States, we had had relatively little, in fact, almost nothing, in terms of relevant training. On the average, we were losing close to one thousand American military lives each and every month, for what proved to be a total of thirty-seven months. Our combat wounded averaged over four times that number for each month that this "not much of a war" continued.

I also knew, although most of my 95th Bomb Squadron comrades did not, that our chances of survival were minimal, particularly zero, if captured by North Korean civilians who lived along the MSRs that we had been raiding almost nightly for a period of well over two and a half years. If captured, it was almost certain that we would be immediately stripped of our warm and durable winter clothing and footgear and then slowly and painfully punched, jabbed, kicked, and clubbed to death, assuming Colonel Bentley's source data was correct.

Our only realistic hope for survival was that if captured we would fall into the hands of communist Chinese military forces who would more likely keep us barely alive for bartering purposes in prospect of a possible exchange of prisoners or, more likely, we would be kept in somewhat better condition so that we could be used as subjects for propaganda purposes by way of photography and its distribution throughout the world.

I had flown a relatively large number of night missions by that time but I realized that I had much to learn about how to perform proficiently in combat operations in order to survive and to succeed in what to me was a very frightening war. And if this strange, stalemated, and deadly war on the far side of the world would escalate into World War III, as many of my older comrades strongly believed and totally expected, I could be there for the "duration," or might even not go home at all.

I remember distinctly these dark and dismal thoughts as some of the most depressing of my then relatively short combat life. So I kept shining and re-shining my black shoes until the gloom and depression slowly faded away.

WORKING ON
THE RAILROAD

I WOKE UP EARLY ONE MORNING IN THE AUTUMN OF 2006 and found myself singing the first line of a song. I lay in bed and sang the entire song, excitedly realizing that I had correctly remembered every word, even though I had not sung that song for over fifty years. And it was effortless—the words just came streaming out one after the other, and I seemed to have supreme confidence that they would. I had first heard that song just after arriving in Tokyo, on my way to Korea. I heard it again one morning in April of 1953 at K-9 AFB.

Bob Crow and I had just walked into the drafty and cold bar at our drab and shoddy officers club immediately after an 0800 hours morning mission briefing. And there they were, four fighter-interceptor pilots of the Royal Australian Air Force (RAAF), rapidly getting quite drunk at that improbable early morning hour. They said they were with us that day because several B-26 pilots from our 17th Bomb Group, several months before, had invited them to drop by and be their guests. It seems that our guys wanted to express in a tangible way their appreciation to the Aussies for delivering superb top cover for a successful daytime formation mission, when our light bombers had almost totally demolished a cluster of railroad and road bridges deep in northeastern North Korea.

Ordinarily it would have been a most unusual time of day for the officers club to be filling up with flight personnel. However, a heavy late winter storm front was just starting to roll in, and the weather forecast was for three or more days of strong winds and heavy snows that would cause all crews to "stand down" for quite a while. Generally we dropped our bomb loads and strafed by visual sightings, and blinding snowfall would put us out of business until good weather and visibility returned.

As in World War II, the Aussies were among our staunchest allies. At the start of the Korean War in June of 1950, the 77th Fighter Squadron of the RAAF, flying our P-51 Mustangs, was at far less than full strength. However, by the end of that year this squadron had been well reinforced and retrained and was fully operational, stationed nearby in Japan. In 1951, the 77th Fighter Squadron was re-equipped with British-built Gloster Meteor jet fighters. From that point on, the Aussies flew competently and courageously alongside our own USAF fighter-interceptor and fighter-bomber aircraft, although the Meteor was overmatched in combat by the Russian-built MIG-15s. In addition to providing proficient and diligent top cover for our 26s and 29s, they aggressively bombed and strafed truck convoys, railroad trains, bridges, viaducts, communication lines, ammunition and fuel dumps, and everything and anything else of strategic or tactical value moving south or north, east or west, as well as delivering determined close frontline support.

So there these Aussies were, laughing, joking, clowning around, and reveling in the sincere admiration and words of appreciation from their many Yankee hosts, while "knocking back" drink after drink of top-quality booze and occasionally entertaining our troops by breaking out loudly into one bawdy song after another. When they started singing that one particular Aussie drinking song, I recognized it and immediately joined in. Frankly, I had never been commended for the finest of singing voices. But in those days, if you knew all the words and you sang softly, good singers would generally tolerate you. In fact, they would encourage you and slap you on the back and drape their arms across your shoulders. Particularly if the free drinks kept coming!

This special song was titled "I Don't Want to Join the Navy." It had been at our sprawling and impressive Tachikawa AFB Officers Club in Tokyo just five or six months before that I had my first contact with the heavy drinking and loud singing Australians. A raucous group of them had sung quite a few vulgar (and often profane) songs that night, but they frequently went back to "I Don't Want to Join the Navy." I'm sure it was because several British Royal Air Force (RAF) pilots were present, and the Aussies always delight in taking verbal jabs at the "Brits" whenever the occasion could possibly justify it. I had been amused ("titillated" might be more accurate) by the words of that song and had quickly learned them. So when the Aussies broke into their favorite song that snowy morning at K-9, naturally I joined in the singing without the slightest hesitation. Here is the way the song goes, being sung in a staccato cadence:

> *I don't want to join the Navy; I don't want to go to war,*
> *I just want to hang around Piccadilly Underground,*
> *Living off the earnings of a highborn limey.*
> *I don't want a bayonet up me arse-ole,*
> *I don't want me buttocks shot away,*
> *I want to stay in England, in jolly, jolly England,*
> *And fornicate me blooming life awayyyyyyyyyy.*
> *Call out the Members of the Home Guard,*
> *They'll keep England free,*
> *Call out the Royal Territorials,*
> *They'll face danger with a smile.*

Call out the Army and the Navy,

They'll keep England free,

Call out me mother, me sister, and me brother,

But for God's sake don't call me!!!

There was immediate and loud applause and shouts of encouragement and we were urged to sing it again by the slowly but steadily growing number of early morning drinkers. So we sang it again, with more and more of the guys joining in as they began to learn the words. And since the Aussies had participated in a number of our missions that involved the destruction of North Korea railroad bridges, it occurred to me that another song was then most appropriate. So during the short lull after the song I began to sing "I've Been Working on the Railroad."

Of course, a lot of our guys knew that one, as well as some of the Aussies, and the volume of the singing became truly awesome. Most of us were not good singers. But we compensated with high volume and enthusiasm so the noise level elevated considerably when we sang it the second and third time. After that song ended, somebody started "That Old Gang of Mine" and more loud and off-key singing followed. After that song had been fairly well desecrated, somebody else started with "The White Cliffs of Dover" in honor of our British comrades in arms, and we unintentionally butchered that one too. The songs kept coming and the booze kept flowing. This singing and drinking session turned into one of the best impromptu parties that I have ever attended, even considering there were no women anywhere in sight!

It was a well-known fact that combat crews were rather close knit, some might say exclusionary. Our flight crew guys tended to socialize very tightly among ourselves and, to a lesser extent, with flight crewmen from other squadrons and only rarely with administrative and non-flight personnel. But this spontaneous song session seemed to draw everyone together, combat crewmen from all three squadrons, as well as some little-known members of our group and wing ground support cadre.

Without notice, the driving snowfall had intensified and seemed to enhance the warm and shared feeling of friendship and camaraderie. So the party rolled on, to the noon hour, when some hungry sorts came straggling in, covered with snow, wondering why there were so many drunken airmen laughing and singing. Not surprisingly, there were quite a few major hangovers the next day or two as the song session merged into card playing, drinking, chess playing, more drinking, darts playing, and so on. But the hangovers were stoically accepted as being well worth it. I came to realize several days later that many of our guys did not learn of this morning marathon of partying until after it had ended: The high wind and heavy snowfall had kept them in their shacks all day, eating and drinking when necessary from their personal "pantries," under beds and in footlockers, where most of us hoarded food and beverages.

About a month later, one of our squadron pilots, a captain close to the end of his tour of duty, walked into our shack and tossed a funny looking cloth cap to Bob Crow and then another one toward me. Several other guys looked up from their bunks, and he said to them, "Only the train wreckers get these; I don't have enough for everybody." He was tacitly recognizing that Bob and I had been regularly flying night missions against communist railroad rolling stock, tracks, and bridges.

He then turned and walked out. My cap had hit my bed and bounced onto the floor. I picked it up and realized what it was. It was a tall, soft cloth cap, with dark blue and white vertical stripes as traditionally worn by railroad engineers and firemen. I later learned that this pilot was the son of a Burlington & Northern Railroad engineer and that he had requested his father to send about a dozen of these caps to him. And he gave them to crewmen who flew frequent "search and de-stroy" missions against enemy railroad bridges, marshalling yards, roll-ing stock, and railroad tracks.

Over the next three or four days we had a series of missions sched-uled and then scrubbed, night after night. Finally, the weather broke and on the morning of the fourth or fifth day after our last flight, the crews who were to fly that night were listed on the Battle Order and scheduled for the early morning pre-flight briefing at Group HQ. Not to our surprise, our crew was posted for a deep "dawn patrol" penetra-tion into the target-rich northeast corner of North Korea. When we walked into the Briefing Room that morning there were among those early arrivals two other 95th Bomb Squadron crews, sitting together and engaging in the normal course of light banter and playful insult. All six members of these two crews were proudly wearing their railroad caps, which now designated them as "Train Busters."

They seemed to be thoroughly enjoying the attention and good-natured ribbing that they were receiving from those not so favored. I must admit this Train Buster gimmick was something that broke the normal routine and quite probably served as a major morale builder for those chosen few who received the railroader caps. It was a significant trigger mechanism for the release of the normal pre-flight tension and anxiety that starts to intensify upon seeing your crew's name and target listing on that next night's Battle Order. However, without any prior discussion or concurrence, Bob, Jerry, and I, individually, had decided not to wear our railroad caps to the briefing.

I observed the captain who gave us the caps glancing repeatedly in our direction with a somewhat puzzled expression on his face. I casually looked away each time and resumed conversation with my crew. I then realized there were other guys in the briefing room who would have liked to be the recipients of the caps, and I was sure that the captain believed that we had agreed among ourselves, as a crew, not to wear them for some negative reason unknown to him. I immediately felt badly for his justifiable feeling of rejection and disappointment. I made mental notice to seek him out later and explain that there was no intended rejection or disapproval of him, his excellent idea, and his efforts and expense in getting the shipment of the caps from home.

I already knew why I left my railroad cap in my footlocker that day. I later gave it, without once putting it on my head, to Kim to give to her young brother who was fascinated by anything American, and particularly things related to planes and trains.

I surmised that Bob and Jerry left their caps behind for the same reason. And a later discussion confirmed the fact that all three of us, individually and for the same reason, logical or not, simply did not want to succumb to any additional superstitions or rituals that could prove deadly if overlooked or ignored. The hard lesson learned from Captain Doolittle's forgotten orange cap was more than enough warning and caution for each of us.

RIDING WITH
THE COLONEL

FOR SOME LOGIC-DEFYING REASON, THE COMMAND-ing officers of Douglas B-26 light bomber squadrons in South Korea, at least during the time of my tour of duty in 1952–1953, could not, under military regulation or directive, fly more than four combat missions during any calendar month. Therefore, these colonels and lieutenant colonels did not have their own flight crews. The inevitable consequence was that squadron commanders generally selected ("drafted") from the ranks of their respective squadrons certain bombardier-navigators and gunners who had trained with and had been assigned to their own crews and had acquired substantial combat experience, and some measure of proficiency, as well as the confidence and trust of their peers.

Prior to my arrival at K-9, our 95th Bomb Squadron Commander, Colonel Delwin D. Bentley, had drafted Captain Robert Abelman as his designated bombardier-navigator. Bob had flown with the colonel, as well as his own crew, until he had completed the magic number of fifty missions and had departed for the ZI for a thirty-day leave of absence and then his next duty assignment stateside. By the time this occurred, I had flown over thirty missions with my own crew, Robert Crow and Jerry Davis, and we had steadily and easily blended into a cohesive and combat-effective team, achieving somewhat better than average mission results but nothing that could be considered exceptional.

So on an unusually sunny morning in late April or early May of 1953, I was startled when Colonel Bentley informed me that I was "riding with sergeant (whoever he was) and me the next night." I had "filled in" for Captain Abelman several months prior and was relieved of that burden when Bob belatedly returned from a Tokyo R&R. Of course, this declaration, being presented as a simple statement of fact, was immediately perceived and accepted for what it was, a direct command but, inferentially, as an implied compliment as well. But it was of very questionable desirability to me; it was generally recognized throughout the 95th that riding with the colonel was more a curse than a blessing. I do not recall my specific response. I think it was something both immediate and insincere, but necessary under the circumstances. Probably it was simply "Yes, sir! That would be great, sir!" Then I realized something further: Just a few days or weeks before I had received a "spot" (in-theatre) promotion from second lieutenant to first lieutenant that meant basically a fifty-dollar monthly pay increase as long as I remained on flight status within the theatre of operations. That was then considered a substantial pay increase. And now I would be expected to justify that promotion by mission performance under close scrutiny!

Frankly, I was amazed and honored to be chosen by the colonel (as if I really had any choice in the matter!), but before and throughout each and every mission that I flew with him, probably no more than nine or ten, I existed in a constant state of apprehension, fear, or sheer terror. It was then, and remains to this day, my considered judgment that Colonel Bentley assumed far too many risks in his solidly entrenched status and image as the squadron's "total warrior." This judgment was confirmed by multiple eyewitnesses, who agreed that he frequently stayed over a "hot" target area too long in expending too many rounds of .50 caliber machine gun fire while on what seemed like too many dangerously low strafing passes.

The colonel seemed to have a totally uncontrollable compulsion for living on the edge. He would make these attacks all too frequently at minimum speeds, far too deep into narrow Korean valleys at but fifty to two hundred feet of terrain clearance, all too frequently under adverse weather conditions, with limited visibility, and sometimes under combinations of intense triple A, machine gun, and small arms fire.

Another major disadvantage in riding with the colonel was that each time I flew with him I got one more mission ahead of my crew. Bob, Jerry, and I wanted to finish our tours of duty together and travel home together, as we really enjoyed and felt comfortable and secure in crewing with each other. And we wanted to fly our last mission together as a crew, which meant that I would have to "stand down" while both Bob and Jerry played catch-up with an unassigned, and quite possibly an inexperienced and not fully qualified standby or newly in-theatre bombardier-navigator. However, no aspect of this dilemma did I ever discuss with the colonel. He might have felt that I should consider it to be an honor and a privilege for a temporary first lieutenant to be crewing for a command pilot who was also his squadron commander.

And, of course, it was. In fact, several of my colleagues expressed some measure of ill-concealed jealousy, mainly because they believed that I was racking up missions faster than they were and that these more frequent "rides" would enable me to complete my tour and get out of Korea before them, and possibly before the next major war broke out (referred to fearfully by some as World War III), a broadly held misapprehension within our squadron and group. If in fact that happened, combat tours for all crewmen would have been extended "for the duration." I should mention that the older, married crew members most often expressed this nagging concern about the ever-present threat of extended tours of duty brought about by any significant expansion in the scale of warfare that we were beginning to observe. In any case, it was apparent that we were seeing much heavier movements of men and materiel by truck convoys south from Manchuria and Russia to the front line.

My first ride with the colonel in my new assignment proved to be a pleasant surprise. We were flying one of the coastal routes (to the best of my recollection) east-northeast of the port city of Hungnam along the Sea of Japan and approximately 150 to 200 miles from the Russian border. We were searching for rolling stock, either road or railroad, but with very few target sightings. Wanting to prove myself to the colonel, I was desperately searching for a string of trucks, a southbound troop train, or some other choice target of opportunity to home in on. Inbound to the target area, the colonel and his flight engineer, an older NCO (who, I subsequently learned, had crewed for the colonel in flying similar missions in Martin B-26 Marauders over France and Germany in World War II), frequently exchanged observations and comments as they sat side by side (the flight engineer occupied what would have been the co-pilot seat), as they had apparently done on previous missions. I did not engage in their easy and casual conversations. I simply gave the colonel headings, both inbound and over enemy territory, while I continually rotated my head and upper body "on a swivel" from wing tip to wing tip, and up and down, in searching intensely for moving targets and/or incoming flak or small arms fire. Fortunately, we had a full moon and zero cloud cover so the colonel needed minimal verbal guidance from me to follow the intersecting main rail line and the primary highway weaving down from Russia and its huge port facility at Vladivostok.

I frequently observed two to four pairs of headlights in close proximity coming down the roadway from the northeast. However, by the time I was about to initiate an attack, by calling for a gliding descent from three thousand feet with minimum power, the truck drivers would extinguish their running lights in the rising moon's shadow or they would turn off the roadway, frequently in multiple directions, dousing their lights as they scattered. This went on for half an hour, and I could sense that the colonel was growing impatient. But I had no intention of wasting ordnance on marginal sightings, colonel or no colonel in the left seat. Finally, and fortunately, we came upon a uniquely configured estuary of a river that I knew quite well. It constituted a very reliable landmark for accuracy in navigating this coastline route. I had been on this route just two or three nights before, when I had observed that there were three low bridges across the river close to a point where it emptied into the Sea of Japan. However, on this night there were *five* bridges across the river, meaning the rapid and recent addition of two bridges, either actual or, more probably, dummy bridges. I quickly reported to the Colonel the unlikely possibility of construction of two new fully operational bridges within but a few days!

Of course, the colonel was then thinking faster, more effectively, and more creatively than I was. While I was fixated on moving targets and small rewards, he was thinking about more important stationary targets and long-term benefits.

The colonel described a plan, and it was good one. Our discussion went basically like this, with the colonel asking the questions: "Can you identify the two new bridges?"

"Yes, sir, they are side by side and closest to the coastline."

"How much spacing between the three old bridges?"

"Five to ten yards."

"What minimum altitude do you need to make a Norden drop on the three old bridges as a cluster target?"

"Three thousand feet will do it if we go straight upwind at 180 knots."

"With a likely bomb scatter, if you aim at the middle of the three existing bridges will we get a tight enough cluster effect?"

"Yes, sir."

"What's your best guess as to wind direction and speed?"

"Forty to fifty knots, dead on the nose on this heading, 040 degrees, sir."

"Do you have a sufficiently precise aiming point?"

"I know this area very well. The edge of the moon shadow now directly intersects the bridges. With a slightly longer run-in I will have enough sighting time to line up on the middle bridge."

"Okay, let's do it, I'm going to do a long 360 out over the water. Let's dump everything."

I had just enough time to set up the bombsight. The colonel made a perfect or near perfect alignment on target after coming around on track. I am sure that he kept airspeed at 180 knots and altitude at three thousand feet as planned, although I had no way of verifying these input numbers at the time as my eyes were continually going from the bombsight to the target area through the clear Plexiglas panel in front of it. And the bombsight was now directing the plane's heading and automatically establishing the release point for a salvo release of all ten five-hundred-pound demolition bombs. The bombsight was automatically making minute adjustments in our heading as I manually kept turning the drift knob to keep the middle of the middle road bridge directly in the middle of the etched and illuminated cross hairs. With the direct headwind, we were actually flying only 135 to 140 knots over the ground below, although our indicated airspeed was 180 knots. Luckily, as planned, there was practically zero crosswind drift left or right. The Norden bombsight, a masterpiece of scientific invention, had also taken into account the specific ballistic coefficient (the degree of streamlining) of the powerful tritonel GP bombs that we were carrying.

I had never Norden-bombed at such low altitude before, either night or day! The lowest was when I was an aviation cadet at Mather

AFB in Sacramento, California, the year before when we bombed fixed targets located at the nearby Beale AFB bombing range, and then, it was from six thousand to ten thousand feet of altitude and only during broad daylight. But for some strange reason, there did not seem to be that much difference. In fact, I was able to quickly pick up the bridges visually, find them in the optical field, and accurately anticipate the Norden's automated release of all ten bombs simultaneously so that I did not bang my head against the Plexiglas as the nose rose sharply with the sudden release of this five-thousand-pound dead weight, and as the colonel quickly shoved the yoke forward to regain level flight to ensure accuracy of target photography.

At such low bombing altitude the simultaneous explosions of all ten bombs occurred not more than ten or fifteen degrees directly behind us, so at the time of impact I had excellent visual target sighting downward and backward. The bombs appeared to me to be right on target. We collectively felt the slightly delayed and cumulative concussive effects of the bursts, and as the colonel turned sharply out to sea and toward home base, a few well off-target tracers passed beside and behind us.

All on board were relieved, relaxed, and elated!

The colonel appeared to be gleeful and exuberant, which was un-usual. He made a few joking remarks, and his flight engineer and I laughed nervously and excessively. It was certainly no surprise to me that the colonel came up with this attack concept, which I would never have considered. It was a perfect solution. We had been high enough so that we easily cleared the mountaintops at straight and level flight required for precision Norden bombing. Visual target identification and sighting was near perfect with a unique and well-defined aiming point (both sharp configuration and color contrast) well familiar to me. The direct headwind resulted in little or no drift left or right of the target, and it provided a slower ground speed and therefore a longer time period for target sighting. If we had gone in low, between two hundred to five hundred feet of terrain clearance, as we would in our normal attack mode, ten five-hundred-pound GPs in salvo release could have caused very substantial fragmentation damage to our aircraft as the massed bomb bursts would be almost directly below us at the time of impact.

What a night! At mission debriefing the colonel and I described his new concept in some considerable detail to the two attentive intelligence debriefing officers. As the colonel had banked and turned sharply and immediately after bomb impact, all three of us aboard had adequate opportunity to evaluate the extent of damage. To us, the bombs' impacts seemed to be right "on target," and all of us consistently so reported it. Now all that was required for full BDA (bomb damage assessment) confirmation was the pictures from our plane's belly-mounted target camera. The colonel further suggested that the navy's Task Force 77, customarily patrolling off the east coast of North Korea, be requested to get daytime photography of the strike to provide further confirmation of our own visual BDA and that provided by our aircraft's photography.

Later the following afternoon, we got the word from 17th Bomb Group HQ that two of our bombs were direct hits, three did substantial damage, two did partial damage, and the remaining three hit the water but could well have caused structural damage to the bridges' foundations. It was indeed a good night's work. And we now had a new SOP for slow mission nights with poor moving target sightings.

Simply stated, it was Colonel Bentley's conclusion that if very little or no rolling stock was moving along a main supply route after an extended period of target search, or if it was too difficult to bomb with any reasonable degree of predicted accuracy due to inclement weather, heavy flak, and so on, then the logical plan of attack was to simply climb to three thousand feet, select a finite and easily discernible aiming or off-sight aiming point, fly straight and level, salvo the full bomb load with one punch of the little red button, continue straight and level flight through bomb impact to get a photographic record of bombing accuracy (or lack thereof), get as much visual post-impact target sighting as possible consistent with crew safety, and then simply get the hell out of there!

It seems that every time I flew with Colonel Bentley I learned something valuable and insightful about flying and bombing. I acquired genuine appreciation and respect for his creativity, aggressiveness, and courage: he was a constant innovator, a relentless and fearless combatant, and a coldly calculating risk-taker. And he handled our B-26 as if it was normal and natural for it to be totally under his command and control. He actually flew this highly powered, and then state-of-the-art, twin-engine light bomber just as he would a fighter plane! The problem for me was simply that while bombing I was not strapped to the airplane like he and the flight engineer were! So I was bounced around the nose compartment of the aircraft, on occasion sustaining minor bruises, whenever the colonel executed sudden and frequently violent evasive maneuvers in avoiding enemy radar-controlled triple A and/or small arms fire, as well as in avoiding cloud-shrouded and snow-covered mountainsides. In conclusion, it was an honor, and a privilege, and a pain to crew with Colonel Bentley.

However, in cold retrospection and with all honesty, the tangible and intangible benefits and values in riding with the colonel never adequately compensated for the apprehension, fear, and raw terror that preceded and accompanied me from pre-mission briefing through the end of the landing roll back at K-9 Air Base.

NOBODY'S WAR

I HUNG UP THE SQUADRON'S LARGE AND UNWIELDY telephone, walked to the colonel's desk, extracted the large and heavy padlock from the right top drawer, glanced around the cold and empty operations shack, stepped out the front door, slapped on the padlock, and walked briskly to my shack through the hardening mud, dirty snow, and heavy slush that was again freezing during the last dim hour of late winter sunlight. Another nine hours of my "day job" was behind me. I had flown with my own crew the night before, so I knew that I would be assured an open evening with plenty of time for an uninspired dinner at the so-called officers club, a small pitcher of insufficiently cold beer, and several games of chess with an excellent chance to win a bottle or two of Courvoisier VSOP, Cherry Herring, or Johnny Walker Black Label with each game won, as several new and willing "guppies" had just arrived from the States.

When I reached our shack, I was surprised to see that Major Brown was sitting on my footlocker, visiting and chatting with three or four of the guys. Major Brown was a highly regarded senior pilot with the 95th, but I had rarely seen him in our shack before and I wondered why he was there. After the usual and perfunctory greetings I stretched out on my narrow bed and listened as they resumed their discussion about the usual pilot stuff: the flight characteristics of different B-26s flown and maintained by our squadron such as fuel consumption rates, electrical system malfunctions, unexplained and erratic manifold pressure readings, and the like.

I was annoyed by Major Brown's continued presence because I wanted to share with the guys some potentially good news that I had just learned while talking with my "covert contact" at our 17th Bomb Group Headquarters, a fellow Chicagoan who had gone through Basic Training at Shepherd AFB at the same time I did. But I did not want to interrupt. Their meandering and technical discussion appeared to me to be very similar to those that I had overheard many times before, only this one was dominated by Major Brown, who was recognized as being one of the most experienced and competent bomber pilots in our squadron. I knew that he was one of the few crewmen to have received a regular commission, which meant that he was probably a West Point graduate and completed extensive formal pilot training thereafter. This I had gleaned by working in Squadron Operations, where I handled personnel documents. We lower forms of military life were mere college graduates, not of the prestigious Academy type, and we had earned our commissions after completing ten months of Aviation Cadet Training, or had been commissioned second lieutenants via the ROTC route upon graduation from some college or university and then had completed formal flight school training. I had heard that Major Brown had flown a tour of combat duty in the Army Air Corps' B-26 Martin Marauder over France and later more combat missions over France, Germany, and Eastern Europe in the arguably much improved Douglas B-26 Invader, then commonly identified officially as the Douglas A-26.

At that point in my young life I could fall asleep anywhere and anytime, with noise never seeming to be a problem. So, even fully dressed and with Major Brown sitting practically at my feet and talking loudly, I quickly dozed off, as it appeared that this familiar pilot talk would continue interminably. Then, unexpectedly, the major reached back and shook my lower right leg to gain my attention. I was rather startled by this sudden movement so I opened my eyes as I raised my head and shoulders to stare directly at him. Surprised that I had fallen asleep so quickly, and he said, "Sorry to wake you, lieutenant, but where did you say Colonel Bentley has gone?" Somewhat annoyed, my smart-ass reply was, "I don't think I said where the colonel had gone."

And in fact I hadn't.

With some visible measure of angry but controlled exasperation, Major Brown's response was: "Okay, lieutenant, so where did Colonel Bentley go?"

My now more respectful answer was: "Major, I do not know where the colonel went as he did not tell me where he was going. He simply told me he would be 'off base' today and tomorrow. Quite frankly, he rarely ever tells me where he is going: he simply calls in from time to time when he's gone to inquire about any significant developments or problems, and it is then that he may tell me his approximate ETA (estimated time of arrival) back at K-9."

Major Brown's protracted silence and the expression of annoyance upon his face told me quite clearly that he did not believe a single word I said! After just a few more moments of awkward silence, I added weakly, "It may seem strange, but that is the way the colonel operates. I simply cannot tell you where he is, as I don't know where he is."

To end these unpleasant and stressful moments, I suddenly realized that there was no reason why I should not share the good news that I had intended to withhold until after Major Brown had departed our shabby living quarters. So to change the subject and divert attention, I announced to the small group assembled that I had just learned, not more than thirty minutes earlier, that the 95th had been selected to receive the Republic of South Korea's Syngman Rhee Presidential Unit Citation. I further volunteered that the source of my good news was my covert contact at Group HQ, without identifying him by name, rank, or responsibility.

Major Brown immediately asked if the other two squadrons in the group were to be equally recognized. I replied that I had not thought to ask that question but I would call the next day to seek the answer.

It then occurred to me that the fact that the colonel had not told Major Brown of his destination might have been an embarrassment to the major. To make matters worse, several lower grade officers in his own squadron were now informed of his lack of "inside" information, which he would logically have been privy to had his relationship with the colonel been as close and friendly as might be expected. So I asked Major Brown how frequently such presidential commendations were awarded. I might add that I had not even known of the existence of such military citations given collectively to service personnel until I got the telephone call from Group HQ earlier that day. Major Brown proved to be very knowledgeable about presidential unit citations, as well as individual military awards and decorations. And he then displayed his willingness to share his extensive knowledge with us.

The major continued, answering several related questions from us about other awards and decorations. He then surprisingly and angrily expressed his displeasure as to the total absence at our K-9 Air Base of any kind of formal presentations of individual awards and decorations, such as the Distinguished Flying Cross or the Air Medal. These presentations, he argued, should be made by the group commander or at least a squadron commander, at scheduled formal ceremonies on the base and conducted within relatively short periods after the combat activities that justified the awards.

He expressed these strong convictions forcefully, making clear his belief that meritorious combat actions justified and fully warranted timely and public acclamation appropriate to the courage and flying skills displayed by the aircrew members involved, and that such recognition would inevitably elevate morale and motivate other airmen to strive to so perform and to be so honored. He observed that this had been the standard operating procedure in the U.S. Army Air Corps' Eighth Air Force at his base for missions flown out of the Midlands of England, and later in France during World War II, pointing out that the morale of our airmen during those difficult and very stressful months and years was remarkably high despite the sustained and devastating losses in men and aircraft caused by Luftwaffe fighter-interceptors and heavy antiaircraft fire.

I began to realize that the major had possibly consumed far too many drinks at the officers club before he arrived at our shack. I had never known him to socialize with company grade officers, as he was doing now, sitting among us and sharing his beliefs, convictions, emotions, and experiences. Surprisingly, he then directed a question to me: "Lieutenant, how long have you been working in the operations shack?"

I replied that I had been there since my first day at K-9.

He asked me how many war correspondents or combat cameramen had come to our squadron headquarters since then. My answer was none. And how many of the "big brass" had come down to our squadron at K-9 from Far East Air Force Headquarters in Tokyo since I had arrived? Again, my answer was none. He asked me if I was aware of the worrisome and continuing shortages of aircrews, aircraft, ordnance, and materiel. I acknowledged that these shortages existed and did present major problems in getting adequate and effective target coverage simultaneously in interdiction and close support.

He observed that our UNC air forces had more than "air superiority," that we had in fact "air supremacy" due to the dominance of our F-86Fs and our fighter-interceptor pilots over the Russian-built and often Russian manned MiG-15s, with our innovative and better trained American fighter pilots amassing a more than twelve-to-one kill ratio against them. (The USAF actually lost only seventy-six F-86Fs while destroying at least 993 MiG-15s during air-to-air combat extending over the course of the war against communist North Korean, Chinese, and Russian pilots.)

The major bitterly lamented that the American public could not accept "either long wars or high casualties" except when our national security was immediately and directly threatened. He contended that we could and should drive the "commies" back across the Yalu River into China and Manchuria and "give the Korean peninsula back to the Koreans" or we would end up fighting them again and then quite probably on their terms and under adverse conditions. I distinctly remember him saying that we were fighting "the wrong war at the wrong place at the wrong time with the wrong enemy."

I learned years later that this often-quoted pronouncement was first made by General Omar Bradley. At that time I was truly fascinated by the major's spontaneous and rather embittered discourse, as I then knew little about international affairs or geopolitics. Before entering the USAF in 1951 I had been a business major with continuing emphasis upon finance and accounting. I had been working almost full time while completing an intensive MBA program and had had little time for or interest in international or military affairs. My father had served in France in World War I and my brother had fought with the Second Marine Division in the South Pacific in World War II (with both of them sustaining major combat injuries), and I unthinkingly had considered it my civic duty to enlist and serve in Korea when this UN-sanctioned defensive war suddenly erupted. But until this extended discussion with Major Brown and my squadron buddies, I had never seriously thought about the complexities of this so-called Korea Conflict, the justification for it, or the limited recognition and support that it had received from our civilian population and the rest of the free world.

Major Brown suddenly realized that he had been talking for some time without any one responding. And I think he mistook our collective and total silence for unspoken disagreement with the beliefs and sentiments that he sincerely expressed. I believe that all or almost all of us basically agreed with just about everything he said, but he did not know this. So he abruptly rose, momentarily lost his balance, and started for the door. He then turned and said to us, "This is nobody's war. The only people who know or care are our families and us. This damned war happened just too soon after World War II." Then he turned toward me and said, "I wouldn't count on any presidential unit citation for the 95th."

Major Brown then walked out the door without saying another word. When I left K-9 two months later, in late July 1953, no formal documentation had yet come through from Group or Wing Headquarters regarding the award of South Korea's Syngman Rhee Presidential Unit Citation to the 95th Bomb Squadron. However, I subsequently learned, more than five decades later, that Major Brown was wrong in two significant respects.

I learned during November 2006 that the 17th Bomb Group, comprised of the 34th Bomb Squadron, the 37th Bomb Squadron, and our 95th Bomb Squadron during the Korean War, *was* awarded the highly regarded South Korea's Syngman Rhee Presidential Unit Citation for "superior military achievement" for combat operations conducted from May 24, 1952, through March 31, 1953. And I also learned that the 95th Bomb Squadron had been awarded two Distinguished Unit Citations for its "meritorious combat service" during our crew's tour of duty. It's just that we servicemen never knew about it.

PART IV
OVER THE HUMP

LITTLE WHITE
FELT BOMBS

DURING MY STAY WITH THE 95TH BOMB SQUADRON most of our flight and ground crewmembers wore dark blue baseball caps. But only we flight crewmembers wore around our necks light blue silk scarves closely matching the squadron "color" displayed upon the painted wing tips, vertical stabilizers, and engine nacelles of our B-26s, which were otherwise painted a dull or glossy black. The soft silk scarves were made from the fabric used in the manufacture of parachute canopies and provided comfort and protection from the roughly stitched collars of our coarse woolen winter flight suits. Also, flight and ground crews frequently wore impressive and comfortable blue gabardine Eisenhower jackets and highly shined black high-cut combat boots.

But for most of us the most significant item of apparel was the dark blue baseball caps, and for a very good reason. Actually, it was what was *on* the peaks of the baseball caps that had major significance. Simply stated, it was a matter of status.

As frequently expressed in the military, rank has it privileges. But privileges (higher pay, better food and housing, etc.) meant little to many of us when compared to the status derived from the number of actual combat missions completed and displayed. Every accredited mission flown was represented by a small white piece of felt in the shape of a bomb, roughly three-fourths of an inch in length, which was firmly affixed to the cap's peak the morning after each mission. The backside of each felt bomb had an adhesive substance that made it easy and convenient to attach it to the cap by simply positioning the bomb in place and then applying pressure. The general idea was that upon completion of fifty combat missions, the peak of a flight crewman's cap was fully and evenly covered by fifty miniature white bombs, establishing for all to see that the wearer had completed, and had survived, a full combat tour entitling him to a plane ticket "back to the world!"

My long-delayed perception regarding the significance of these little white bombs was that the indefinable status one achieved by the number of missions flown was as important, if not more important, than the level of military rank achieved. Such an easily recognizable measure of a crewman's combat record almost without exception resulted in his own projection of a certain quiet confidence and a subjective, covert feeling of pride of accomplishment. Furthermore, our bomb-laden baseball caps confirmed that we were resourceful, durable, and most importantly, genuinely lucky, as all of us believed more strongly with the addition of each felt bomb that we would survive and that we would relentlessly fill our caps' peaks with fifty small but very meaningful indicia of our destiny to survive. This feeling almost blocked out the ever-nagging worry and anxiety about the close proximity of death that those little white bombs also signified.

In fact, upon flying our twenty-fifth mission, we considered ourselves to be "over the hump" and we figured that the road home was downhill and therefore would be much easier. Of course, this was blatant self-deception and we inherently realized it, but we were all in an unconscious state of perpetual denial in this regard. When our thoughts turned, as much too often they did, to being shot down, it was always "the other guy" who would be "buying the farm," or "plowing the paddy," or "riding a one-way ticket to North Korea," and almost always that dreaded and fleeting thought was accompanied by a small and silent prayer for deliverance.

I woke up with the worst hangover of my entire life in the early afternoon of the day after the night that our crew flew its twenty-fifth mission. We had started drinking at mission debriefing, where we were indulged by the debriefing officers with a few extra shots of Old Methuselah, a poor substitute for bourbon whisky that had apparently been passed off as high-quality booze upon some unwitting purchasing agent of the USAF. I continued the celebration by drinking in the back of a parked crew transport truck with five or six other guys in our squadron, doing more than my share by ingesting a truly impressive quantity of really good stuff, including Johnny Walker Black Label, Drambuie, and Courvoisier VSOP, that I had won playing mediocre chess against abject losers and rank beginners. This impromptu party group slowly faded away, one inebriate after another, so it was close to sunrise when I finally stumbled off to bed alone.

The next thing I knew, brilliant early afternoon sunlight was streaming into our shack, nearly blinding me. Kim was sitting on the next bed with a broad smile on her face while holding my blue baseball cap in both hands and extending it toward me. She had attached twenty-five little white felt bombs to the peak of the cap that covered exactly the entire right half of its top surface. I did not know that she was going to do that, so I was surprised and pleased that she had thought to expend the effort. Most crewmen started the ritual early by attaching a bomb to their cap immediately after every mission flown. For some inexplicable reason, I had not done so, causing the display of an empty peak until Kim got the process going for me that morning. I should have accepted Kim's offer, made the morning after my first mission, to attach the first little white felt bomb. To this day, I do not know why I declined. I recall she never made that offer again. Nor did I ever ask her to perform this simple task until she gratuitously began to perform it the morning after I went "over the hump."

I should add that I felt fully justified in wearing my properly adorned baseball cap whenever and wherever it was acceptable. To make matters progressively better, with the passage of time, Kim meticulously adhered an additional little white bomb to my cap's peak the morning after each and every mission I completed thereafter, much to an excessive, but hopefully well-concealed, measure of pride and personal self-satisfaction.

COUNT THE FIREFLIES
AND MULTIPLY BY THIRTY

EIGHT OR TEN OF US WERE LOLLING AROUND THE drab K-9 Officers Club one stormy early afternoon in May in our accustomed lounging area near the end of the bar. We were all company-grade flight officers: pilots and bombardier-navigators. All of us were captains, first lieutenants, or second lieutenants assigned to the 95th Bomb Squadron. It had been raining steadily, often heavily, for three or four days. As there was no chance for a better weather forecast, we were going absolutely nowhere, fast. All bombing missions, as well as junkets back to Japan for aircraft repairs and incidental R&Rs, had been indefinitely postponed, and we were bored, restless, and frustrated.

Most of our crews had been briefed the early morning of the day the rains began.

My crew and another 95th Bomb Squadron crew had been assigned to fly a "hunter-killer" mission, one of the first of its kind to be scheduled by 17th Bomb Group HQ within a number of months, to the best of my recollection.

The hunter-killer mission profile and technique had been conceived and first executed during the summer and fall of 1952 by B-26 Night Intruder crews of the 731st Bomb Squadron, 3rd Bomb Group, then stationed close to the west coast of South Korea and near the Yellow Sea, at K-8 AFB, Kunsan. The 3rd Bomb Group had entered the Korean War within two months after the initial penetration by overwhelming numbers of North Korean troops across the common border between South Korea and North Korea. Within six weeks, the communist forces had advanced relentlessly to within forty miles of the city of Pusan near the southern tip of the Korean peninsula, before the UNC pushed the enemy back and well to the north of Seoul, the capital of South Korea, in late 1950. The 3rd Bomb Group had the distinction of flying the first UNC bombing mission as well as the last UNC bombing mission of any air group, tactical or strategic, engaged in the Korean War. It was the recipient of numerous and well-deserved awards, citations, and commendations, including three Presidential Unit Citations and the Korean Presidential Unit Citation. And its 731st Bomb Squadron was the first unit in the 5th Air Force to be trained specifically for low-level, night bombing operations. In fact, a number of our 95th Bomb Squadron crewmen were later assigned on temporary duty to the 731st Bomb Squadron at K-8, specifically to acquire the training to qualify for such hazardous low-level night missions that had never before been attempted by any unit of the 5th Air Force, in any war.

Now six of us, including our two gunners, had been ordered to remain after that briefing for additional instruction and mission preparation. The two briefing officers, a senior pilot and a senior bombardier-navigator from Group HQ, detailed the assigned mission profile of our squadron's variation of hunter-killer. The other crew had been designated as the "hunter," to carry ten five-hundred-pound GP demolition bombs. They would fly at four hundred feet of terrain clearance to search out and stop troop or cargo trains and truck convoys coming down the east coast route from Russia. As the "killer," our aircraft would carry ten five-hundred-pound napalm bombs and would fly at three hundred feet of terrain clearance and just one to three hundred yards behind the hunter. Our specific mission was to strike the stopped trains and trucks and destroy their troops and/or cargo by splashing flaming jellied gasoline over these vehicles and any foot soldiers attempting to escape from them.

It was a clever idea in concept. But it was hard to execute effectively and safely, and for several reasons. At low attitude over mountainous enemy territory, our navigation was entirely by visual sightings of recognizable and unusual natural (e.g., river estuaries, mountains, lakes, and islands) and cultural (e.g., roads, bridges, railroad tracks, villages) features upon the earth's surface. It should be remembered that in 1953 there was no operational advanced radar and GPS (global positioning system) technology. Moreover, we were frequently flying with very limited visibility caused by strata of low clouds and ground fog, steep and irregularly configured mountainsides, and in the dead of night, with frequently nothing more than a half moon to light our way. We were flying in two heavily laden B-26s to execute a sequence of extended racetrack-patterned attacks on rolling stock, in close proximity one to each other.

Getting to the target area was not the problem, as flying with one plane closely behind the other and traveling at the same speed was very much like two cars, one closely behind the other, driving down a straight or curving freeway or turnpike at seventy miles an hour at night. It is relatively simple for the second driver to maintain a safe and approximately equal distance behind the lead car, by noticing a widening or narrowing of the distance between the cars and making adjustments in speed accordingly. And for me in the clear Plexiglas nose of the trailing 26, it was relatively easy to assist my pilot in maintaining adequate spacing between the two aircraft, as it was my primary responsibility to continually keep in sight the brilliant yellowish-white glow of the two exhaust stacks of the hunter's huge Pratt-Whitney eighteen cylinder engines and to warn my pilot if we were getting too close or too far back. However, after a steam train or truck convoy was visually located and our coordinated attack began, with the two aircraft circling in a racetrack configuration, coordinated operations became much more difficult and hazardous.

Then, we silently lived in constant and justifiable fear and dread of a mid-air collision that today would be described by military analysts as a likely consequence of the "fog of war." We quickly learned, by dire necessity, that our pilots would need to periodically adapt strike efforts by direct radio contact. They would alert each other as to their location and direction by activating their running lights (the flashing green light on the right wing tip and the flashing red light on the left wing tip) at precisely the same time for just two or three seconds. Of course, this commonly labeled "Christmas Tree" procedure would often draw immediate and concentrated enemy triple A and/or small arms fire, but that hazard was considered a necessary evil.

I remember distinctly a segment of that rambling mid-day conversation at the officers club. One of our bombardier-navigators had referred negatively and scornfully to a particular intelligence debriefer's insistence that we acquire and record more complete and accurate BDA data from the visual sightings of the targets we attacked. This young and vocal lieutenant then observed that a napalm bomb's burst of flaming jellied gasoline would upon impact saturate an area roughly the size of a standard baseball diamond, generally circular in coverage but elongated along the line of flight. He reasonably questioned how anyone could possibly estimate, with any degree of accuracy, the "body count" of foot soldiers riding in a closed wooden boxcar, or killed fleeing from it if escape was possible. At this point, one of the older squadron bombardier-navigators, a "retread" from World War II with a notoriously sick and dark sense of humor, spoke up. All we had to do, he blandly suggested, was to "count the fireflies and multiply that number by thirty." His statement brought forth a small burst of nervous laughter followed immediately by a loud groan shared by almost all except him; he just sat there and grinned with smug satisfaction.

The reason for our delayed but deeply and immediately felt revulsion to this smart-ass solution was that "fireflies" was the much too accurately descriptive name placed by some of us upon the enemy soldiers running, or futilely attempting to run, out of the rapidly spreading flames of the napalm bursts.

To this day, whenever I hear the word "firefly" or "fireflies," I am once again down upon my knees as I lean forward and over the bombsight, staring fixedly and morbidly downward and backward at the "fireflies," the swarming communist soldiers engulfed in flames, desperately fleeing or attempting to flee from the huge whitish-yellow splashes of raging fires that I had created. These images are seared into my mind and memory: I see them at unexpected times almost every day or night of my life, although with the passage of the decades, these images are progressively less frequent and intense.

Simultaneously, I realize that I must continue to try to look back upon that human carnage, that immolation of multiple lives and burning flesh, in a dispassionate and objective manner. After all, our efforts, our lives, and those of our crews were totally invested in saving the lives of our own and other UNC foot soldiers, then most often greatly outnumbered in trenches, dugouts, and foxholes below as they fought for their own survival, day after day after day. With this perspective, I can and must tell myself that the psychological necessity, and ultimately the only logical conclusion, must be the reason, or rationalization, that there is no morality in war, nor can there ever be. But I am still inexorably impelled to project myself directly into that gruesome scene, as a victim rather than as an assailant, and so to experience vicariously the blinding and searing heat and horrendous pain, suffering, and terror of those long past moments in time.

DOWN IN THE VALLEY

"Down in the valley, valley so low,
Hang your head over, hear the wind blow."

I USED TO SING THESE FIRST TWO LINES OF THIS PLAIN-
tive old song, over and over again, as I leaned forward and over the
bombsight, intensely scanning the darkened valley below, searching for
the telltale pairs of dimmed headlights of a truck convoy or the wispy
white-gray plume of smoke trailing behind a steam engine of a troop
or munitions train that could be too easily perceived as ground fog. My
crew could not hear me unless I carelessly depressed the intercom button. And this I rarely did. I sang to myself to find comfort and some
measure of normality and security in a cold and hostile environment.

I would have sung more of the song but I could not remember the
words. This memory loss really bothered me at the time. I had always
been able to quickly learn and long remember almost all of the words of
the dozens of "old songs" that we used to sing in local Irish and German
bars and taverns on the northwest side of Chicago.

At that time I was well aware that a B-26 crew could fly an entire
fifty-mission combat tour, during the hours of darkness over North Korea, *without ever going down into the valleys of the enemy.* There probably
were a small number of combat crews that did exactly that! I knew that

it could be done simply by flying "straight and level" at a minimum altitude of three thousand feet, as the old, weatherworn mountains of our target areas along the eastern coastline of the Korean peninsula generally "topped out" at 2,750 feet. Thus, it was possible and safe at that altitude to hit stationary targets, and even some moving targets such as freight trains or truck convoys moving along segments of straight track or roadway. But use of this altitude made unlikely the reasonably required levels of bombing accuracy. Consequently, most of our B-26 crews regularly made deep and effective penetrations into the valleys of North Korea to perform both bombing and strafing runs against assigned targets or targets of opportunity, with their aggression and proficiency increasing progressively with acquired experience and success.

Simply stated, the cumulative and negative effects of a multitude of variables dictated aircraft penetration deep into the valleys in almost every situation. These ever-shifting variables had a major negative impact upon bombing accuracy because at altitude we were required to use the conventional Norden bomb sighting techniques or those of its more simplistic and inaccurate reflex (fixed angle) sight appendage.

The first variables that come to mind that significantly reduced bombing accuracy were the varying speeds and directions of the trucks and trains being targeted, as they necessarily followed the twisting and turning roadways and railway tracks that in turn usually paralleled the winding rivers and streams flowing down the valleys, contoured generally in a southwesterly direction toward the Yellow Sea.

The next set of variables was the winds, which varied both in their own ever-changing directions and speeds and, further, in the sudden changes of altitude of the aircraft. We also carried varying combinations of bomb loads: 500-pound GP or tritonal bombs, clusters of small antipersonnel/fragmentation bombs (MIA2s), 260-pound and 500-pound napalm bombs, five-inch rockets, etc. Each type of bomb had its own unique configuration and resultant ballistic coefficient that affected its streamlining and the resulting and varying measures of distance behind the aircraft at time of impact.

The quantities, types, and locations of cloud decks and ground fog covering and concealing targets and approaches to them presented additional sets of variables. And with the clouds came snow cover that constituted a much more worrisome variable: when the moonlight reflected off the snow, the mountain slopes looked an awful lot like clouds. Thus, the wry references to a downed crew as having probably struck a "hard cloud," with that actually and deceptively being a rocky mountainside covered by its own light-reflective, snow-covered surface.

On the upside, however, with the brilliant light of a full or near full moon free of intervening clouds, I could quite easily "pick up" targets and quickly set up successful strike patterns. In fact, there were occasions when bright moonlight would enable me to actually read the print on an aeronautical chart quite easily.

Compensating or offsetting errors frequently constituted a substantial factor in reducing the impact of multiple variables and contributed to more successes in hitting targets of opportunity, both stationary and moving. For example, if our aircraft was actually closer (read lower in altitude) to the target than I had estimated, and the targeted truck was carrying munitions, gasoline, or other flammables, it could still be utterly demolished if I triggered off the bomb "too early," and, consequently, it did not impact behind or "short" of the truck.

Therefore, with retrospection, detached analysis, self-critique, and "learning the hard way" by missing numerous targets, one's self-confidence and bombing accuracy improved. At least that's how it was for our crew, as we gained collective confidence in ourselves, in our own judgment, in each other, and in our trusted B-26s. These quick, maneuverable, responsive, and durable machines took us down in the valley, sometimes as low as fifty to one hundred feet of terrain clearance, whenever conditions were optimal, and safely back out again, mission after mission after mission.

MOMENTS OF MADNESS

I WAS STRAPPED IN SECURELY FOR IMMEDIATE TAKEOFF on runway 15 in the Plexiglas nose of a bone-chillingly cold B-26C. We were first in line, with our engines idling, at the end of the taxiway on the approach to our single runway. Bob and Jerry were behind and above me, as ready and eager for departure as I was. We were anxiously waiting for voice clearance from the control tower to begin trundling onto the asphalt runway for the start of our downwind takeoff roll on its south-southeasterly heading of 150 degrees. We were hauling a maximum bomb load of ten highly explosive tritonal bombs, total weight five thousand pounds, with two bombs racked under each wing and three more hanging vertically on each side of the bomb bay. The ammo cans were fully loaded for all ten .50 caliber Browning machines guns (500 rounds each), with three of them imbedded in the leading edge of each wing and four more in the top and bottom turrets. We carried a topped-off main tank of high-octane aviation fuel, as well as full wing and auxiliary fuel tanks, as our target was a recently rebuilt and strategically critical railroad bridge located in the far northeastern corner of North Korea, along the coastline of the Sea of Japan and about fifteen minutes of flying time from North Korea's common border with the USSR.

As we idled the engines and waited with increasing impatience and anxiety, the gusting winds from the north were noticeably growing stronger: from observation of the streaming windsock, my rough estimate was that its velocity was in the vicinity of thirty to forty knots. Takeoff from K-9 downwind at night with heavy wing loading was always a daunting adventure, but with ever-increasing wind speeds off the tail the cumulative effect of these multiple, negative factors made this particular takeoff a truly challenging assignment.

As I sat there, securely strapped in with my back flat against the bulkhead, set back from the Norden bombsight and the Plexiglas nose of the aircraft by five or six feet, and with my electrified flight suit plugged into the aircraft to conserve needed body heat, I knew that we were being kept waiting much too long in receiving the required "cleared for takeoff" instruction from the tower. Therefore, we were wastefully burning off too much of our reserve fuel supply, which might be critically needed to get back to K-9 in the event of the loss of an engine or a break in a fuel line.

I finally reached out for the intercom button to ask Bob about our departure status but he clicked in simultaneously and informed Jerry and me that the tower had instructed him to delay takeoff until a slowly approaching MATS (Materiel Air Transport Service) C-54 on the far taxiway had passed us for entry upon and clearance for take up ahead of us. I released my safety belt and leaned forward to look back through the Plexiglas. I saw for the first time a huge four-engine aircraft slowly approaching us while we were stopped close to the end of runway. This lumbering C-54 seemed to be just crawling along the taxiway as it passed by. I looked upward and into the cabin of the aircraft and observed a number of older men, all of them well dressed in business suits, talking and laughing among themselves. They seemed not to have a care in the world!

The C-54 slowly turned and came to a full stop at the very end of the runway. And then it appeared to us that its pilots performed the most deliberate and painstaking preflight takeoff procedure in the history of K-9 Air Base. These pilots spent fifteen to twenty minutes in completing instrument check, engine run-up, and then, finally, revving up to max power, releasing brakes, and initiating their takeoff roll.

On all of our missions we were required by FEAF regulations to take off on the exact minute and second assigned to us at preflight briefings for tactical departures, both day and night, and here we were, burning up precious fuel reserves and increasing the risks and anxieties of combat so some high-ranking diplomats could get back to the safety, security, and comfort of Tokyo or Washington D.C., or wherever else they were heading, being moved ahead of us and thereby getting back just a few minutes earlier.

Then and there, and quite suddenly, a strange thing happened to Bob, Jerry, and me at almost the exact same moment in time. We began to shout and swear at these "fucking civilians," at these complacent and relaxed "black suits" in their customized and comfortable C-54, although we knew quite well that there was no way they could hear us. And then, quite suddenly, I panicked and became quite claustrophobic as I found myself sweating profusely despite the bitter coldness of the uninsulated and unheated B-26 on this clear, moonlit night. It was simply one of the weirdest phenomena that I had ever experienced.

There we were, by our own free will and voluntary commitment, isolated from the rest and best of civilization, shouting and swearing collectively for about two or three minutes at total strangers who could neither see nor hear us and who could not have possibly been responsible for our predicament. This unusual form of collective hysteria evidentially had been the cumulative result of insidious and slowing mounting strain, anxiety, and fear inherent in fatigued combatants. We had already flown approximately thirty to thirty-five combat missions at this point in our respective tours of duty, but apparently we were much closer to emotional burnout than we had thought possible.

Finally, after receiving clearance from the tower to proceed, the C-54 began lumbering down runway 15 and finally lifted off into the darkness at the far south end of the runway. Bob received immediate clearance. He quickly rolled the B-26 off the PSP and onto the black asphalt and into position for takeoff. He set the brakes. He steadily advanced both throttles to achieve required manifold pressures and revolutions per minute, and our huge Pratt-Whitney R2800 engines' roar rose to a deafening decibel level. He eased off the brakes and the B-26 began to lurch forward, bounce rapidly, and then charge down the center of the cracked and undulating runway. This sudden burst of acceleration pinned me back against the firewall. But Bob's takeoff was smooth and uneventful: I could hardly tell when the weight of the aircraft came off the wheels. I leaned forward and looked downward at the illumination created by our extended landing lights. I stared at the large whitecaps and the churning and turgid yellowish-brown waters of Suyong Bay. I felt that we were so close that I could just reach down and touch them.

With maximum loads of bombs, machine gun rounds, and high-octane gas, our gains in speed and altitude were so slow it seemed that our climb-out would never end. But our southward passage further out over the Korean Straits and then northward and back over the shoreline was made safely and uneventfully.

We had been informed at preflight briefing that there was a recently spotted flak trap recessed in or near a railroad tunnel approximately a quarter mile southwest of our targeted railroad bridge, and that this tunnel would be our secondary target should we take out the bridge and still have unexpended ordnance. However, we were instructed en route that another B-26, scheduled to hit the bridge about an hour before our ETA, had succeeded in dropping it into the water with that aircraft's full load of five-hundred-pounders. So we were instructed to proceed directly to the railroad tunnel as our new primary target and attempt to take it out and, hopefully, destroy the flak trap as well.

Bob and I decided that we should drop all four wing bombs in train (i.e., one after the other in close sequence) on the first bomb run, with the center of the tunnel mouth my aiming point (provided that I could locate and target it), and that we should approach the tunnel at an approximate 5 degree angle of incidence, dropping "two short" and "two long" in bracketing the target on a generally west-to-east heading. And if we achieved a good visual BDA, we would proceed to the other side of the mountain using the same angle of approach, except that the first bomb would be "short," the second "on target," and the third "long." The third and last run would be a replica of the second, by the use of a racetrack pattern back over the tunnel mouth in dumping our last three GPs. In each run, our aiming point would be a direct hit on the railroad tracks precisely at the tunnel mouth, having high hopes but reduced expectations of collapsing the heavy wooden beams above and supporting the roof of the tunnel mouth, as well as destroying the wooden railroad ties that supported the tracks at their point of entry into the tunnel.

Our crew had had a collective "bad feeling" about this mission, even before it began, as one of the other two squadrons of the 17th Bomb Group had lost a 26 and its entire crew several nights before and the general consensus was that they "went missing" at this specific target site. And our encounter with the C-54 before takeoff didn't improve our mood. So our shared conviction was that we would be in the target area within less than two hours and that the North Korean (or Russian) triple A crew manning the guns would reasonably expect that we would be coming. So would we be predator, or prey? Probably both.

With the aid of brilliant moonlight, I was able to quickly locate the target. As originally planned, we made our first run on the tunnel mouth west-to-east, dropping all four GPs from the wing racks, with close spacing and with surprising accuracy. Actually, if a target is clearly identified at five hundred feet, great accuracy is not imperative, as narrow bomb spacing will compensate for some measure of inaccuracy. And there was no returning fire from the presumed flak trap. Nor did we see anything resembling a flak trap on or near the tracks. We also had the benefit of superb visibility, with no clouds above and no ground fog or mist below. We did not see any flatbed railcars or anything that could be deemed to resemble the rumored flak trap in or near the tunnel mouth. We proceeded to the east side of the low mountain that contained the railroad tunnel and I dropped the first three bombs from the bomb bay as planned, releasing the first short, the second "on target," and the third long. My alignment was slightly off but we could call it a partial hit, as the right edge of the bomb burst area seemed to reach and penetrate the tunnel mouth.

We came around again, on approximately the same heading and parallel with the line of craters from the first run. Our alignment was slightly to the right of the first three-bomb sequence, and my release point for these last three bombs was almost the same. Just after release, Bob tipped the left wing down and we could see the first bomb hitting the tracks somewhat earlier than the first bomb of the first run from the east side of the mountain, but with the second and third seeming to "walk up the tracks" and over the tunnel mouth. Bob and I talked about taking another look at the strike area, but two streams of tracers from the side of another small mountain close by prompted a quick change of mind so we immediately headed for home base.

All the way back to K-9 our crew seemed to be unusually talkative on intercom. It was a good mission and we generously celebrated it. The bad feeling we had had about the mission had been proven to be unfounded and we were very glad of it. And our brief moments of madness back at the north end of runway 15 had apparently been quickly and totally forgotten, as that strange incident was never discussed or mentioned among us, then or thereafter. I think all three of us were simply too embarrassed to even want to think about it again. But I am sure that we did. I know I did. And these thoughts were, in retrospect, truly frightening.

THE STRANGE BLACK BIRD AT THE FAR END OF THE FLIGHT LINE

BY THE TIME BOB, JERRY, AND I FIRST CAME TOGETHER as a cohesive bomber crew, the role of air gunner had been steadily and very much diminished by circumstances beyond anyone's foresight. By January of 1953, comparatively few daylight bombing missions were being scheduled for our 17th Bomb Group at K-9, whether formation or single ship. Intensive pressure had been placed upon daytime enemy ground transport by the heavy, relentless, and frequently effective attacks by United States Air Force, Navy, and Marine aircraft and concentrated and accurate bombardment by the cruisers and destroyers of Task Force 77 upon North Korean rail tracks and roadways running along or relatively close to the eastern shoreline of the peninsula. More and more, enemy shipments of men and materiel by train and truck were being conducted during the hours of darkness.

Further, our increasing numbers of low-level bombing and strafing sorties were conducted at night at such close terrain clearances that a B-26 air gunner's .50 caliber Browning machine guns were practically useless. Now, the gunner simply did not have the time to visually locate and identify targets, nor did he have sufficient reaction time to aim and trigger his weapons. The direct consequence of these realities was that he was now occupying the right seat in the cockpit throughout the entire mission, functioning as co-pilot and bomb strike recorder. He also served as observer to alert his pilot as to the direction to take to best avoid the streams of flak that could come at any time and place while over hostile territory.

Jerry adapted and excelled in now performing in all three of these capacities. And he was always able, ready, and eager to take on any other duties as assigned. There were several times that Jerry sighted "incoming" green tracers before I did when the reverse should have been true. There were other times when I was looking through the Plexiglas panels on the left side of the B-26's nose for prospective targets coming toward us as we roared over the valley floor at fifty to five hundred feet of terrain clearance, and a stream of tracers would suddenly erupt on our right side, slightly behind the aircraft. Jerry would catch their illuminated flight path and shout for a "break left." Bob would react without the slightest doubt or hesitation, breaking hard left and climbing sharply out of the valley and the diminishing stream of triple A fire. He did likewise when I made the call. Bob always trusted our perceptions and the judgment calls we made under close time constraints when he himself could not possibly see the cause or causes of sudden danger.

JUST PRIOR TO TAKEOFF, JERRY PLACED HIS AND BOB'S gear atop the fuselage and just behind the open clamshell canopy while Bob did his thorough visual inspection of the B-26, circling it slowly in a counterclockwise direction with flashlight in hand. After that task Jerry really had nothing else to do until Bob had finished his "walk around." One night Jerry asked me if he could help "pull the pins." I was quite surprised by this offer as I always wanted to stay as far away from live ordnance as possible, and for as long as possible, as all of the various types of bombs we hauled into North Korea were World War

II surplus and were considered by many to be "unstable." (In fact, our ordnance officer early on informed me of the importance of having minimal contact with payloads of any composition, and I never saw any advantage in conducting myself otherwise.)

If our roles were reversed, I am sure that I would not have volunteered, as pulling the pins was always considered the "bombardier's job." I reluctantly agreed and showed him the precise manner of pin removal. He learned this simple procedure quickly and we worked each bomb together. I worked the front end while Jerry worked the back end. Before moving to the next bomb he walked to the front end and handed me his pin for the purpose of maintaining control and accuracy of count. By working together we finished the task much more quickly and we would then have a few minutes to stand and talk together before Bob arrived back at the nose of the aircraft.

One early evening of a rather dark and chilly night, Jerry and I were waiting for Bob to finish his walk-around when Jerry noticed some movement near the front end of the long protective revetment, constructed of sand-filled fifty-five-gallon oil drums, stacked side by side two levels high, that separated each aircraft's parking and servicing area from the others. We were at the far north end of the flight line with the last B-26, or so we then thought. As enemy infiltration and sabotage was always a concern, I pointed to where Jerry was staring. He nodded his head in quick accord and together we walked slowly and silently to that end of the long straight row of stacked oil drums.

As we turned the corner, some type of security guard confronted us. He was a tall Caucasian wearing black coveralls. He stood perfectly still. Jerry and I were quite startled when we saw him. At just that moment a departing B-26 turned sharply onto runway 15 and revved up to maximum power for takeoff, back-lighting both him and a B-26 some distance behind him and wide of his left shoulder. Nobody spoke or moved. Actually, we could not have heard each other even if we tried, as the roar of the engines' warm up and full-power takeoff roll would have overpowered any voice. As the B-26 roared down the runway, lifted off, and passed out over the water's edge, this quiet stranger said in a soft and friendly mid-American voice, "Why don't you guys go back to what you were doing and forget about what you saw and heard here."

Jerry and I just stood there, perplexed. We had never before seen a B-26 there, parked out in an open area usually totally vacant of any and all aircraft and activity. We were baffled by this security guy who spoke with such calm and quiet assurance. The logical things for us to do seemed to be just to turn and walk away. And that is exactly what we did.

When we got back to our B-26C Bob was waiting for us with a question: "Where were you guys?"

Jerry said: "There's a weird looking hard-nosed 26 over there with some guy guarding it."

"Yeah, what makes it so weird?"

"It's painted totally black, no markings at all, and its got a funny looking nose extension that looks like radar equipment."

Bob was silent for too long. Finally he said something like, "It must be one of those special flights. They come in after dark, refuel, and fly out the same night."

He then simply turned away and climbed up the side of the 26.

I had not noticed anything different about the aircraft, as I had been staring at the security guard. I only knew it was a 26, assuming it was one of ours.

Jerry brought up the subject of the "special mission B-26 from some other base" several times thereafter. Bob would usually respond hesitantly and evasively, and then change the subject. But Jerry and I continued to be intrigued by the strange black bird at the north end of the flight line. Subsequently, we talked and speculated about it and the soft-spoken security guard a number of times, but just between ourselves. We agreed there was much more to the story. We concluded that Bob knew all about it, since he was an assistant operations officer and, therefore, knew just about everything that happened on or near the flight line. Jerry and I were totally convinced that he simply was not going to tell us. We assumed that Bob did not think, and rightly so, that we had any official "need to know." So we dropped the subject and never did mention it to Bob again.

But still we were very curious. We had many unanswered questions: How often did these B-26s spook in and spook out? Where were they coming from? Where were they going? What was their mission? Would we ever get answers?

For well over fifty years after leaving South Korea, I never gave a deliberate thought to the mystery of that strange black bird. However, during the summer of 2007, a friend, Don Moler, who served in the USAF as crew chief on B-57s and who continues to work as a crop dusting pilot throughout the Central Sacramento Valley, gave me a book by Felix Smith, *China Pilot/Flying for Chennault during the Cold War.* It describes a specific type of clandestine night penetration into Manchuria. These special missions were flown for the purpose of dropping off and picking up Manchurian patriots who resisted, and to this day, continue to resist, the oppressive Communist Chinese who conquered their country before the Korean War and still occupy it today. I now think that is what Jerry and I saw on the flight line that dark night at K-9 Air Force Base.

RUNNING OUT OF
HORSESHOES

I WAS ALONE IN THE 95TH BOMB SQUADRON'S OPERA-tions shack on a cool and dismal Tuesday morning. At least I think it was a Tuesday morning, but at K-9 they all seemed like Tuesday mornings. As I was hanging up my heavy, clumsy telephone unit Captain Grump walked in. I vaguely recall that he was either an assistant ar-mament officer or an assistant maintenance officer. I never did know his first or last name; most everyone in the squadron who knew or knew about him referred to him as "Captain Grump." Or simply as "Grump," which seemed to be accurately descriptive and appropriate. I think he was from Brooklyn.

Grump was a little guy, five-five or five-six tall, slight of build, with a long, gaunt, and vertically lined face. My guess is that he was thirty-five to forty years old. He seldom spoke and rarely smiled. And it seemed that he had little if anything to smile about. His segment of the work force was reported to be burdened by an excessive number of chronically unhappy and troublesome self-described "grunts." These flight mechanics or bomb and gun loaders or ordnance truck drivers labored long and hard, and often under dangerous working conditions, in the cold and wet snow and rain as our Douglas B-26s were parked in a long row, sixteen in number if they were all there, along the east side of our single runway, out in the open and well distanced from any type of hanger or shelter.

Grump's ground support troops seemed to generate a disproportionately large number of personnel problems and situations that required his attention, vigilance, and disciplinary action. Unfortunately, his inability to address and resolve these sometimes difficult and sensitive matters would worsen with time, and some of them would then be escalated to the attention and final decision-making level of Colonel Delwin Bentley for resolution. On such occasions the displeased colonel would come down hard upon the indecisive Captain Grump. As a result, this justifiably apprehensive little man tried to avoid our squadron's operations shack, and especially the colonel, if at all possible. Therefore, when Captain Grump entered our worksite that morning and strolled casually and confidently across the rough wooden floor of our Quonset hut and stopped directly in front of my desk, I was rather surprised. Then I realized that the absence of the colonel's vehicle from its accustomed parking spot just outside the front door probably explained Captain Grump's unexpected visit during normal duty hours.

Before I had a chance to inquire what I could do for our long-suffering captain, he announced, with a wide and unlikely smile upon his face, "Lieutenant, you are definitely running out of horseshoes."

Having not the foggiest idea as to the meaning of this declaration, I simply sat there staring at him. He stared back at me, apparently puzzled by my failure of response. Belatedly, my brilliant reaction to his pleasant silence was, "Well, what?"

"The wing damage, what else?"

"What wing damage?"

"The 927 (or some such number)"

"The 927 what?"

"The last three numbers on the tail assembly of the B-26 you guys took out last night."

"Captain, I still don't know what the hell you're talking about." (I did not address him as Grump as I was still a temporary first lieutenant and he was a captain).

Only then did I realize what this was all about. Each Douglas B-26 had its own six-digit serial number to specifically identify it. That number was painted white on both sides of the black vertical stabilizer of that aircraft, and the last three digits of that serial number were generally used when that plane was being orally identified to someone else. Apparently our crew had flown 927 on an early night mission the day before in executing a deep and long low-level armed reconnaissance penetration up along the east coast of North Korea.

I never paid any attention to an aircraft's number, as it had no significance for me. If a B-26 had a "soft nose," that is, a nose compartment covered with clear panels of Plexiglas, a well functioning Norden bombsight, and a small and fully operational bombardier-navigator's instrument panel, I was "fat, dumb, and happy," being totally indifferent as to the identification number on the aircraft from which I bombed and navigated. On the other hand, to a B-26 pilot the number designation of an aircraft had considerable meaning, as each plane had certain unique flight peculiarities, and our bomber pilots would often discuss among themselves differing operational characteristics of different aircraft that were assigned permanently to our squadron.

Captain Grump's next question: "Do you have a couple of minutes? I'll show you what I mean."

He then turned and walked out the door. By now my curiosity was fully aroused so I rose and followed him out the door and locked it behind me. I felt no reluctance in leaving my assigned work station, as the colonel had informed me but a half hour earlier that he would be off the base "for the rest of the morning." Therefore, my absence from the operations shack for ten or fifteen minutes would most probably not be noticed by anyone in a position of authority. So I climbed into Captain Grump's jeep and he aimed the vehicle toward the flight line, where a long row of B-26s were parked, almost wing tip to wing tip.

Near the far north end of the flight line stood a B-26C, right where we had left it in the darkness earlier that morning. Grump braked to a stop in front of the right wing and within several yards of the nose of the aircraft. He suggested that I climb up the right side of the aircraft and step out onto the wing. I did as instructed and saw with shock and amazement just what he had been referring to.

There in plain sight was a gaping circular hole in the upper surface of the wing roughly six to eight inches in diameter and about a yard or so outboard of the right engine nacelle. The rough and jagged metal of the upper wing surface was bent upward from the curving black aluminum "skin" of the aircraft. I took a long, awkward step over the engine nacelle and then another. Leaning forward, I looked straight down through the hole. And there was the grinning face of Captain Grump, who was squatting directly beneath me.

All sorts of disturbing thoughts raced through my mind as painful sensations of horror, fear, and apprehension suddenly began to churn within me. Then I realized that during the course of the previous night's routine mission over North Korea I had not seen, nor heard, nor felt, anything that came close to being enemy ground fire. Nor had there been any curving arcs of tracers from triple A batteries, no noticeable difference in the feel or vibrations of the aircraft, no unusual sounds in the performance of the B-26's massive Pratt Whitney R-2800 twin engines, nor any unusual aspects in the aircraft's flight performance.

A large-bore triple A shell, fortunately equipped with a high-altitude sensing fuse and not a contact-sensing one, had gone right through the wing without detonating, and not one of us had any idea that something very dangerous had happened to our aircraft!

I reached down and touched the rough and jagged edges of the protruding metal, realizing for the first time just how thin the aluminum skin of a bomber's wing actually was: it was no more than an eighth of an inch thick. I became more upset and agitated by the inevitable inference that arose in my mind: if the wing surfaces had been as thick as I had previously thought they were, it is likely that this high-velocity shell, meeting greater resistance, would have most assuredly exploded in close proximity to a large gas tank imbedded in the right wing nacelle. By happenstance, two or three days before, I had overheard several of our pilots discussing problems in switching gas tanks and one had mentioned that each main wing tank held 300 gallons of high-octane aviation fuel, each auxiliary wing tanks carried another 100 gallons, and the bomb bay tank carried an additional 125 gallons. In any event, if any of these tanks had been struck by the unexploded shell the entire wing, or the fuselage, would have most assuredly exploded and disintegrated in flames.

Captain Grump walked out from under the trailing edge of the wing, squinted up at me, and asked the question that I was also thinking about: "Do you know where the wing tank is located?" I always assumed it was in the engine nacelle or very close to it. But I answered in the negative, with a shake of the head.

He then informed me that the hole in the wing was just beyond the outer edge of the right wing tank, located just outboard of the engine nacelle. He smiled and said, "Lieutenant, as I told you before, you are running out of horseshoes."

At this point, my stomach contracted involuntarily and I released a stream of partially digested bacon, eggs, and toast that I had consumed about an hour before, narrowly missing Captain Grump below. I remember hearing him laugh nervously and telling me if I did that again I would not be riding with him again but that I would be taking the long walk back to the squadron's operations shack.

BY GUESS AND BY GOD!
(NAVIGATING OVER
NORTH KOREA)

DURING THE LAST PHASE OF THE KOREAN WAR, there were a number of us who flew the USAF's light bomber, the Douglas B-26, in making deep penetrations into North Korea in total darkness. We pursued and attempted to destroy, damage, or at least delay, the relentless flows of troop and supply trains and trucks heading southward with their vital cargos needed by the communist Chinese in launching or sustaining any major attempts by them at significantly advancing and holding their front line.

Over South Korea there were masses of lights illuminating its two major cites, Pusan (now called Busan) and Seoul, and many smaller cities, towns, and villages. The major roadways flowing north and south were also clearly defined by the moving and bright headlights of the heavy flows of men and materiel by truck and train. And along the front lines there was an intriguing phenomenon: the frequent and bizarre use of searchlights that were constantly moving and probing the night in search of enemy operations, both ground and air. However, upon passing over the front lines we literally plunged into a very different kind of world, a world of total darkness that was, and still is today, the bleak and menacing world of North Korea. This darkness resulted from the total "blackout" ordered by governmental edict, an edict that was continually and brutally enforced.

And for us, as B-26 bombardier-navigators, getting "lost" in the vast and black skies over North Korea was a major and ever-present worry and nagging concern, as we were very much on our own. We were forced to rely upon ourselves. We operated as "a single ship" attack force in a hostile environment where there were no navigational systems, devices, or aids to enable us to determine our present, and continually changing, position. Consequently, we were frequently challenged in our ability to provide our pilots correct course headings or course corrections in getting to our assigned target area, in remaining in that target area, and getting back to home base upon mission completion with some margin of safety and fuel reserve. In 1952/1953, we had no systems or devices or equipment to "get a fix," that is, to locate with certainty our present position over the surface of the earth, as are so readily available today by GPS, LORAN (long range navigational equipment), and the like. To further compound our navigational problems and anxieties, we had no way of determining in advance wind speeds and directions to accurately compute estimated times of arrival or compass headings. Furthermore, all weather stations, where present and prevailing winds blowing over the Korean peninsula from China, Manchuria, and Russia could be determined, were within enemy territory or under enemy control, so we had no dependable weather forecasts to help us determine compass headings and ETAs. Therefore, we were required to attempt to accurately measure wind speeds and directions after becoming airborne, by use of crude dead reckoning procedures and devices.

At 0800 hours the day before every night of combat missions, crews from all three squadrons gathered at 17th Bomb Group Headquarters for a pre-flight morning briefing. The weather briefing officer's portion of the briefing was always met by all those assembled with a loud and discordant chorus of boos and catcalls, as the "metro data" (wind speed and direction) almost always was later determined to have been inaccurate, and sometimes grossly inaccurate. So the prudent bombardier-navigator began to compute his own evolving metro data upon gaining inbound altitude and speed and, time permitting, re-computing it as penetration into North Korea was achieved.

Depending upon where the assigned armed reconnaissance route (most frequently referred to as the "recce route") was situated within the eastern half of North Korea, about two hours, or more, were generally required to get to and enter the assigned target area. If the bombardier-navigator was both diligent and effective, the critical factors of wind speed and direction were by then accurately, or at least approximately, established in his mind. These data were essential in achieving some measure of precision in making bomb runs visually from and below the customary minimum altitude of three thousand feet required to clear with safety the many peaks and ridgelines of the seemingly endless and closely spaced coastal mountain ranges extending northeasterly and southwesterly, and roughly parallel with the eastern shoreline of the peninsula.

During the earlier months and years of the Korean War, piston-driven P-51 Mustangs and jet-powered F-84 Thunderjets so effectively and efficiently bombed and strafed the trains and trucks of the enemy during daylight hours that by the time of my crew's arrival in Korea almost all train and truck traffic moved solely during hours of darkness. Their collective successes provided our Douglas B-26 Invader crews with almost continuous night-time business activity. And when the sky was clear on moonlit nights and the moon was anywhere within its half moon-to-full moon-to-half moon sequence, B-26 night-time "hunting" was especially exciting, challenging, and rewarding.

Whether I was crewed with Colonel Bentley or Captain Crow, I was always pleased when I learned at morning briefings that we had been assigned to patrol one of the purple routes that ran along North Korea's east coast, numbered in sequence from the port city of Wonsan north to the port city of Hungnam and then extending generally northeasterly to the Russian border. On one of these purple routes we always knew we had a good chance of encountering a munitions or troop train, coming down the line from Vladivostok, Russia, hauling a full load of choice targets. I had another very good reason for liking such a choice assignment: it was much more difficult to get lost along the North Korean coastline. Here there was a barely sufficient (but desirable) distribution of recognizable landmarks, such as estuaries, rivers, and islands, to be used as visual references. These natural features were frequently essential in getting literally "back on track" in the event of heavy cloud cover when I became disoriented after multiple bomb and strafing runs on steam-powered trains coming down the line, where they spurted from tunnel to tunnel to avoid detection and destruction. For example, there was a fairly large and generally rectangular coastal island (Mayang-do) located about forty nautical miles east of Hungnam that was an excellent "fix" in making landfall and/or in determining present location and fairly accurate course headings.

I usually tried to assist my pilot by helping to keep the B-26 "down moon" of the railroad tracks. That is, by my voice direction, I would attempt to keep the plane slightly north of the tracks. With North Korea in total darkness, the light of the moon reflecting off the railroad tracks was surprisingly easy to see and was most helpful in keeping the B-26 in close alignment with the tracks. In fact, there were many times when I could read, solely by moonlight, the smaller print on my aeronautical maps and charts and navigate accordingly. It was also advisable to keep the plane north of the tracks because winds were generally from the northwest, north, or northeast and being north of the tracks would enable fairly accurate compensation for wind draft.

With a "good moon" and good low-level visibility due to the absence of ground fog and low cloud strata, both pilots I crewed for were absolutely fearless and unrelenting in "going in low," meaning as low as fifty feet of terrain clearance. At that altitude, they could shoot up both railroad tracks and adjacent roadways after I had completed my bomb drops at the absolute minimums of 500 to 750 feet of clearance needed to avoid aircraft damage from our own bomb bursts.

For me, and for many other flight crews, inland MSRs were dreaded assignments, as navigational and bombing problems multiplied the further inland the assigned MSR took you. Simply stated, there were no navigational or electronic devices or aids to assist us in navigation, and inland targets were fewer and more difficult to locate and bomb. Inland there was mountain range after mountain range, indistinguishable one from the other, and they were far more menacing and dangerous because the mountain peaks inland were at significantly higher altitudes. Of great concern was the fact that there were no cities, no towns, and few villages that did not appear from the air to be in any way different from the next village. And to make matters worse, there were few discernible natural features that would help the bombardier-navigator in performing his job.

I remember distinctly a morning briefing when our crew was assigned an inland recce route that was well west and north of Wonsan, and where I felt uncomfortable and insecure about flying. As the briefing ended, I asked an old and experienced bombardier-navigator sitting beside me how he navigated such a mission. His laconic reply: "By guess and by God." Upon sober reflection, those few words could well be considered the mantra of the Korean War.

THE BOOM MIKE

THE KOREAN WAR OF THE WINTER, SPRING, AND SUM-
mer of 1953 was progressively more a war of short supply for our
95th Bomb Squadron. Even though the war was in its third year, we
were almost always out, or running out, of something of either major or
minor importance, or more usually, out of many things somewhere in
between. One memorable thing somewhere in between was a standard
government-issue headset with a boom mike (microphone) for use by
B-26 crewmen in combat operations. These boom mikes were then in
short supply and therefore much in demand.

Unfortunately, most of us upon our arrival at K-9 had been issued
headsets (voice receivers) with separate throat mikes. Throat mikes are
a little hard to describe and much harder to remember. They were ex-
pandable, elasticized fabric bands three quarters of an inch wide and
approximately one-sixteenth of an inch thick that were wrapped around
the neck, with their ends fitted together with easily closed metal snaps.
Once one climbed into the B-26, throat mikes were affixed and left in
place until landing and mission completion. Embedded in this neck-
band were two small voice transmitters, roughly three inches apart.
These transmitters were manually positioned over the voice box, on
both sides of the throat, and were intended to remain there at all times
to enable the pilot, bombardier-navigator, and air gunner to keep in

direct voice contact with each other at all times. To communicate, the user's intercom button would be manually depressed, he would speak simultaneously in a normal tone and volume, and his words would hopefully be heard clearly by the other crewmembers. Unfortunately, these transmitters frequently slid off the voice box due to perspiration and/or the sudden and often violent movements of the user.

On the other hand, a headset with an attached boom mike was constructed with the voice transmitter positioned conveniently just a fraction of an inch in front of the user's lips. It was connected in place at the other end by a pair of curved wires extending across the lower portion of the left side of the face and forward from the left earpiece. Because of its rigid and durable construction, the mouthpiece did not move relative to movement of the lips. The earpieces looked and functioned like earmuffs worn by snow skiers, and they had earmuffs' beneficial effects; the engines' roar was substantially blocked out, making voice messages much more easily understood while also providing protection for the ears from the intense cold often experienced in flight.

I knew of only one bombardier-navigator in the 95th who had a headset with an attached boom mike, and that was Captain Robert Abelman. When I arrived at K-9, Bob was Colonel Bentley's "personal" bombardier. He continued to possess that highly respected status until he completed his tour of duty. Simply stated, being the colonel's personal bombardier-navigator meant that Abelman flew with the colonel whenever he flew. This was not as frequently as the colonel desired since he, as squadron commander, could fly only four missions per calendar month because of a mission limitation imposed by a recently promulgated FEAF directive. It seemed that Korea was considered by FEAF to be a superior training opportunity for squadron commanders with "high rank potential," and commanding a squadron in intense combat operations was the kind of experience such officers should possess.

Colonel Bentley intensely resented this mission restriction and could not restrain himself from vocalizing his hostility to it. I could not help but overhear him when he loudly complained about it in several telephone conversations with the two other squadron COs within the 17th Bomb Group.

Initially, the colonel's opposition to this directive did not affect me, so I listened to his sometimes-profane complaints about it with little interest or concern. However, after a successful daylight-bombing mission against a complex of railroad bridges at Majon'ni in May or June of 1953, when his crew flew as lead ship in a twelve B-26 formation, with our crew being among them, I was suddenly made very much aware of its imminent and negative impact upon me.

That daytime group mission was a very sweet one: a break-of-dawn drop time with moderate cloud decks but with a clear opening over the targets for Bob Abelman's visual Norden drop: several steel reinforced concrete bridges destroyed with numerous visual sightings and total photographic confirmation, surprisingly light to moderate flak, and an uneventful return flight followed by the gathering of numerous flight and ground crew personnel opening and guzzling expensive French champagne from oversized bottles upon a cool and pleasant forenoon. I remember standing under the wing of our 26 thoroughly enjoying the friendship and camaraderie of happy and relieved airmen eagerly celebrating a successful operation, with laudatory words and bad jokes flowing in all directions.

That day we were also appropriately celebrating Bob Abelman's fiftieth and final combat mission. Bob was an extremely well liked and highly regarded bombardier-navigator, and for good reasons. He was appreciated for his considerable technical abilities and skills, character, sound judgment, and personality. He was also viewed with admiration as he was reputed to have been a star football player at West Point. With the colonel and Bob Abelman in the lead position in the formation and with our B-26 in the number two spot, I had been on my bombsight "shadowing" Bob down the bomb run as a precautionary measure in the event anything adverse would happened to the colonel, Abelman, his bombsight, or their aircraft.

As we drank and basked in our fifteen minutes of glory, I felt a strange upwelling of positive energy and emotion. It was precisely then and there that the colonel instructed Bob to give his boom mike to me, as he "wouldn't be needing it any more." Bob hesitated, for the briefest of moments, obviously with mixed emotions. He then leaned toward me and softly tossed the headset with boom mike to me. I did not know what to say. I looked up and directly at him. I mumbled an almost inaudible "thank you." That gesture was so meaningful to me that I choke up whenever I recall those brief moments in time and place.

For Bob Abelman, whom I did not know well at the time, this was the end of an era. I am sure that he had the desire, possibly the intention, to take the boom mike home with him as a treasured memento of his Korean combat tour of duty. Of course, as government-issued equipment it rightfully should never have been considered his personal property. But as in every war, combatants become emotionally attached to certain types of government owned and issued articles of clothing, weapons, and so on, and, consequently, there is frequently an uncontrollable urge to take such items home in a duffel bag.

Quite obviously, the colonel had his own personal reasons for his instruction: I was going to be around for another two or three months and the colonel would continue to need an experienced bombardier-navigator. Apparently, I was among several being considered by the colonel to be sufficiently competent to qualify for the job. He also knew that some of the guys in the squadron considered me to be "lucky" as well.

My immediate reactions were mixed and inexplicably intertwined. I was honored, surprised, and pleased to be in contention as Bob Abelman's successor, but I was also quite apprehensive about being so selected. The colonel was a demanding and relentless taskmaster: he expected perfection in job performance. I was genuinely fearful that I could not deliver what he wanted and needed. He was a high-ranking career officer and I was a low-ranking citizen soldier. And so continued a most interesting and frequently terrifying professional relationship.

IN THE CATBIRD SEAT

I WALKED INTO THE K-9 OFFICERS CLUB AND GRABBED the choice stool at the end of the bar just as it was being vacated. On the next seat was a stocky and compact air force captain, a senior pilot as evidenced by the pair of silver wings with star worn upon his chest. He had reported for duty with the squadron just the day before, and we recognized each other immediately. Now we quickly identified the other's rank and AFSC (Air Force Specialty Code), establishing my lower status in the military hierarchy: he outranked me by a pay grade and was a senior pilot, while my bombardier-navigator classification was one notch down the totem pole from the top ranking of pilot.

He then opened the conversation: "When I saw you sitting in the 95th's operations shack I thought you were a paddle foot. How many missions ya got?"

The label "paddle foot," identical in meaning to "ground pounder," was a put-down then used by just about every combat crewman to describe any and all categories of air force personnel not on flight status, irrespective of military rank or occupational specialty. When I replied "thirty-seven," my status not unexpectedly went back up considerably in his mind, as evidenced immediately by his more positive and friendly facial expression and body language.

"What kind?"

"Mostly single-ship night bombing and strafing."

Another small, upward movement in my social status. Now I really had both his interest and curiosity.

"So why are you riding a desk when you are flight crew?"

"Because that's where the colonel put me."

Now I really had his attention!

"What are you doing there?"

"Anything the colonel tells me to do. I'm his assistant to his non-existent administrative officer."

My response both satisfied and puzzled him, but he moved on. It was obvious that he now considered me a potential member of the private intelligence network he was in the process of developing. In other words, I was a possible or probable source of useful information. The USAF, like any other hierarchy with a definitive order of rank and responsibility coupled with specialized job functions, is a highly structured institution where information and knowledge equate directly to power and prestige.

He then went right for the jugular with two trenchant questions, one right after the other. He knew I had no right or intention to answer either one of them, as he knew they involved classified information. So I looked directly at him and replied: "I really can't say, to both questions."

He didn't give up however: "You can't say or you won't say?"

I did not respond but silently waited. He stared at me for a full thirty seconds. I stared back but with a pleasant and innocuous smile on my face. He finally turned away and reached for a flight officer's favorite beverage of the day, a "7&7" comprised of Seagram's Seven Crown Whisky and 7-Up over ice. He then turned back and laughed heartily. The tension was broken. Then he said: "No harm trying. I guess the sign means what it says."

"What sign?"

Before he could speak, I remembered the large red on white sign inside and above the only exit door in the 95th Bomb Squadron's operations shack that commanded—"What You See Here, What You Hear Here, Stays Here When You Leave Here"—a familiar wartime admonition about confidentiality and security matters carried over from World War II. So I quickly and quietly answered: "Yes, I guess it does."

"Well, kid, you're in the catbird seat."

I had no response to that declaration as I had no idea what a catbird seat was. In fact, I didn't even know what a catbird was, and I so informed him. He then advanced my continuing education: "Kid, the catbird seat is a position of power and influence, and that is where you are when you are sitting in the 95th's operations shack."

He added: "Rank doesn't make that much difference. You are where the action is. You hear and know what's going on in the squadron at all times. You're right there, right in 'the catbird seat.'" He went on to inform me that Red Barber, the famous play-by-play broadcaster for the New York Yankees, whose name I had vaguely remembered, had regularly used that term on the radio in calling the Yankee games during the years of the thirties and forties whenever the Yankees were in an overwhelmingly favorable position to win a ball game, such as when a walk, a single, a deep fly ball, or an error would score the winning run in the bottom of the ninth inning. He took great pride in the fact that both he and Red Barber were born and raised in one of the Carolinas where the catbird was the dominant bird throughout the region's wooded areas, literally at the top of the pecking order.

Until this conversation I had never considered my secondary (and unofficial) daytime duty assignment as assistant administrative officer to be one of either power or prestige. In fact, I had considered it to be a royal pain in the ass, as I was required to be at my miserable little desk in the corner of the operations shack every day except the day following a night combat mission. This daytime obligation included my being there on Saturdays and occasionally, even on Sundays. This ground pounder assignment had continued relentlessly even after Jerry Davis and I were crewed up with Robert Crow. At that time Jerry was relieved of his crew transporting duties, but I was not so benefited by being relieved of my burdensome, but quite frankly, rather interesting desk job.

So when the other flight crew guys were regularly enjoying time off for two or three or four days and nights between missions (and even longer when bad weather prevailed), playing chess or poker or pinochle; drinking excellent and inexpensive beer and liquor; writing and reading letters; or otherwise engaging in similar and relaxing and/or frivolous activities, I was punching out documents, reports, and statistics for the colonel in his seemingly constant "paper war" with the brass at the 17th Bomb Group Headquarters across the base.

It might be mentioned that neither combat crews nor ground support personnel ever "hung out" in the operations shack of the 95th Bomb Squadron, as they tended to do in the other two squadrons of the 17th Bomb Group. People only went there when ordered or requested by the colonel to be there, or when they were conducting significant military business. To the colonel, the squadron operations shack was exclusively for serious military business, and that admonition went out to newcomers very quickly. As a result, I was there alone much of the time, holding down the phones and recording and conveying messages for and to the colonel and other squadron officers. The colonel would come and go, the operations officer would come and go, the ordnance officer would come and go, the maintenance officer would come and go, but I was always there—well, almost always—typing away and cursing my old malfunctioning manual Royal typewriter, with its keys that

kept getting stuck against the roller. Korea was a war well before personal computers; it was back when carbon paper was required to make
file copies of documents, and getting the originals, and often multiple
carbon copies, properly aligned on a manual typewriter was a constant
chore and a maddening frustration.

Being "in the catbird seat" caused other problems, concerns, and
complications. I had been commissioned a second lieutenant in August
of the prior year upon completion of bombardier-navigation training.
It seems that I had received, to my surprise, a "spot promotion" from
second lieutenant to first lieutenant just four months after arriving in
Korea. And this promotion, although fully appreciated, did not appear
to some of my peers to be fully deserved. I then preferred to believe
that it was earned because of several of our notably successful bombing missions (when I had been drafted by the colonel to fly with him),
flown both in daylight formations and on single ship night bombing
and strafing runs. But in retrospect, I must acknowledge that the colonel probably caused it to happen because of my clerk-typist proficien-
cies and my quiet service in the drafty corner of squadron operations,
laboriously punching out paperwork that he could not or did not wish
to draft himself.

In any event, I detected some resentment emanating from several of
my younger colleagues, there being several occasions, usually during a
night of heavy drinking, when I regretted having received the silver bars
on my shoulders and the additional fifty bucks or so in monthly base
pay. But, with the perspective of a long view back in time, I realize that
the advantages of an early and temporary promotion exceeded its disad-
vantages. For example, I found myself flying more interesting and challenging missions, getting deeper penetrations into North Korea along
more heavily trafficked MSRs. Also, our crew seemed to be scheduled
for more frequent missions than the average crew. This may not seem

to be an advantage, but the worst part of any mission was the waiting period preceding it. Every morning at 0800 the so-called Battle Order for the following night's missions was posted, and every crewman would dutifully trek to squadron ops to learn if his crew was listed for the next morning's 0800 preflight briefing at 17th Bomb Group Headquarters. If your crew was not listed, you knew that you probably would not fly the following night and, therefore, you could have a few or more drinks that night. So the waiting, and the resulting uncertainty and anxiety, would begin again.

For me, another advantage, and probably a major one, in being "in the catbird seat" was the character and location of my next duty assignment. Although I have no way of proving that it was helpful in my career development and potential, what I observed, what I learned, and what I did in the operations shack, being there day after day, gave me seven months of administrative experience and insight that was, cumulatively, most valuable in developing judgment and discretion. So rather than being reassigned, upon completion of my Korean tour of duty, to the Air Training Command (ATC) or Tactical Air Command (TAC) back in the States in some more traditional peacetime flight training or operational capacity, I was assigned to an obscure unit in an arcane division of Air Force Headquarters in a facility located in a pleasant mid-western city. Here my primary focus was as a project officer coordinating efforts and equipment of military aviation personnel and federal civil service administrators and technical specialists in developing and testing innovative navigation and bombing devices and techniques in the execution of low-level, high-speed strategic and tactical attack profiles.

There I duly performed the last two years of my three-year contract term of commissioned officer status, functioning additionally as a USAF Project Officer to NATO (North Atlantic Treaty Organization), in working closely with experienced and highly qualified American and Canadian military and civilian experts in such fascinating and diverse fields as photogrammetry, optics, cartography, and weaponry. This choice assignment was so engaging that I was almost impelled to stay in the air force and make it my lifelong career.

COLLATERAL DAMAGE

WE ARE HEARING AND READING MUCH THESE DAYS about "collateral damage," in both print and electronic media, often from individuals who know little or nothing about the stark and brutal realities of military combat, be it in past, present, or future tense. What these generally well-meaning media types must accept, but seem to be genetically unable to accept, is the brutal reality that in warfare there always has been and there always will be actual or apparent non-combatants who shall suffer injuries or death because they just happen to be at the wrong place at the wrong time. Another way stated, there simply is no such device as a totally surgical weapon.

It was that way in Korea when we were there, bombing and strafing surface military traffic, and it is still that way today. In those long past Korean War days, and long before that deceptive euphemism "collateral damage" came into common usage, the human life below us was comprised simply: uniformed allies or enemies.

The stark reality is that collateral damage is inevitable; if there is combat there will be collateral damage. This is particularly evident in modern-day warfare involving weapon-bearing terrorists and their nebulous support structures where there is no discernible front line, no wearing of uniforms to identify them or their enablers as the enemy, and no differentiation in the minds of the terrorists between our armed military personnel and defenseless civilians, as terrorists believe that both categories are to be equally targeted for death or destruction.

Every reasonable precaution can and must be taken by our forces to minimize collateral damage. But it cannot be totally eliminated. That state of fact exists particularly when terrorists deliberately melt into civilian populations to avoid their own detection and destruction. To demonstrate this point, during the Korean War we generally flew up and down the deep valleys of the mountainous eastern half of North Korea on "search and destroy" missions at minimum altitudes, at minimum speed (180 mph—approximately one-half of the B-26's maximum speed), and frequently under cover of almost total darkness. Our window of best opportunity generally extended from a half moon through full moon and back to a descending half moon, as it was considered much too dangerous during the dark of the moon to descend sufficiently low into the North Korean valleys to be able to see, target, and strike tactical targets. Most frequently, we were limited to visually searching for and identifying truck convoys and supply trains coming south from China, Russia, and Manchuria, generally heavily laden with the men and materiel of ground warfare.

Our Chinese and North Korean enemies were masters of cover and concealment. In the winter when the winding MSRs were covered by heavy snows, they would drape their supply trucks with white canvas coverings to well blend them into the snow-packed roadways. And during summer months, these vehicles would be covered with brown or olive drab nettings into which tree branches were thickly woven to provide a primitive but effective camouflage, as their many unimproved earthen roads were generally very close in protective coloration.

The communists also had primitive but effective early warning systems. As we dropped into a valley upon observing the bright glow of a string of oncoming truck headlights, with our pilot cutting back power and muffling engine noise for the preferable northbound (and upwind) bomb run, a well-concealed anti-aircraft battery would frequently fire off a few short bursts of its distinctly colored tracers (usually green and sequenced as every eighth round) vertically so that they could easily be seen by the drivers of the convoyed trucks, up ahead as they proceeded southward. If this happened on our approach or actual bombing run into these moving targets we would observe the trucks turning off the roadway, both left and right, while simultaneously extinguishing their running lights. Many times the truck drivers drove their vehicles under trees or behind and/or under heavy brush or bush to gain protective cover. Alternatively, they often parked right next to the many straw thatched earthen structures that heavily lined just about every north-south road, functioning in the dual capacity as rest shelters for the rice farmers by night and rest shelters for the truck drivers and their contingent of foot soldiers by day.

Additional protective coloration was provided these military vehicles by the placement of camouflaged wooden panels leaned against the sides of the trucks when stationary. This made their silhouettes very difficult to detect by visual sightings, as our B-26 bombers were traveling at three miles per minute at minimal altitude with little if any time to see, recognize, and line up such well-hidden vehicles for targeting.

The obvious and necessary solution: generally identify the rough parameters of the segment of MSR where four or more vehicles had found cover, request and assist in causing your pilot in executing a 180-degree reversal of course, come back over the target area by closely paralleling or intersecting the roadway, and drop two or four GP bombs or napalm bombs at very close intervals to bracket the targets. Fragmentation of such a 500-pound GP bomb would propel jagged chunks of hot metal through the earthen walls and often take out multiple trucks, their occupants, and their cargos. Equally or more effective was the detonation and splash effect of the flaming jellied gasoline, which often caused flames to engulf the highly flammable straw roofs on these earthen structures, resulting in total destruction or major damage to the transport vehicles within or beside them.

There were occasions when, upon ducking down and entering the B-26's bomb bay before takeoff, I would find to my surprise a maximum payload of small and clustered anti-personnel (fragmentation) bombs. When combined with four external 500-pounders, these anti-personnel bombs further enhanced the aircraft's potential for higher levels of death and destruction. These weapons were rigged to scatter over large areas, with some of these twenty- to one-hundred-pound fragmentation bombs being fused to detonate upon impact, with the balance timed to explode at randomly spaced intervals thereafter. Some of these nasty little bombs were time-delayed in detonation for as long as three to five days, causing multiple and dangerous problems of clean up of the target area by our enemies, and further obstructing and delaying their resumption of traffic flow and cargo movement. These fragmentation bombs were usually dropped last in sequence and particularly when the targets were rail or road bridges or viaducts, as their visible presence would cause major delays in reconstruction efforts to replace or repair the targets destroyed or damaged.

The positive impact and result of this innovative strike and weapon combination: the total destruction of or substantial damage to enemy truck convoys (and their logistical support systems and structures) and their critically needed cargos well behind the front line, as well as destruction or major damage to bridges, railways and roads. The concomitant and inherent evil of this mission profile: unknowable but obviously substantial "collateral damage."

BYE, BYE, BLACKBIRD

IT HAD BEEN A LONG MISSION AND A LATE ONE. OUR crew was part of the "dawn patrol" that took off at 0300 for a deep, low-level, low-speed penetration into the northeast quadrant of North Korea to bomb and strafe targets of opportunity on or adjacent to the main rail and road supply lines zigzagging down along the edge of the Sea of Japan from Russia. We achieved moderate successes but nothing exceptional. I am sure we had good hits on several moving targets, but there were no secondary explosions or sustained fires to provide photographic proof. I was reasonably sure that we created several track and road cuts, but such conjecture generally did not mean much to the intelligence guys at post-flight debriefing.

As pre-dawn light was starting to illuminate the eastern horizon, we left the target area with an empty bomb bay, very few .50 caliber ammo rounds unexpended, and an adequate but not overly reassuring supply of fuel for the long trip home to K-9 AFB. So I calculated a course heading well out over the Sea of Japan and east of Wonsan Harbor and the hordes of hostile North Korean and Chinese communist forces at and near the front line. Bob Crow nicely "cut the corner" at a gas-conserving airspeed so that our return trip turned out to be a calm and uneventful one.

By the time we got back to base and Bob had greased another perfect landing on our battered asphalt runway, the Asian sun was well above the horizon and another hot and humid June day had begun. We found ourselves tired, somewhat relieved, but also impatient as we waited in the shade of a wing of our B-26 for pickup by the crew truck for the bumpy ride to debriefing and then back to the 95th Bomb Squadron's housing area for much needed sleep and the start of another three-day life cycle. Two other returning aircrews had been picked up before us. They slid forward along the side benches in the back of the open truck to make room for us and our gear.

At that moment, Bob remembered that having just completed our fortieth mission, each of us would be placed "on orders" later that day and, as a direct consequence, we would be airlifted back to the States thirty days later, it being the understanding that we would fly our last ten missions within that time frame. I still remember the wide smile spreading across his open and suntanned face as he needlessly reminded Jerry and me of this happy forty-mission reality as the heavily loaded truck slowly gained speed and we passed in front of the B-26 we had just vacated. I gazed up at the weather-beaten and chipped black paint that covered the entirety of the aircraft's fuselage. I wondered how many missions this battered old black bird had flown over North Africa, Italy, and Rumania; over Normandy and across France and Germany, as well as over Poland and the Balkans, before the end of World War II less than five years before the Korean War erupted in June of 1950.

The other crews overhead our conversation. They congratulated us on our good fortune and express their good-natured envy. We were then recognized as legitimate members of the "Lucky Bastards Club." They made some funny and raucous comments and predictions about our likely nocturnal interests and activities on our return to the land of the "round-eyed jossans," meaning white women, back in the United States. I fondly remember those moments of levity and camaraderie with crystal clarity.

Suddenly, there came to mind an appropriate song that I had learned in Chicago, as a teenager while World War II was still very much in progress. I began to sing the song softly as we slowly bounced along. The words easily came flowing back to me as I sang them:

Pack up all my cares and woes,
Here I go, singing low,
Bye, bye, blackbird.

Where somebody waits for me,
Sugar's sweet, so is she,
Bye, bye, blackbird.

No one here can love or
Understand me,
Oh, what hard luck stories
They all hand me.

So I'll arrive late tonight,
When I come, she'll delight,
Blackbird, bye, bye.

As I sang, several of the other guys joined in, singing the refrain, "Bye, bye, blackbird." Somebody requested that I sing the song again. So I sang it again and more of the guys, remembering the words, sang them along with us. We sang this song two or three more times, emphasizing different words, so by the time we reached debriefing it seemed that everyone had either remembered the words or had learned them.

After our crew had finished debriefing we climbed onto the back of the same open truck where one of the other two crews was waiting for us. Collectively, we urged the driver to head back to our squadron area as another truck, an empty one, had just pulled into the group's crew loading area. As we passed the long row of parked B-26s of the 34th and 37th Bomb Squadrons somebody began to sing "Bye, Bye, Blackbird" again. Within seconds everybody joined in. For some reason, singing this simple old song seemed to cause everybody aboard, including the driver, to feel sadness, nostalgia, relief, happiness, and elation, probably in different progressions, but in any event, the positives were much stronger collectively than the negatives. When we jumped off the back of the truck and cheerfully went our respective ways within our squadron area, it seemed that each of us had an elevated level of morale and a genuine feeling of joy and good cheer that had not existed before.

This song briefly spread within the squadron. And it was almost always sung just after completion of a mission. So it was not unusual for me to hear a returning 95th Bomb Squadron crew singing it while riding into the space between our operations and maintenance shacks after an early morning mission debriefing. So, as I sat at my old beaten up metal desk, drafting and pounding out drab reports and relatively uninteresting correspondence for our good colonel, I would smile quietly to myself, being stupidly proud and self-satisfied at having started what could evolve into a minor tradition that might bring pleasure and a sense of relief from tension to us and to those who follow. And for some of us, fond memories of a far less dangerous time and place: a time and place where fear and anxiety were not ever-constant and unwelcome companions.

FIXED BAYONETS

IT WAS REPORTED THAT LITERALLY THOUSANDS OF communist spies and saboteurs had been pouring into democratic South Korea from North Korea even before the start of the Korean War in June of 1950. They moved easily across the border by commingling with the tens of thousands of refugees from North Korea who were continually fleeing from the tyranny of President Kim Il Sung, the grandfather of the present and rotund young dictator of North Korea. As a direct consequence of the ever-present dangers that these covert insurgents presented, military security efforts at K-9 Air Base were constantly being reviewed and evaluated, and occasionally augmented or replaced.

It was an unusually hot and humid Sunday afternoon during the early summer of 1953. Sunday was my only assured day off from my daytime confinement in the 95th's operations shack. I had walked across the perimeter road and beyond the south end of the runway, where a wide, sandy, and frequently crowded beach provided swimming opportunities for those of us who ventured into the waters of Suyong Bay. Our flight surgeon had advised us that unknown kinds and quantities of deadly bacteria and hazardous waste materials contaminated this busy harbor. He advised that if we were crazy enough to swim off this beach it was imperative that we keep our mouths, noses, eyes, and ears clear of the water at all times. However, this caveat was generally ignored.

I had these repeated admonitions in mind as I carefully entered the water and performed a slow and careful breaststroke, heading out to deeper water. My objective was to swim out far enough to clear a barbed wire fence that extended into the water and separated K-9 AFB from the land to the east and to head for a long, relatively clean and totally unoccupied beach beyond the fencing. Once I cleared the perimeter fence, I swam steadily back to shore but at a wide angle from it. The fence extended into the bay well beyond my expectations and I had to swim much further out from shore than I had anticipated, so I was breathing heavily.

As I labored up the sloping bank I was looking downward to avoid tripping on some partially concealed rocks and other such obstacles near the water's edge. Sensing movement ahead, I looked up. There were three uniformed South Korean soldiers not more than twenty feet away, staring at me while advancing with fixed and lowered bayonets. Without saying a word, and without taking their eyes from my face, they continued to slowly approach, forming a progressively tighter semicircle before me. With upward thrusts of their weapons they signaled for me to move back into the water.

I did not want to display any shock or apprehension at their sudden appearance, nor fear or terror at being confronted in such a menacing manner. As I backed into the water their quick and jerky thrusts of their bayonets were now toward our beach beyond the fence. I took their implied command, turning and swimming out and back around the barbed wire fence and then toward the K-9 beach. As soon as I had cleared the extended fence and was heading back, I located and stared at the spot where these three angry soldiers had appeared. They had disappeared as easily as they had appeared, without being seen nor heard. They must have had a well-concealed foxhole dug into the dunes above the high-water line to which they had returned. After struggling up the bank I sank onto the warm sand, exhausted from swimming and straining to keep my head well above the choppy water as well as by the stress caused by the confrontation.

Over the following week I did not describe this disturbing experience to anyone. However, one quiet afternoon in the operations shack, when Colonel Bentley and I were alone and he appeared to be in a particularly relaxed and talkative mood, I brought up the subject of base security. I asked him whether there had ever been any penetrations of our base perimeter by saboteurs or any destruction or damage done to our aircraft, ordnance, or other military property or personnel by such intruders.

His response was that there had never been any destruction or damage to our base or any of its properties, although there were several incidents of suspected or attempted sabotage. He added that the primary reason that our security was so effective was that if such destruction or damage ever occurred "the entire South Korean base security force" would be immediately replaced and that every one of its soldiers would be sent directly to the front line for hazardous and indefinite combat duty.

I later learned that the beaches on both sides of our K-9 swimming beach were reportedly laced with land mines. Of course, I never did mention to Colonel Bentley, or any one else for that matter, my scary and wordless confrontation with the belligerent and silent South Korean soldiers with fixed bayonets.

BRING BACK
THAT AIRPLANE!

I WAS SLOUCHED DOWN ON A WORN WOODEN SIDE bench in the back of an open truck, waiting impatiently but quietly for Colonel Bentley to come out of the debriefing shack. It could not have been later than 0800 to 0900 hours, but the sun was well up in the Korean summer sky and the smell of Korea was pungent and strong in the humid, early morning air. The colonel's gunner had stretched out on the long bench on the other side of the truck and was already asleep with his head on his heavy body-length "back pack" parachute. I always thought that I held the record for falling asleep quickly, but he had me beaten by a country mile.

The colonel had exited the debriefing shack when we did but had returned to tell the debriefers "one last thing" about something he had forgotten to mention. He sure did love mission post mortems: it seemed to many of us that debriefings involving Colonel Bentley took more time than that required to complete the missions preceding them. He simply loved to analyze, to strategize, and to devise innovative and alternative tactics.

The door to the debriefing shack burst open and the colonel came bounding out and down the wooden steps. He jumped into the back of the truck as I slid over to make space for him. We had had a successful mission working over the railroad tracks extending northward from Wonsan, and the colonel was indeed a happy man. As the colonel was happy, I was reflectively happy, or at least relieved. Probably in my case, the word "relieved" is more accurate since riding with him was always stressful for me.

This mission was close to the end of "hostilities," somewhere in middle to late July 1953. The communist crazies were willingly and wantonly sacrificing the lives of large numbers of foot soldiers in exchange for small gains in land acquisitions in their anticipation of the signing of an armistice, the timing of which they controlled. The lands so acquired would presumably remain permanently in their possession and under their dominion. And, in fact, they did become permanent components of North Korea by way of the ceasefire agreement of July 27, 1953.

The major reason for the colonel's elation was that our bombing efforts had been highly effective. He had then exhibited his exceptional ability and skill in gunnery by chopping up a heavy contingent of communist troops assembled in and near a railroad marshalling yard just after the break of dawn. His gunner and I had simultaneously sighted multiple small clusters of foot soldiers as we headed northeast, almost directly up and nearly parallel with two sets of railroad tracks and an adjacent roadway. We were literally "right on track," and the colonel just drove right on in. I dropped all four GPs off the wing racks on that first run, and on the quick reversal of course I dropped all six from the bomb bay in close sequence: six quick punches of the little red button. As we were probably at little over 750 feet of terrain clearance, the closely timed concussions were jarring and the visual sightings of death and destruction overwhelming.

Colonel Bentley wasted no time. He executed a quick and immediate 180-degree turn and hit anything and everything that moved or might move. It was mass devastation from no more than fifty feet of terrain clearance. I watched from the nose with awe and amazement at the agility and proficiency of his flying and the viciousness and accuracy of his shooting. Although he executed no more than five or six firing passes, I lost count and became dizzy and disoriented from the sudden and steep turns.

I still remember the expressions of shock and terror on the faces of the soldiers as they scattered in every direction in their futile attempts to escape the six searing streams of hot lead splashing around and through them. Many of the soldiers appeared to dive toward the ground and to crawl for whatever little cover they could find. However, some young uniformed boys among them seemed so shocked and terrified that they just stood motionless while staring fixedly at us as they were cut down and chopped up by the awesome firepower of the colonel's perfectly functioning .50 caliber machine guns.

I later tried many times to remember the color of their uniforms. But all that I can remember about them are their faces—faces strained and blank, simply staring at us as we roared toward them. At times I had thought their uniforms were brown, at other times, green or ochre. I simply did not know and I had never attempted a search to learn what color they were until quite recently, when I had an opportunity to ask some marines of the First Marine Division, who were heavily engaged in ground combat throughout the Korean War. Their consensus was that the summer uniforms of the Chinese soldiers were an earthen color, brownish yellow. I still could not remember. Still only the faces, the faces of undersized twelve- to fourteen-year-old boys being sacrificed upon the barren altar of a cruel and cold-blooded communism.

Despite the total and obvious success of his efforts, Colonel Bentley was reluctant to leave the target area. I don't think the colonel ran out of ammunition, but he must have been very close to empty. Although ground fire increased progressively and substantially, we amazingly did not take a single hit, as was later confirmed by our careful inspection of the aircraft on the flight line.

I was greatly relieved when he finally executed an accelerating and climbing turn (a maneuver well known to fighter pilots as a chandelle) and headed south-southwest. He didn't ask for a heading: he knew exactly where we were. And then he and his gunner began chatting away like it was just another day at the office! I could hardly speak. I depressed the mike button, but I didn't know what to say. So I quickly released it, saying nothing. I was shocked and stunned by the precision and brutal efficiency of his multiple firing passes and the horror of the death and destruction that we had caused. And I had seen it all too clearly and memorably from the nose of the 26 on this warm, early summer morning.

As we continued to climb rapidly to exit altitude, everything seemed so calm, clean, and peaceful. We crossed over the bomb line and then the front lines without incident. As I knelt behind the bombsight, forearms crossed over the gyroscope casing of the Norden bombsight, I gazed down at the multiple shades of green and brown and yellow of the rugged mountainous terrain of the Korean peninsula. I was awestruck by the sudden and drastic contrasts between the horror and death of close air-ground combat and the tranquility and beauty of the earth in summer and as seen from a safe distance.

As we glided through the cool morning air, I stared fixedly through the Plexiglas nose at symmetrical rows of puffy white clouds building up to the south. Suddenly I was startled back to reality by the colonel's strong and clear voice on intercom, asking me to contribute in calculating the statistics for the strike report to be delivered at mission debriefing. There was some discussion and disagreement in determining the numbers, but we quickly came to the collective judgment that we had destroyed or damaged fifteen to twenty boxcars, six to eight flatcars, three or four trucks, and several roadside buildings. We figured that at least two hundred and fifty soldiers had been killed or wounded. We also estimated that we caused six or seven rail or road cuts. There should have been a steam locomotive there, or somewhere in the vicinity, but none of us saw one, so none was reported.

As the colonel and I sat side-by-side in the open truck bound for our squadron area, we laughed and joked about his old gunner ("old" meaning somewhere around thirty-five or forty years of age), now snoozing loudly, and his amazing ability to sleep throughout the bumpy ride back to our side of the runway. As our truck came to a stop in front of our operations shack, the colonel lit a long cigar. Another 95th Bomb Squadron combat crew had just finished loading, and the truck carrying them slowly accelerated and started to pull away for its short run to the parachute shack and then on to the flight line. Recognizing the pilot of the other crew, Colonel Bentley rose up from his seat, leaned over the side of the truck, jabbed his cigar at the other pilot, and jokingly admonished him by saying, "Captain, you better bring back that airplane! You hear me? We need every single one we've got!"

I knew what the colonel was really saying, and I am sure the other pilot did too. He was, in effect, saying, "Captain, don't take any needless chances, we need you and your crew."

I have often wondered what that other pilot would have thought had he known the gruesome specifics of Colonel Bentley's extremely aggressive combat performance just a few hours before, one that some could easily characterize as excessive, even reckless.

UNSEEN AND UNSUNG

The B-26 Crew Chiefs, Flight Mechanics, and Flight Instrument Technicians of the Korean War

MANY OF US HAVE SEEN MOVIES AND READ STORIES of World War II and the massive and deadly air war over Europe during the first half of the 1940s. Much attention has been justifiably directed to the heroism of the combat crews who flew the Army Air Corps' B-17s, B-24s, Martin B-26s, and the Douglas A-26s in day and night operations over France and Germany, and of the ground crews who so ably supported them. The friendships and camaraderie between air and ground crew members have been frequently portrayed, and their true stories of mutual respect and confidence are indeed heartwarming and most gratifying. The dramatic story of the famous "Memphis Belle" comes to mind at this point. As well, most combat crewmembers formed strong bonds with the bombers that were assigned to them for the full duration of their combat tours. Similarly, most of the ground crewmembers formed similar emotional bonds and, some would add, irrational attachments to their assigned aircraft, and they maintained them in the very best condition that they were capable of achieving.

A typical crew chief and his ground crew would begin to assemble at the assigned location along the flight line several hours before "their" plane was scheduled to return from the target area in Germany. Repair and maintenance work would begin almost as soon as the plane touched down and taxied to a stop. Frequently, the crew chief would not leave that hardstand from takeoff until landing, nervously "sweating out" the safe return of his "baby."

During World War II, the aircraft was usually identified not just by its assigned number, painted in black in several different places upon its wings and fuselage, but, more interestingly, by its name, painted on the left side of the nose and most frequently accomplished by a cartooned picture consistent with its given name. This picture, in multicolor, was usually of a voluptuous pin-up girl (for example, Bette Grable or Lana Turner) or an animal (a snarling tiger, a kicking mule, a warhorse, etc.). After each mission, the crew chief would paint an additional bomb symbol in close proximity to the aircraft's name and picture so that a passerby would know at a glance the number of combat missions that that plane had flown to date. Although combat crews came and went, each aircraft stayed with its squadron until it was destroyed in combat or damaged to such an extent that its components and parts were cannibalized and used in the repair of other aircraft.

The experience of bomber ground crews in Korea was considerably different. Throughout the entirety of the Korean War, these unique relationships between and among bomber aircrews and ground crews, as well as between aircrews and aircraft, just simply did not develop. One reason was that no B-17s or B-24s were entered into combat over Korea, as they had been superseded by the more advanced B-29s flown out of Okinawa into North Korea six hundred miles from the south. Furthermore, soon after the B-29s entered into combat over North Korea their use in daylight strategic bombing operations was drastically reduced because of heavy losses of crews and aircraft caused by deadly high-speed attacks by increasing numbers of MiG-15s, coupled with the drastic and rapid reduction of sufficient numbers of strategic targets in North Korea. Thus, the four-engine B-29s were quickly replaced by Tactical Air Command's Douglas B-26s (with their two powerful 2000 horse powered Pratt-Whitney R2800 engines), which operated with just a three-man crew (rather than ten-man crews in the B-29s) and flew many more and far shorter bombing missions out of South Korea, either from our 17th Bomb Group at K-9 AFB at Pusan, or from the 3rd Bomb Group at K-8 AFB.

At both K-8 and K-9, no specific B-26 was ever assigned to a specific combat crew, planes being assigned to specific missions based upon their configurations of navigational and/or bombing systems and equipment, as well as their airworthiness and availability at the time, and whether the mission required a bombardier-navigator in the Plexiglas nose or not. Instead, at the morning crew briefing each pilot was given a specific three-digit tail number (the last three numbers of the six-digit serial number for that specific B-26), which he recorded in his flight data for the following night's mission. And, except when the pilot happened to be either the squadron's engineering officer or the assistant engineering officer, there was no reason for any pilot, or any other crew member, to personally know the crew chief assigned to that designated B-26 for that night's mission or to develop close relationships with the crew chief assigned to that plane. Since there were far more combat crews than aircraft assigned to each B-26 squadron, it was simply a matter of random chance as to which aircraft would be assigned to any particular crew for any particular mission.

In any event, whenever our crew was driven to our assigned B-26 prior to take-off, day or night, its regular crew chief was already there, waiting to inform our pilot about any repair or maintenance work that had recently been performed upon that plane. However, if he were sick, injured, or otherwise unavailable, another 95th Bomb Squadron crew chief would be there to function in his place. But other aircrew members, usually bombardier-navigators and gunners, never had either reason or motivation to meet and get to know the men who kept their aircraft in superb operational condition and repair and upon which their very lives depended. In fact, my recent and best efforts to recall a single significant conversation that I ever had with a B-26 crew chief (or with a flight mechanic, flight instrument technician, or bomb loader, for that matter), even one that lasted for just a minute or two, during my seven-month tour of duty in Korea, did not prove successful. Nor did I ever feel any sort of emotion or relationship with any particular B-26. If the aircraft had a Plexiglas nose, a functional Norden bombsight, the small and customary control panel, and a full bomb load, I was as satisfied and happy as I could expect to be.

Most generally, our bombing missions were single ship, night bombing "search and destroy" operations that really began when the driver of one of our squadron's crew trucks dropped off Bob, Jerry, and me near the nose of the numbered B-26 assigned to us. After stowing my gear on the plane, I would begin removing the safety pins from the bombs while Bob and Jerry began their customary visual walk-a-round pre-flight check of the B-26. By that time, the truck driver and his truck would have disappeared into the night. About then, a crew chief would appear out of the darkness and engage Bob in conversation, usually about the current condition and peculiarities of that specific light bomber. By the time Bob and Jerry's walk-a-round was completed, I had pulled all the pins and had climbed into the nose compartment and the crew chief had disappeared into the darkness of the night to take a position well forward and in front of the tip of the left wing, at an angle where he could observe both engine nacelles simultaneously, and there he would wait and watch as the fireguard, holding a fire extinguisher.

After Bob brought both engines to life, the left and then the right, and each was running smoothly, the crew chief would lay the fire extinguisher on the tarmac and wait for the pilot to signal him to remove the heavy wooden chocks from fore and aft of each of the two large front wheels. He then returned to the front of the aircraft and picked up two long light wands, one in each hand, and waited for the pilot to signal him at the assigned and exact minute and second for the start of taxi and subsequent take-off from the north end of runway 15, also begun upon the assigned minute and second. Upon receiving an affirmative signal from the pilot, the crew chief would face the pilot from a safe distance in front of the nose of the B-26, and he would elevate the two wands and, in rapid and successive movements, direct the pilot to taxi slowly forward until the plane's tail assembly was clear of the revetments on both sides. At this point, the crew chief would point the light wand in his right hand at the left engine, while quickly and rapidly gesturing with the wand in his left hand for the pilot to add power to the right engine to start a left turn to aim the plane northward on the taxiway that ran parallel with the flight line. Then we'd be off.

Upon our return to base, always the plane's crew chief, or his designated replacement, would be waiting with his light wands to guide Bob into the same tight space reserved permanently for that plane. A squadron crew truck and driver would usually be waiting to give us our rapid ride to mission debriefing at the 17th Bomb Group HQ on the west side of the runway. By the time I descended from the nose compartment, burdened with my parachute pack and an array of charts, maps, and navigational aids, the crew chief was reviewing with Bob his Form 5 report, which described any unusual occurrences or problems during the flight related to the performance of either engine or any other component of the aircraft. Occasionally, the crew chief would be off and away before my feet had touched the ground. It seems that no one involved in the total exchange of control of the aircraft from aircrew back to ground crew seemed to have any desire or inclination to linger and converse out there on the usually cold and windswept hardstand.

Among the veterans who served in Korea that I have met in the last several years, several were members of the 95th Bomb Squadron's ground crew. For example, Gordon Cooper of Aleto, Illinois, after enlisting in the air force, completed flight mechanic's training and jet mechanics school before arriving at our flight line at the age of twenty-one in late 1952. Gordon gave me one of his photographs of #449, the 95th Bomb Squadron's Douglas B-26 for which he was crew chief. Captain Ken Doolittle and his bombardier-navigator flew #499 into North Korea on the dark night of April 25, 1953, and they never returned.

I also met Donald Eaton of New York City, who enlisted in the air force at the age of twenty and was assigned to the 95th Bomb Squadron in 1953 as its only flight instrument technician. He had completed flight mechanic training at Sheppard AFB in Wichita Fall, Texas, and the flight instrument technician school at Chanute AFB in Rantoul, Illinois, but had no training or experience whatsoever in the installation, repair, or servicing of the instrumentation of Douglas B-26s. However, he became so proficient so quickly that he was assigned to service the B-26s of the two other squadrons of the 17th Bomb Group as well.

These are but a few of many other officers and airmen who served in our ground units at K-9 Air Force Base from June of 1950 through July of 1953. They were and remain to this day the unseen and unsung heroes—among them the armament and engineering staffs, the truck and equipment drivers, and the bomb loading teams.

WHILE DRAFTING THE PRECEDING THREE OR FOUR PARA-graphs, I suddenly remembered fragments of a conversation that I had with Colonel Bentley in an otherwise empty 95th Bomb Squadron operations shack on the afternoon before our memorable daylight formation-bombing mission on the wide steel-reinforced concrete bridge over the river in the center of the industrial and dockage facilities of Wonsan, the largest seaport on the east coast of North Korea. He stated to me that he and I were going to be the "tip of the spear" the next morning, meaning that we, he as lead pilot and me as lead bombardier, would be vital to the success or failure of the entire operation. I also remember being speechless, and embarrassed for being speechless. I was already apprehensive and fearful about my ability to perform adequately in such a responsible capacity at such an early point in my new duties as a recently commissioned second lieutenant. But I am sure that Colonel Bentley did not intend to terrorize me by his use of that metaphor. He merely intended to emphasize that unless we both functioned effectively, the efforts and energies of many people at K-9 would have been totally in vain. These included the many others who had engaged in getting the formation's required aircraft, and the related ordnance, fuel, equipment, and supplies, shipped to K-9 and ready for action.

Unfortunately this was indeed the case with every other mission, because we, as combat crewmembers, rarely ever considered that reality, being too preoccupied with our own anxieties and concerns regarding the task at hand and our own survival. Fortunately for Jerry and me, our own pilot, Bob Crow, was fully aware of the importance of the work of the ground crew.

NO ABORTS!

WITH ANOTHER B-26 CREW, WE WERE BEING bounced around in a crew transport vehicle well after sunrise, circling the runway on our way to the 95th Bomb Squadron area. The distinct smell of Korea was rising with the sun. The words "aroma" or "fragrance" would not be accurate in this context, although "stench" could have been used were it later in the afternoon, as the summer growing season, with fertilizing done with human excrement, was well upon us.

The other crew's pilot, a constantly complaining first lieutenant, was once again voicing his frustrations: "I don't know how you guys do it! No aborts! No aborts after forty-five missions!" He continued to stare directly at Bob Crow, who was sitting directly across from him. He knew that Bob was an assistant operations officer. Bob simply looked back at him with a benign and friendly smile upon his wide and open face. He did not utter a word in response.

Lieutenant Big Mouth's lament continued: "We have been scheduled for sixteen missions so far and three were aborts! Radio problems, manifold pressure, whatever! And you guys just keep rolling along."

We rode the rest of the way in total silence, too tired to talk or too bored to listen.

After Jerry and the other crew vacated the vehicle, I rose and made a sweeping and exaggerated gesture with my right arm, extending it across my body and toward the back of the truck while saying, "After you, captain—rank must have its privileges."

Bob chuckled and gave me a broad smile. The guy had a world-class smile. It brings tears to my eyes when I think about him and his sincere sense of happiness and mirth. But Bob didn't move from his side seat directly behind the driver. He simply said, "Art, you go ahead, I've got a few things to do."

Then and there I realized for the first time that he always stayed on the vehicle after each mission briefing and rode off alone with the duty driver. And then, like a revelation, I knew why his crew never had an aborted combat mission. Nor would we have an abort while flying our last five penetrations into North Korea.

I knew that Bob had just acquired at the briefing the last three digits of the serial number (often called the "tail number") of the aircraft that we would be flying on our next mission. He was now on his way to the flight line and to that B-26 to perform a preliminary pre-flight inspection and to talk with its crew chief about the present condition and flight characteristics of that plane. By that point in our tour of duty Bob probably knew, and knew well, each and every crew chief and flight mechanic on the flight line of the 95th Bomb Squadron. In fact, because of his naturally friendly and outgoing personality and his humility and innate respect for everyone as a human being, he was probably the most well-liked and respected pilot on our side of the runway.

Several days later I came upon the same duty driver sitting idly in his vehicle while parked in front of our operations shack. No one else was around at the time, so I struck up a casual conversation with him. He was a young guy with two stripes on his sleeves. I asked him where he was from. In the military this question was always a good conversational wedge. He said he was from around Amarillo, Texas. I replied that my pilot was from Gonzales, Texas. He said he knew where that was; it was down toward the Mexican border. Now we had a conversation going! I mentioned that it was an honor and privilege to be a member of Captain Crow's combat crew. He said, "You sure are lucky. Captain Crow is a great guy."

Soon I had the whole story. The driver volunteered that Bob would ride to the far end of the flight line and start working his way back on foot to the squadron area, talking with just about every crew chief, flight mechanic, and bomb loader along the way. I am quite sure that Bob personally checked out our designated 26, while chatting at length with its crew chief. After all, he had come up through our enlisted ranks, as they had, so the beneficial effect of shared experiences was undoubtedly in play.

Although the quality of repair and maintenance of all our aircraft in the 95th was exceptionally good, one can assume that Captain Crow's 26s consistently received the highest level of attention and care because of the invaluable personal relationships that he created and nurtured with the ground crew guys directly responsible. Fortunately for us, Jerry and I were the coincidental beneficiaries of that extreme concern and high level of quality of technical services rendered.

STAYIN' ALIVE

URING A TORRENTIAL RAINSTORM THAT SEEMED never-ending, I had just spent an enjoyable but unhealthful and wasteful evening at our so-called officers club at K-9: gambling too much, drinking too much (how could you stay sober with mixed drinks with high-quality booze costing 25 cents and a bottle of Budweiser going for only 10 cents?), and inhaling too much secondhand smoke.

I departed the OC and sloshed through sheets of cool rain and huge mud puddles in getting to our shack. I had just learned about the arrival at our base of Lieutenant Perly Elbridge Eaton III, whom I knew from Air Force Cadet Training days. One of the guys from one of the other two squadrons had said the unusual surname "Perly Eaton," and I asked him if he was referring to Perly Elbridge Eaton III from Athol, Massachusetts. I described Perly as a short, chunky, and cocky second lieutenant. He concurred that it probably was him, adding that the new guy had a pronounced New England accent.

When I met Perly at Ellington AFB, Houston, Texas, I did not like him at first. He had attended an upscale preparatory school and then an Ivy League university where he participated in their ROTC Program. Perly was subsequently designated as the flight leader of our small contingent of thirteen aviation cadets when our B-26 segment of Cadet Class 52–06 first arrived at Mather AFB, near Sacramento, California, to begin an advanced navigation, bombing, and radar training program.

Perly had been so selected because of his training and experience in performance of marching drills, knowledge of proper military attire, and other such matters that many of us from non-military schools found tedious or simply uninteresting.

Our original cadet class of forty-eight cadets had completed primary navigation training at Ellington. While there, we were among several hundred other aviation cadets at different levels of training. We attended ground school, flew day and night training missions, engaged in vigorous and frequent physical training sessions, slept in open bay barracks, and marched in military formation from one activity or location to another all day long. However, at advanced training at Mather AFB we were the first class of cadets on base since the end of World War II. We lived in bachelor officers' quarters and we took our meals at the officers club. However, we were still required to march ceaselessly in tight formation around the base, and all of us, except Perly, were most unhappy about it. Perly, as flight leader, marched along at our side, called cadence, and loved every minute of it.

As time passed by, I got to know and like Perly very much, as he was a person of intelligence, character, and considerable charm. In fact, we became good friends. So I was thoroughly delighted to learn that he might be assigned to K-9 as "permanent party" and now might be residing as a B-26 crewman just across the runway, and I decided to seek him out, right there and then.

I caught a crew transport truck to the other side of the base and began to make inquiries about the previously sometimes pompous and pretentious Perly Elbridge Eaton III. Following directions, I finally found the numbered shack where he presumably was now residing. I pushed open the heavy wooden door and stepped into dark and dismal sleeping quarters that appeared to be totally deserted. Startlingly, from the middle of the shack came a booming voice with a very annoyed and annoying tone, "Don't any of you guys ever take your boots off before entering?"

My immediate and unthinking response was, "Look, I've got to take a step or two into this garbage dump, and sit on a footlocker before I can even start to take them off."

And this I proceeded to do without further comment, although I was not yet even reasonably sure that Perly resided there.

As my eyes grew accustomed to the darkness of the shack I could see that the unwelcoming voice belonged to a tall, gaunt captain, later determined to be a bombardier-navigator, sitting in his skivvies on a footlocker just beyond the potbellied stove. I asked him if one Lt. Perly Elbridge Eaton had recently moved into the shack. He did not reply for quite a while. Finally, as I was about to say something else he stated, "A little pudgy bombardier-navigator moved in about a week ago. He was on a trip north but something happened to their 26 and they diverted to some base up north and it hasn't returned yet."

I was elated: now I simply knew it was Perly!

I told the captain that I was sure that it was my old friend. I added that he would soon come to like Perly. The captain's brusque response was that he was not particularly interested in "making any more new friends" and that he just wanted to "get the hell out of this stinking Korea."

As he spoke, I noticed that he had a distinct accent, probably having been born or raised in the State of Minnesota or one of the Dakotas. He seemed surprised that I had picked up on his state of birth (in fact, Minnesota) so quickly, so I mentioned that my brother had married a Minnesotan and moved to Minnesota. I told him I had visited there and liked the country and the climate. I added that I was considering permanent residency in Minnesota after my release from the air force. I told him I particularly liked the long and superb pheasant-hunting season! He shared my enthusiasm for bird hunting.

Pleasantly and steadily, the captain's attitude and tone of voice had changed. He seemed more relaxed and became quite talkative. He said he was close to the end of his "involuntary servitude" in Korea and had "served his time" in combat operations during World War II in the European and Pacific theatres of operations in medium bombers. I assumed that he was probably referring to the Mitchell B-25 and the Martin B-26 Marauder, the latter having been classified as a medium bomber during World War II, and as the Douglas B-26 Invader was later classified as an attack bomber (i.e., an A-26).

After World War II, he had been summarily RIFed (released due to "reduction in force") and later joined a reserve USAF unit in Minnesota. He flew on Douglas C-47s on routine training flights on weekends and for two weeks each summer to maintain navigational proficiency and to earn a few bucks to help support his new and growing family. (Little did he, or anyone else for that matter, anticipate the explosion of a distant war on the Korean peninsula so soon after Japan's unconditional surrender in August of 1945.)

Then he suddenly stopped talking. Neither he nor I spoke for several minutes. So to break this awkward silence I offered an apology for the sarcastic response that I had made when I had entered his shack. He in turn belatedly expressed regret for his abrupt question. This verbal exchange phased into a somewhat strained conversation about the "shitty" weather and our dim prospects of flying missions any time soon.

With the ignorance and lack of tactfulness that hopefully I can now attribute to comparative youthfulness, I asked why he was sitting alone in total darkness. I clearly remember his belated two-word answer, "Stayin' alive."

This succinct reply really startled me. I had never in my life heard that thought so accurately and concisely expressed. I then thought that I was invincible. I would live forever. When conscious thoughts of death occurred to me I could always quickly and easily push them away.

About a week later, just before my departure from K-9, I returned to the west side of the runway. I easily located the shack of the thin, gaunt bombardier-navigator from Minnesota, and was told that he had departed with his crew on a bombing mission a few days after I met him and that they were now probably dead or still missing in action. It had happened during a short break in the weather and during a flurry of air and ground activity in anticipation of the signing of the ceasefire agreement.

I did not think about this tired old captain for many years. More correctly, I had tried consciously *not* to think about him for these many years. And I thought that I had substantially succeeded. However, late one night, being unable to sleep, I got up from bed, put on a bathrobe, and turned on the TV set. I "surfed" through the channels, hit Channel 6, our public television station, and got a fund-raising campaign. The campaign featured the Bee Gees, who were then singing "Stayin' Alive."

Since then, whenever Channel 6 utilizes the Bee Gees to generate funding for their programming needs and I happen upon that channel, I am illogically and relentlessly impelled to continue to listen into the night, sometimes for several hours, until that song is played again. The unique sound of the Bee Gees singing that song inexorably brings me back, in time, place, and emotion, to that rainy evening and that lonely and unhappy old soldier who quite probably did not stay alive long enough to ever see his family again.

Nor did I locate Perly Elbridge Eaton III, who apparently never did get to K-9 AFB after all. But I wonder if he is still with us.

PART V
COMING HOME

THE LAST MISSION

WE FINISHED OUR TOUR OF DUTY TOGETHER A few days before the long and bitterly negotiated armistice agreement was signed at Panmunjom on July 27, 1953. Bob and Jerry had caught up with me in mission count, as I had taken several extended R&Rs on Kyushu, the southern island of Japan. So we flew our fiftieth mission as a well-integrated and smoothly functioning team flying a typical mission profile as part of the dawn patrol. We were glad it happened that way. We returned to base as three good friends who sincerely appreciated and trusted one another.

We destroyed several small clusters of supply trucks that late night, one smack in the middle of a road bridge right along the coastline northeast of Songjin, leaving a sustained fire burning behind us. We observed relatively little small arms fire and there was no triple A response. We then "cut the corner," heading south-southwest out over the Sea of Japan to bypass Wonsan Harbor and the front line, making landfall thirty miles south of the front line near the city of Sokch'o.

We returned to base without incident with a shared sense of accomplishment that could never be denied us. While stationed in South Korea we rarely gave a thought or were even slightly concerned about how little the world knew or cared about our efforts. In fact, we rarely were even curious about what was happening "back in the world" during our shared Korean tenure. Our reality was always right there in Korea; our focus—to fly and survive each mission, one by one by one. We knew that we were doing our jobs and that we were doing them responsibly and honorably. So we returned that early morning with a deep sense of satisfaction upon completion of the task.

I will never forget the blinding glare of the rising summer sun over the edge of the Pacific just before Bob began a gradual descent, executing wide and sweeping turns before heading northward again and easing the wheels of the tired old Douglas B-26 Bomber back onto the worn and rubber-stained surface of runway 33.

Once again, the landing was as smooth as silk, without bouncing or jarring, with just a little squeaking noise as the rubber gently kissed and held the asphalt. It was another perfect Bob Crow performance to demarcate the end of one phase of our lives and the start of another. Or so I thought at the time. Unfortunately, for me there has been no ending, no closure, no finality, as our "small, regional war" has been with me every subsequent day of my life. However, I cannot speak for either Bob or Jerry. Once we made it back to the United States, I never had any contact with either of them, not even a short letter or brief telephone conversation.

IN THE MIDDLE OF ONE OF UNCOUNTABLE SLEEPLESS nights, over four years after I wrote the first draft of the forgoing narrative of our last combat mission over North Korea, I suddenly realized what was conspicuously missing from my recollection of that memorable but puzzling experience. It was something that Bob, Jerry, and I had silently shared just after that last touchdown on runway 33 at K-9 AFB.

Bob had smoothly decreased speed as our B-26 rolled to the end of the runway, and he had turned right onto the narrow off-ramp leading back to our flight line, just north of our living quarters. Within fifty yards he made a second ninety-degree turn, again to the right, paralleling the runway, until we reached the first revetment where our light bomber was regularly parked and serviced. When Bob neatly maneuvered the B-26 into its assigned slot and cut the power to the engines, there was absolutely no one in sight, not even the aircraft's assigned crew chief or a truck driver from the Motor Pool, who would usually be waiting to take us on our fast and bumpy ride to the other side of the runway, for mission debriefing at 17th Bomb Group HQ.

Usually, before the second prop even stopped turning, I would store my navigation charts and tools in my brown leather, government-issue briefcase, pocket my gloves and other personal flight gear scattered within the close confines of the nose compartment, collect my parachute chest pack from behind my right foot, and descend through the exterior drop-door to the tarmac below. Ordinarily, before I began my exit from the aircraft, Bob and Jerry would already be standing on the tarmac, talking and laughing.

However, during the final phase of this last mission, I did not hear any voices above and behind me, nor did I receive any indication that Bob and Jerry were exiting the cockpit. So I hesitated and listened. Only silence. I continued to wait and listen. Nothing. I refrained from making any movement that could generate any kind of noise. And the sound of silence continued: it was mesmerizing. I slowly turned my head left and right and then left again. Nothing was happening anywhere.

I had just completed my tour of fifty combat missions, almost all of them flown during hours of total darkness. Now, under the brilliant sun of a July morning, I began to examine closely the small black rectangular control and instrument panel, located just behind my left shoulder, as well as the Norton bombsight before me. I leaned back and flipped multiple toggle switches on the panel, simulating the opening and closing of bomb bay doors and the release of single bombs, single bombs in close sequence, and then the entire bomb load at the same time. Then I leaned forward and looked into the eyepiece of the sight with my right eye (my dominant eye), while slowly turning the rate and draft knobs with my right and left hands, respectively. It seemed as though I was seeing and manipulating these familiar devices for the first time! It was indeed a strange sensation.

Suddenly, a startling realization came upon me: I began to fully comprehend that most certainly I would never again engage in air combat operations, in this or in any other war. I felt elation, fear, sadness, joy, guilt, and many other emotions too fleeting, numerous, and nuanced to identify. I also knew that I did not want to leave the aircraft so long as this flood of vivid memories of the past seven months were rolling over me. The temperature and humidity were rising steadily in the cramped nose compartment of the B-26, with the greenhouse effect of the surrounding Plexiglas increasing the flow of perspiration and intensifying my physical discomfort. And yet I could not end the moment; I felt a desperate need to hold onto it for as long as I could. Then I sensed that Bob and Jerry were most probably experiencing the same flow of thoughts and emotions that I was. So the sounds of silence continued.

It seemed that two or three more minutes passed by before I saw and heard the rumble of an open crew truck coming up the flight line. Still there was no movement or sound within the aircraft. As the truck decelerated and passed, from right to left across the nose of the 26, its young redheaded driver, probably a new gunner on temporary assignment, looked directly up at me as I stared down at him. He came to a stop in front of the left engine nacelle and looked up at Bob in the cockpit. Surprisingly, no one moved or spoke even then: we were four blocks of stone. The eerie silence continued for another minute or two until the driver slowly and deliberately stepped from his vehicle. It was then that I heard the sounds of movement from the cockpit. So I lifted the inner half door and followed Bob and Jerry from the aircraft. We climbed into the back of the truck, looking at and then away from each other, all the way around the perimeter road to the debriefing room. Only when the debriefing officer greeted us did the situation return to normalcy with the resumption of casual conversation.

EPILOGUE

THE REPUBLIC OF KOREA, THE UNITED STATES OF America, and the cause of democracy and freedom won the undeclared but never-ended Korean War (1950–1953), which brutally and abruptly took the lives of 36,940 American military servicemen, as well as the lives of literally millions of Korean and Chinese soldiers and civilians. But relatively few people anywhere in the world at the time knew the cost, or really cared. Sadly, that deadly and fiercely fought regional "police action" simply happened too soon after the end of World War II. Korea was a regional war, fought too far away, on the far side of the planet, to be of major interest or concern to average Americans, who were then much more interested in getting back to living normal and secure civilian lives.

It must be emphasized that the Korean War was won by the United Nations forces and lost by North Korea. The limited mandate of the UN charter was basically to restore to South Korea the land that had been taken by North Korea's unprovoked invasion of South Korea on June 25, 1950, and that targeted result was achieved and formalized as of the effective date of the ceasefire agreement, signed and effectuated thirty-seven months and two days later, at 2200 hours (10:00 p.m.) on July 27, 1953. Suddenly and finally, the seemingly endless sounds of gunfire along the front lines faded away and an eerie silence prevailed.

This uneasy but highly desired silence has been perpetuated to the present date by the presence of thirty to forty thousand uniformed American armed forces along South Korea's northern border under the long-continued U.S.-ROK Mutual Defense Treaty between the Republic of Korea and the United States, an agreement of major and ongoing benefits to both countries, as well as to Japan, the Philippines, and other countries in the Far East.

These benefits were outlined in the Brookings Institution's Northeast Asia Commentary in October 2008:

> The U.S.-ROK Mutual Defense Treaty, signed in October 1953, two months after the end of the Korean War, has guaranteed South Korea's national security. The security alliance counts as one of the most important of America's alliances, not only serving to deter another North Korean attack on South Korea, but also providing a continental base for U.S. forces to face China and Russia and to provide a front-line defense for Japan. The alliance has also augmented South Korea's military forces and provided a nuclear umbrella, thus enabling the South Koreans to pursue economic progress with relatively low military budgets.

ABOUT A WEEK BEFORE THE CEASEFIRE AGREEMENT WENT into effect, Bob, Jerry, and I were returning from a typical armed reconnaissance mission deep into northeastern North Korea, where we had been patrolling one of the purple routes. I remember, with surprising clarity, that the sky was exceptionally clear of overcast that late night, and visibility was unlimited. As we approached the bomb line and the main lines of resistance ten miles beyond, the innumerable and startlingly brilliant and beautiful night-lights and sky glow of Seoul and South Korea became progressively more discernible to the naked eye.

With every passing second, the terror and tension of the hidden hazards of air-to-ground combat diminished and faded away as we silently left behind a country of near total darkness. At that defining point in time and space, I stared downward and backward, behind and beyond the trailing edge of our right wing, shocked and saddened by the emptiness and desolation of North Korea.

On many other occasions, our crew would begin our return to K-9 AFB on a line of flight further to the east and much closer to the coastline that parallels the Sea of Japan. On those nights, gazing back and beyond the right wing, I would have a clear but disturbing and depressing view of the much smaller and far less visible cluster of the night lights of Pyongyang, the capital city of North Korea and its only major and surviving city, inhabited by several million people living at or close to starvation and in near total isolation from the civilized world. I could easily see the many blinding searchlights in and around Pyongyang and the heavy concentrations of artillery fire that their sudden illumination would almost instantly trigger. But that defined and concentrated nightglow was surrounded by nothing but darkness, in all directions, except for an occasional and faint flash of a single vehicle's headlights.

As I abruptly turned my head and upper body back to the nose of the aircraft, the impact of the innumerable lights of Seoul, South Korea's capital, would be overwhelming in their collective number, variety, and intensity. Radiating from the city of Seoul, as the absolute center of that emerging economy, culture, and democracy, to the east, south, and west, were undulating and seemingly endless streams of headlights and tail-lights of the trucks, buses, tanks, cars, jeeps, and other various forms of surface traffic moving to and from the smaller cities, towns, villages, and military installations located throughout South Korea. As we moved slowly southward, at three nautical miles per minute and usually from eight to nine thousand feet of altitude, this ever-changing and encompassing wide-angle sighting was a virtual sectional map of South Korea—this evolving, striving, and democratic country now commonly and more appropriately known as the Republic of Korea.

On this particular night, late in the war, this wondrous sight created within me a spontaneous and uncontrollable emotional response that caused tears to stream down my face. These were simultaneously tears of pure joy and tears of deep sadness: my joy for the optimistic and soon-to-be freed people of South Korea and my sadness for the poverty, privation and hopelessness of the enslaved people of North Korea, a militaristic tyranny now ironically known as the Democratic People's Republic of Korea.

Almost sixty years later, it seems that I am not simply remembering these visual sightings and the stark contrast between the two major cities of these two still-hostile countries, moment by moment, and recording them just as I remember them, but that I am actually reliving them, and I experience the same strange amalgam of thoughts and feelings. Uncontrollable fear and anxiety diminish progressively as they are replaced by spontaneous feelings of freedom from the constant threat of imminent death, along with an upwelling of sheer exhilaration and joy, as we inch over and across the bomb line and the main lines of resistance just beyond, with a dark and serene mile and a half of comforting airspace protecting us from the ever-lurking danger below.

The President of the Republic of Korea

September 1, 2011

Mr. Haarmeyer Lee Arthur

▆▆▆▆▆▆▆▆▆▆▆▆▆▆▆
▆▆▆▆▆▆▆▆▆▆▆▆▆▆▆

Dear Mr. Arthur:

On the occasion of the sixtieth anniversary of the Korean War, we honor your selfless sacrifice in fighting tyranny and aggression. We salute your courage in enduring the unimaginable horrors of war. We pay tribute to your commitment in protecting liberty and freedom.

We Koreans made a promise to build a strong and prosperous country that upholds peace and freedom so that the sacrifices that you made would not have been in vain. We have faithfully kept that promise. Korea today is a vibrant democracy with a robust economy and we are actively promoting peace and stability around the world. Korea transformed itself from a country of received aid to one that provides aid to others. We are proud of what we managed to accomplish and we wish to dedicate these achievements to you.

We know that the Korean War is often referred to as "the Forgotten War" despite the tragic great cost of millions of lives. We, however, have never forgotten. Korea is a free and prosperous country because of you and your nation. You will no longer feel "Forgotten" when you witness our love and appreciation and the modern Korea. You deserve our unending honor, respect and appreciation. We also remember those who did not make it home and were taken from their loved ones.

Please accept, once again, our warmest gratitude and deepest respect. You will always remain our true Heroes and we assure you that we will continue to do our best to make you proud. On behalf of the Korean people, I would like to say "Thank you."

Sincerely yours,

Lee Myung-bak
President, Republic of Korea

GLOSSARY OF MILITARY ABBREVIATIONS, ACRONYMS, AND MISNOMERS

LONG BEFORE THE DAWN (OR DARKNESS, DEPENDING UPON your perception) of political correctness, USAF personnel frequently used abbreviations, acronyms, and misnomers. This is an alphabetical listing of a number of these convenient devices and their plain language definitions that I unthinkingly had merged into my everyday vocabulary while stationed in South Korea in 1952 and 1953.

AAA   Incoming and outgoing anti-aircraft artillery fire, used interchangeably with "triple A."

ABORT   A mission that resulted in returning to base without achieving its objective, usually caused by engine and/or equipment malfunction or adverse weather conditions.

AFSC   Air Force Specialty Code. Every job in the USAF had and still has a specific multi-number designation to identify the primary work functions performed under that designation. It is not uncommon for USAF personnel to have a primary AFSC and one or more secondary AFSCs.

AGL   Above ground level. Synonymous with TC (terrain clearance). Distances are measured in feet.

ANTI-PERSONNEL BOMBS   Deadly types of small bombs ranging in weight from 20 to 260 pounds. These bombs were frequently released in clusters and scattered over large areas. They were sometimes fused to detonate upon impact, while others exploded randomly over varying periods of minutes, hours, or days to impede the enemy's efforts to replace or repair the ground targets destroyed or damaged. Also referred to as fragmentation or frag bombs.

AP   Aiming point. The specific spot that identified the center of the chosen target that a bomber pilot selected in firing his wing-mounted machine guns, or that his bombardier- navigator maintained in the center of his bombsight's crosshairs throughout the bomb run in striving for accuracy in placement of his bomb load. See also "IP."

AP-I   Armor piercing-incendiary. The type of .50 caliber machine gun rounds generally used in the interdiction of enemy tanks, trains, trucks, bridges, viaducts, etc. Whenever the gunner was "on target" during hours of darkness, the impacts of these rounds appeared as small silver or white sparks when striking a metallic surface. Interspersed, usually every eighth round, was a tracer that illuminated the trajectory of the rounds being fired.

ARMED RECONNAISSANCE MISSION   An attack by a single aircraft intended to destroy men and/or materiel. This was the innocuous phrase used to describe the military action performed during the course of flying low-level, low-speed B-26 bombing and strafing missions over North Korea.

Also called "road recce" or "train recce" depending upon the target pursued. ("Recce" is pronounced "wreck-ee").

BDA   Bomb damage assessment. A determination of the nature and extent of death, damage, and destruction to the enemy as established by visual sightings of the target area by one's own flight crewmembers or by another crew's members, or by visual sightings by forward air controllers or other ground personnel, or by photographic evidence at or after the fact.

BG   Bomb group. Generally a bomb group was comprised of the personnel, aircraft, ordnance, trucks, ordnance carriers, equipment, housing, and repair and maintenance facilities of three bomb squadrons, operating and quartered at the same air base, along with its command, control, and support personnel.

BOMB LINE   The bomb line was initially fixated at 10,000 meters north of the front line of the UNC's ground forces and parallel with it across the peninsula of Korea from the China Sea or Yellow Sea to the Sea of Japan. All of our bomber crews were required to secure prior approval from UNC Ground

Control before firing or dropping ordnance of any kind within this narrow corridor of enemy territory to minimize the chance of bombs falling upon friendly forces. During the spring of 1953 this distance was sharply reduced to 3,000 meters, making our close ground support for UNC forces consistently hazardous, and particularly risky during periods of inclement weather.

CE   Circular error. The primary measure of a bombardier's accuracy in performing bombing operations, irrespective of the type of bombing equipment used, whether by a complex mechanical device (e.g., the Norden bombsight), a manually operated device (e.g., the simplistic hand-operated reflex sight), or electrical/electronic (radar/sonar) equipment.

CLOSE SUPPORT MISSION   A combat mission flown either day or night, and specifically against enemy frontline ground forces. Such targets were frequently selected by on-the-ground forward air controllers (FACs), who directed attacking aircraft to them. Enemy troop concentrations or stores of munitions in close proximity to the front lines were also frequently targeted.

COMMAND PILOT   A USAF pilot who has completed three thousand or more hours of military flying time.

DIVERSION   Redirection, ordered by responsible authority such as Ground Control HQ or forward air observers, of a bomber crew while airborne and inbound, from one target to another, or from initial destination to an alternate. Most frequently, a road or train recce (see "armed reconnaissance mission") was diverted by a FAC to assist in repelling a massive night-time attack by communist ground forces.

DOLLAR RIDES   The first two or three missions flown by combat crewmembers before they began to fly missions "in the rotation" with their own crews. "Dollar riders" participated in combat operations primarily as observers of the flight activities of seasoned veteran crews in order to gain needed knowledge, information, and combat experience.

DOUGLAS B-26   A quick, fast, and highly maneuverable two-engine bomber flown during World War II, the Korean War, and the Vietnam War by the USAF. It had varied configurations and applications but was used primarily for bombing and reconnaissance missions. This tactical bomber was commonly known as an A-26 during World War II and until 1947.

FAC   Forward air controller. An observation post, involving the efforts of generally two or three Marine or army personnel and a combat-experienced

USAF pilot on temporary duty in coordinating the delivery of close air support. It was sufficiently well positioned in advance of the front line or along the front line so that it could assist by directing accurate and immediate attacks by UNC aircraft to specific ground targets along or close to the front line.

FEAF   Far East Air Force. Collectively, all USAF squadrons, groups, and wings, as well as the air force units of our allies comprising the UNC, stationed in South Korea or Japan during the Korean War, and operated under the control, direction, and jurisdiction of FEAF Headquarters located in Tokyo, Japan.

FLAK TRAP   A flak trap was comprised of clustered anti-aircraft artillery weapons, often mounted on railroad flatcars or large truck beds. Flak traps could be quickly moved in and out of concealed locations, such as tunnels or caves carved into mountainsides. Concentrated firepower from these multiple weapons was frequently directed vertically, particularly when truck- or flatcar-mounted, so that any attacking aircraft flying directly overhead could more likely be destroyed or seriously damaged.

FRAGMENTATION BOMBS   This type of airborne ordnance, also known as anti-personnel bombs, weighed most frequently from 100 to 260 pounds. They were often commonly identified as "deadly little fuckers." See "anti-personnel bombs."

GOLF BALLS   Anti-aircraft artillery rounds, generally referred to as "triple A," were unseen and deadly streams of hot metal that were sometimes interspersed (usually every sixth to eighth round) with luminous tracers of various colors. These tracers visually appeared most frequently as streaming and upward arching sequences of brilliantly white "golf balls." They were used by the triple A gunners in targeting and sighting in on over-flying UNC aircraft.

GPs   General-purpose bombs. These TNT-loaded bombs (with or without a tritonal component) comprised the most frequently carried bomb load of tactical USAF light bombers (B-26s) and fighter-bombers (F-84 Thunderjets and P-51 Mustangs) in Korea. Usually 260, 500, or 1,000 pounds in weight, this ordnance was mostly left over from large inventories of bombs produced before and during World War II air operations.

IDIOT SEAT   The small, uncomfortable, and confining space directly behind the right seat in the cockpit of a Douglas B-26. The idiot seat was usually occupied by a newly arrived aircrew member who was being provided orientation and training in a combat crew's customary air-ground operations. It was more formally known as the jump seat.

INTERDICTION   This convenient and seemingly harmless word referred to day or night bombing raids conducted by bombers or fighter-bombers beyond enemy lines and against any and all methods of ground transportation or communication or other enemy structures (e.g., trains, trucks, ammunition/fuel/supply depots, railroad marshalling yards, facilities, equipment or supplies, bridges, dockage, or viaducts).

IP   Initial point. The specific and finite location on the earth's surface selected and used by a bombardier as the starting point of his bomb run upon a pre-selected target and upon his pre-selected heading. In visual bombing with the Norden bombsight, it was preferable to select a natural feature (e.g., the convergence of a river and a major stream or an offshore island) or a cultural feature (e.g., the intersection of two major roads), three to five minutes of flying time from the IP to the aiming point, where the bomb or bombs are intended, for optimum destruction potential.

KPA   Korean People's Army. The official designation for the totality of the military forces of communist North Korea.

MARTIN MARAUDER B-26   The most effective and efficient tactical two-engine USAF bomber utilized during World War II against Germany and Italy until the arrival of the twin-engine Douglas B-26 Invader. This aircraft was most effective in bombing while in straight and level flight at altitudes around 10,000 feet. Its successor in air-ground operations in Korea was the Douglas B-26, based and used by the Tactical Air Command with the 17th Bomb Group at K-9 AFB, just east of Pusan, South Korea, and the 3rd Bomb Group at K-8 near Kunsan, South Korea.

MISSION   An air reconnaissance or a combined air reconnaissance and bombing and/or strafing operation that could be performed, day or night, by one or more aircraft.

MISSION CREDIT   Official recognition that a crewman had flown into enemy territory and had encountered sufficient hostile enemy action to justify that action as a combat mission for the purpose of determining the duration of a required tour of duty.

MPC   Military pay certificate. These monetary units, usually in small denominations such as $1, $5, $10, or $20, were used as currency in a combat zone to prevent U.S. currency from being acquired by the enemy in event of a military service member's capture or death.

MSR   Main supply route. Designated target areas centered along major roads and/or railroad lines utilized in tactical air operations over North Korea in the assignments of mission responsibility. Each of them were identified by color and number, such as Red-8, Green-5, or Purple-13. MSRs usually extended from sixty nautical miles to one hundred and forty miles, their lengths inversely related to the volume of traffic they generally carried.

NAPALM BOMB (OR TANKS)   A deadly bomb containing jellied gasoline that ignited on impact and spread over a large ground surface area. Used frequently against attacking enemy ground forces or behind-the-line troop concentrations. Officially designated as AN-M76. Weight, 500 pounds; length, 59.1 inches; and diameter, 14.2 inches.

ORDNANCE   Broadly defined, ordnance included all categories of military ammunitions, weapons, and related equipment and devices. In tactical air operations, the definition was limited to bombs, high-velocity aerial rockets, and ammunition directed at the enemy or expended in bombing orientation and training.

PADDLE FOOT   A playful but derogatory term used by USAF flight crewmembers in referring to anyone who was not a combat crewmember. Has the same basic meaning as "ground pounder."

PAYLOAD   The combination of types of ordnance carried on a particular mission. The most frequent bomb load consisted of ten 500-pound bombs containing TNT or tritonal (with 20 percent more explosive power), or ten 500-pound napalm bombs, or varying numbers of 260-pound GP bombs, or clusters of small anti-personnel bombs, but there were many other combinations of such bombs, depending upon targets. On shorter missions, six five-inch aerial rockets were added to the payload, with three hanging from pylons under each wing.

PSP   Pierced steel planking (a.k.a. perforated steel pavement). A quickly installed and utilized manufactured surface for runways, taxiways, flight lines, and other work areas. PSP was of inferior serviceability as it was originally intended for temporary use only. Slippery when wet, it elevated the dangers and risks of takeoffs and landings.

R&R   Rest and recuperation. A short break away from combat duty, usually extending from three to five days and nights and generally spent in Japan. R&R passes were usually given to individuals or crews of combat or combat support staff when it was deemed by appropriate authority that they might be approaching the point of mental breakdown and/or fatigue.

RECCE ROUTE   An assigned target area for aircrews executing an armed reconnaissance mission. Synonymous with main supply route (MSR).

RELIEF TUBE   A simple mechanical device comprised of a flexible rubber hose with a funnel attached at one end with the other end extending to the exterior of the aluminum underside of the fuselage of the aircraft. It was utilized while airborne to enable a crewmember to void.

ROLLING STOCK   For targeting purposes, the generic term for motorized ground traffic, such as troop trains or truck convoys.

SALVO   A bombardier's intentional release of his aircraft's entire bomb load at the same moment in time, preferably upon a target sufficiently valuable to justify that release. A salvo could also be justified if the aircraft was so seriously damaged that the weight of the bomb load would prevent the plane from returning to base with some margin of safety.

SHORAN   An acronym representing a specific and complex system of electronic equipment and procedures to accomplish SHOrt RAnge Navigation utilized in both navigation and bombing operations.

SMALL ARMS FIRE   Discharge of ammunition from hand-held weapons. Small arms fire was used by communist ground forces in Korea against air attacks. Such weapons included Japanese rifles, Russian submachine (burp) guns and carbines, Russian semiautomatic rifles, Russian antitank rifles, and American-made Thompson submachine guns (tommy guns).

SOP   Standard operating or operational procedure. Well-established and required military procedures and practices consistent with official USAF regulations and directives.

SORTIE   A combat mission by a single aircraft and its crew.

TAC   Tactical Air Command. The division of the USAF responsible for the operation of smaller (single or double engine) aircraft used in attacking smaller or closer tactical targets. The Strategic Air Command (SAC) flew larger (four or more engine) aircraft designed to attack major or strategic targets located throughout the world.

TC   Terrain clearance. Has the same meaning as AGL (above ground level). This distance above ground level was usually measured in feet.

TDY   Temporary duty. An assignment to another facility, usually for specialized training or for providing additional and fully qualified personnel to conduct larger air operations.

TOP COVER   The protection (usually by an elliptical orbit flown overhead) against attacks by single engine fighter-interceptor aircraft provided to bomber crews, particularly while they are in tight formation and flying straight and level during daylight hours, and thereby extremely vulnerable to attacks by enemy aircraft.

TOT   Time over target. One of the major parameters used in measuring the effectiveness of a bomber crew. The longer the period of time a light bomber crew patrolled over the enemy's main lines of transportation, the greater the degree of its success in interrupting and slowing the movement of men and materiel to the front line.

TRACER   A visually identifiable round fired from an anti-aircraft artillery piece, or from a machine gun fired from an aircraft in flight, usually every sixth to eighth round, that in passage is seen as a streaming visual display marking its line of flight. Tracers are used to assist the gunner in correcting his aim in honing in on the target selected. Tracers were of various colors: white, green, red, etc.

TRIPLE A   Another way of saying "anti-aircraft artillery."

UNC   United Nations Command. The UNC was comprised of military forces of sixteen countries from throughout the world to participate in the Korean War in response and opposition to the unprovoked invasion of South Korea by communist North Korea. The UNC had the total and ultimate responsibility for planning, organizing, directing, and coordinating the combat and support efforts of these countries.

ZI   Zone of the Interior. The continental United States.